D1528277

Verification: How Much Is Enough?

sipri

Stockholm International Peace Research Institute

SIPRI is an independent institute for research into problems of peace and conflict, especially those of arms control and disarmament. It was established in 1966 to commemorate Sweden's 150 years of unbroken peace.

The institute is financed by the Swedish Parliament. The staff, the Governing Board and the Scientific Council are international.

The Board and Scientific Council are not responsible for the views expressed in the publications of the institute.

Governing Board

Stockholm International Peace Research Institute
Pipers väg 28, S-171 73 Solna, Sweden
Cable: Peaceresearch Stockholm
Telephone: 08-55 97 00

Verification:
How Much Is Enough?

Allan S. Krass

sipri

Stockholm International Peace Research Institute

Taylor & Francis
London and Philadelphia
1985

UK   Taylor & Francis Ltd, 4 John St, London WC1N 2ET

USA   Taylor & Francis Inc., 242 Cherry St, Philadelphia,
              PA 19106–1906

British Library Cataloguing in Publication Data

Krass, Allan S.
  Verification: how much is enough?
  1. Disarmament—Inspection
  I. Title   II. Stockholm International Peace
  Research Institute
  327.1'74   UA12.5

  ISBN 0-85066-305-9

Library of Congress Cataloging in Publication Data is available

*Cover design by Malvern Lumsden
Typeset by Mathematical Composition Setters Ltd,
Salisbury, UK.
Printed in Great Britain by Taylor & Francis (Printers) Ltd,
Basingstoke, Hants.*

Preface

Whenever arms control issues are raised, the question of the verification of compliance follows close behind. Security is widely assumed to depend on adequate military power. A country which signs an agreement to limit its military capability will therefore wish to make sure that the other parties to the agreement also observe its terms.

There are two main issues here. One is technological: what are the capabilities of various verification techniques—what can they do, and what could they do if they were further developed? The other issue is political. For any particular arms control agreement, how much verification is enough? Total certainty is unobtainable: what scale of evasion would be militarily significant? These questions are not simply issues between governments. They are extensively argued about within governments themselves: disagreements about verification often conceal disagreements about whether arms control is desirable at all.

In this book—written during a sabbatical year at SIPRI—Professor Allan Krass deals with both the technological and the political issues. He is eminently qualified to do so. Arms control is now one of the central issues of our time: this study is therefore particularly opportune.

Acknowledgement is given to Dr Ronald Ondrjeka, Dr James Fraser, Dr Eli Brookner, Dr B. R. Hunt, Dr Tamar Peli, Dr Ola Dahlman and Dr H. V. Argo for their reviews of individual sections of chapter 2. In addition the entire manuscript was reviewed by Professor Stephen M. Meyer of the Massachusetts Institute of Technology, Mr Ralph Earle II of Baker and Daniels in Washington, DC and Dr Valery P. Abarenkov of the Institute of the USA and Canada in Moscow. All of the referees contributed useful and constructive criticism of the manuscript; any remaining errors of fact or interpretation are the responsibility of the author. Editorial assistance from Billie Bielckus and Gillian Stanbridge is also gratefully acknowledged.

SIPRI
July 1985

Frank Blackaby
Director

This book is dedicated to the memory of Ulf Reinius, a valued member of the SIPRI staff from 1978 until his untimely death in 1985.

Contents

List of figures

List of tables

Chapter 1. Introduction

Verification has been called by the United States Arms Control and Disarmament Agency "the critical element of arms control";[1]† not *a* critical element, but *the* critical element. On the other hand an authoritative Soviet statement on verification states that "we are against giving absolute pre-eminence to verification and carrying it to absurd lengths; we are in favour of reasonable, balanced verification on the scale that is truly necessary – no more, no less".[2]

Both of these statements are highly abstract and both permit sufficient latitude in interpretation to allow either violent disputes or congenial agreements between the two sides. And the history of arms control negotiation between the USA and USSR has produced both kinds of result.

There is no logical contradiction between seeing verification as "the critical element" and still refusing to give it "absolute pre-eminence" or carry it to "absurd lengths". Yet there are differences in tone and emphasis in these statements which it is essential to elucidate and to analyse in order to understand why progress in arms control and/or disarmament has been so agonizingly difficult to achieve.

The problem becomes even more complex when it is realized that arms control and disarmament are not either ideally or practically bilateral concepts. Sooner or later all efforts to control or reduce armaments must involve *all* states and not just the few most powerful ones. The question must therefore be asked what role verification plays in existing international arms control agreements and how much it might be expanded and intensified in future agreements.

Given the great importance of verification in arms control it is unfortunate, but probably inevitable, that it is the subject most shrouded in secrecy, technical mystification and rhetorical distortion. On the one hand, over-enthusiastic arms control polemicists reassure us that all is well because satellites can read motor car licence plate numbers from an altitude of 200 kilometres. On the other hand, professional fear-mongers dream up bizarre evasion scenarios capable of defeating even the most sophisticated monitoring

---

†Superscript numbers refer to the notes and references at the end of each chapter.

1

devices and leading to ultimate 'victory' for the ruthless and imaginative cheater.

To say, as is so often said in such cases, that "the truth lies somewhere in between" may have a comforting and responsible tone, but it also misses the point. Even if there existed some kind of 'truth' in this deeply complex and subjective area, it would be neither accessible, comprehensible nor immutable.

Verification is intimately connected with the gathering of sensitive military intelligence, so a high level of secrecy is essential. Verification employs highly complex techniques and devices, so most people will never be able to assess for themselves the capabilities and limitations of most monitoring technologies, even if full information were made available. And rhetorical distortion is the very essence of political debate.

This book does not offer the 'truth' about verification. Instead, its purpose is to review the long record of arms control negotiations in order to identify some of the fundamental problems posed by verification and to derive a few general conclusions about the role that verification has played and is likely to play in the future.

There is a great danger in attempting to discuss verification on an abstract, theoretical level. It is understood by any student of arms control that negotiation of verification provisions only makes sense in the context of a given treaty or agreement. To an engineer, negotiator or political leader the tasks of designing, advocating or accepting a particular form of verification are intimately connected to the particular arms control objective to be achieved. General propositions are of little use in such practical questions.

But most people concerned about arms control are not engineers, negotiators or decision makers and have neither the desire nor the capability to influence detailed practical decisions on verification. Yet such people, for example teachers, journalists, diplomats or political activists, have an essential role to play in both informing and guiding public opinion. It is important that these groups have as clear as possible an overview of the problem of verification in order for them to deal constructively with the mass of arcane technical information and tendentious rhetoric that characterize the political debate over arms control. The question then becomes whether or not there exist some generalizations and propositions about verification which can be useful to such groups. This book is an attempt to derive such propositions using as a data base the history of arms control negotiations conducted and treaties signed since the end of World War II.

This data base is summarized in table 1, which has been organized chronologically to demonstrate the historical evolution of verification provisions in arms control treaties. Except for the first item all treaties listed are post-World War II, and the list includes treaties which, although signed, are still not in force, as well as three embryonic treaties which are in advanced stages of negotiation.

Several features of table 1 merit special attention. For example, the first column of the table reflects the history of *détente* between the USA and USSR: its slow rise up to the late 1960s, its flourishing in the early and mid-1970s, and its rapid collapse at the onset of the 1980s. In particular, it can be seen that no significant arms control treaty has been signed since the SALT II Treaty of 1979.[3] The collapse can also be seen in the second column which shows that no bilateral US–Soviet treaty has entered into force since 1972 and no international treaty since the relatively insignificant (note only 47 signatories) Environmental Modification Convention in 1978.

The failure of recent bilateral US–Soviet treaties to enter into force is attributable entirely to the failure of the US Senate to ratify them. The blame for this must be shared by the Senate and Presidents Carter and Reagan who, since 1979, have not submitted any of the pending treaties for ratification. While it is important to emphasize that President Reagan has publicly committed the USA to abide by the terms of the pending treaties as long as the Soviet Union does so, it is still a very significant measure of the degree of tension and suspicion between the two states that these treaties remain unratified. This situation is also highly relevant for verification, since a number of important verification provisions in the Threshold Test Ban and Peaceful Nuclear Explosion Treaties cannot go into effect until the treaties are ratified. In particular the innovative and precedent-setting provisions for exchange of geological and seismic data, as well as observers for peaceful nuclear explosions, remain untested, even though much might be learned from them that would be relevant to verifying a comprehensive nuclear test ban treaty.

The final eight columns of table 1 list a variety of verification measures and whether they are included in a given treaty. There are five columns of monitoring techniques, which range from the remote-sensing techniques called 'national technical means' to unlimited on-site inspection, the most intrusive form of monitoring. The compliance procedures in the last three columns are means for dealing with ambiguities or disputes over implementation of the agreements and range from the weak injunction for the parties to "consult and co-operate" with each other to the more formal and well defined structures of a consultative commission or an international control organization.

No detailed analysis of the table entries is made in this introduction; such analyses are the subject of later chapters in which the treaties and their verification provisions are used to illustrate trends and general propositions in verification. Here it will suffice to point out the quite apparent increase over time in the variety and intensiveness of verification measures embodied in arms control treaties. This makes very clear the slow but steady increase in both the awareness of the importance of verification by some states and the efficacy and acceptability of a wider range of monitoring techniques and compliance procedures.

The trend to more thorough and effective verification measures is most evident in the last three treaties. The number of provisions already agreed to in principle is quite impressive. Yet these treaties remain unsigned, and by far

Table 1. The historical evolution of verification provisions in arms control treaties

Existing treaties

Year signed	Years in force	Treaty and coverage	Review conference	Number of parties and type	NTM[a]	Information and observer exchange	Black boxes or control posts	Selective on-site inspection	Unrestricted on-site inspection	Consult and co-operate	Consultative Commission	International control organization
1925	1928 →∞	Geneva Protocol — Use of chemical and biological weapons	None	106 International								
1959	1961 →∞	Antarctic Treaty — Military use of Antarctica	Possibly after 1991	31 Regional	Yes	Yes			Yes	Yes	Yes	
1963	1963 →∞	Partial Test Ban Treaty — Nuclear weapon tests in outer space, the atmosphere and under water	None	112 International	Yes							
1967	1967 →∞	Outer Space Treaty — Nuclear weapons in space	None	85 International		Yes			Yes			
1967	1968 →∞	Treaty of Tlatelolco — Nuclear weapons in Latin America	None	23 Regional		Yes		Yes				Yes
1968	1970 →1995	Non-Proliferation Treaty — Horizontal proliferation of nuclear weapons	Every 5 years	124 International				Yes				Yes
1971	1972 →∞	Sea-Bed Treaty — Nuclear weapons on ocean floor	1977	75 International			Yes	Yes	Yes	Yes		
1972	1975 →∞	Biological Weapons Convention — Production and stockpiling of biological and toxin weapons	1980	101 International						Yes		
1972	1972 →1977 (ABM); 1972 →∞	SALT I[b]: 5-year Interim Agreement (offensive strategic nuclear weapons) and ABM Treaty (anti-ballistic missiles)	Every 5 years (ABM)	2 Bilateral	Yes					Yes	Yes	Yes

Year	Treaty	Review	Parties / Type						
1974	Threshold Test Ban Treaty Nuclear weapon tests above 150 kt	None	2 Bilateral	Yes	Yes		Yes		
1975	Document on confidence-building measures and certain aspects of security and disarmament (CSCE Final Act, Helsinki)	1978 1980–83	35 Regional	Yes	Yes		Yes		
1976	PNE Treaty Peaceful nuclear explosions above 150 kt	None	2 Bilateral	Yes	Yes	Yes		Yes	
1977	Environmental Modification Convention Hostile use of environmental modification techniques	1978	47 International	Yes	Yes			Yes	Yes
1979	SALT II Treaty Strategic offensive weapons	1984	2 Bilateral[b]	Yes	Yes		Yes	Yes	

Treaties under discussion

	Treaty		Parties / Type						
—	Comprehensive Test Ban All nuclear weapon tests	—	International	Yes	Yes	?		Yes	Yes
—	Chemical Weapons Treaty Development, production, stockpiling of chemical weapons	—	International	Yes	Yes	Yes	Yes	Yes	Yes
—	M(B)FR Reduction of troops and weapons in Europe	—	Regional	Yes	Yes	?		Yes	Yes

[a] A 'yes' is inserted in this column only if the treaty contains an explicit provision on non-interference with NTM.
[b] The SALT I and II negotiations were originally assumed to be part of a continuing process of strategic arms limitation between the USA and the USSR. Continuation of this process (even under the new US designation of START and the present Geneva negotiations) serves many of the functions that review conferences serve under other treaties.
[c] While the Stockholm Conference is not a Review Conference it is part of the CSCE process.

Sources:

Goldblat, J., *Agreements for Arms Control: A Critical Survey* (Taylor & Francis, London, 1982) [a SIPRI book]; Crawford, A. *et al.*, *Compendium of Arms Control Verification Proposals*, 2nd. ed., ORAE Report R81 (Department of National Defence, Ottawa, 1982); Report of the *Ad Hoc* Working Group on Chemical Weapons, Committee on Disarmament document CD/416, 22 August 1983; SIPRI, *World Armaments and Disarmament, SIPRI Yearbook 1982* (Taylor & Francis, London, 1982), pp. 432-36; *Defense Monitor*, Vol. 11, No. 8, 1982.

the most common reason given (almost always by Western states) for not signing them is that they are not yet adequately verifiable. It seems that the perceived need for verifiability in some states has managed to stay well ahead of progress in finding technically feasible and politically acceptable verification methods. Why this gap remains so wide and what might be required to close it are discussed at length in subsequent chapters.

Terminology

Verification has developed a rich and varied vocabulary derived from the intimate historical connections between science, intelligence and diplomacy. Scientific terms have come from such diverse fields as seismology, electromagnetism, chemistry and biology. Technical terms flow in from photography, radar, computers, toxicology and space travel. The connection between verification and intelligence gathering has given words like 'monitoring' and 'surveillance' highly specific meanings, and diplomacy has produced such constructs as 'national technical means' and 'confidence-building measures'. Before moving ahead with the analysis of verification it is worth pausing to define some of these terms in the way they are used in the balance of the book.

Verification is defined by the Oxford English Dictionary as "the action of demonstrating or proving to be true or legitimate by means of evidence or testimony". When this abstract definition is applied to the particular field of arms control and disarmament, verification can be taken to be the action of *demonstrating compliance* with treaty obligations by means of evidence or information gathered by a variety of technical and institutional means.

The phrase 'demonstrating compliance' immediately raises the question 'demonstrating to whom?' The most straightforward answer to this is to assume that the parties to arms control agreements are unitary actors who demonstrate their compliance with treaties to one another. But in the real world, in which states are not unitary actors but complex political and bureaucratic entities, such an answer misses some essential aspects of the verification process, in particular its domestic political role. When the Soviet Union demonstrates compliance with SALT I does it do so for the US President or for the US Senate? And when the United States demonstrates compliance does it do so for the Soviet Politburo or the Soviet Army?

These are subtle and important questions which are analysed in detail in chapter 3. In the meantime the phrase 'demonstrating compliance' will be taken in the straightforward sense unless otherwise noted.

It is important at the outset to distinguish verification from two closely related concepts: *intelligence* and *espionage*. Intelligence is a general term for the full spectrum of methods by which one state acquires information about another. Intelligence gathering ranges all the way from reading the newspapers and recording the radio programmes of another state to infiltrating secret agents into its most sensitive military, political or economic policy-making structures. Espionage occurs when these methods go beyond those sanctioned by "generally recognized principles of international law".

The last phrase has been placed in quotation marks because it has become a standard feature of the verification provisions of arms control treaties. It is used to distinguish those activities of such remote sensing devices as photographic satellites or radio antennas which qualify as *national technical means* (NTM) of verification from those which constitute illegal or improper intelligence gathering. Most recent arms control treaties contain non-interference provisions which prohibit any party both from interfering with the national technical means of verification of the other parties and from using deliberate concealment measures which impede verification by these means. These provisions explicitly recognize the legitimacy of NTM and make it a violation of the treaty to interfere with them or otherwise impede their use.

Such provisions make it extremely important to draw careful distinctions between legitimate NTM and other intelligence-gathering activities against which it remains legitimate to take countermeasures such as camouflage, deception, physical interference and so forth. But just where this line should be drawn has often been a matter of dispute and is strongly influenced by technological developments and the political atmosphere (see chapter 4).

In summary, intelligence can be seen as an umbrella term covering the full spectrum of information gathering activities, verification can be seen as those legal and proper intelligence activities which are carried out for the explicit purpose of demonstrating compliance with existing treaties and agreements, while espionage can be seen as those intelligence activities which are illegal or improper under generally accepted rules of international conduct. Even the combination of verification and espionage still leaves a vast area of the intelligence spectrum uncovered, and most of the intelligence activities of a state qualify as neither verification nor espionage.

While these definitions imply a satisfying precision of vocabulary, such precision should not be overrated. In the real world of military and political competition all information is potentially valuable, and it is rare that evidence for a possible violation of a treaty comes only from those devices or mechanisms devoted specifically to verification. Conversely, it is virtually impossible to design a device for monitoring compliance with a treaty which does not also pick up other information (often called *collateral* information) as well. And there is no question that espionage activity can help in the verification process and vice versa. So while the various terms have meaningful differences in international law, in practice the distinctions among them are much less important, and there are unavoidable limits to how precisely treaties can be worded or monitoring instruments designed to keep them separate.

The verification process itself consists of a number of activities which it is often useful to visualize as occurring in stages. The process begins with *monitoring*, which is the gathering of data, for example by reading the scientific journals of another state or photographing its military installations from a satellite. Monitoring itself can be divided into two more or less distinct activities: *surveillance* and *reconnaissance*.[4] Surveillance is the systematic observation of some place or activity on a continuous or periodic basis. For example the International Atomic Energy Agency places tamper-proof cameras at sensitive locations in many nuclear facilities. These cameras take pictures on a continuous or periodic (or possibly random) schedule to watch for unauthorized or suspicious behaviour. In contrast, reconnaissance is carried out in the form of missions or *ad hoc* activities, generally aimed at a specific objective which for some reason has attracted attention. For example, high-resolution photographic satellites only take pictures when ordered or programmed to do so from the ground. The areas photographed are chosen for their particular interest at a particular time.

The monitoring step is accompanied or followed by an *information processing* step in which the data recorded by the monitoring device are assembled into some appropriate form. For example, the image of a missile exhaust plume recorded on the infra-red sensor of an early-warning satellite must be converted into digital data on temperature, speed, altitude, and so on, and transmitted back to a receiver on Earth where it is then put into a computer. Photographs taken from satellites or aircraft can be put through a wide variety of image processing techniques to make them more intelligible to photo interpreters (see chapter 2).

Once the data are processed they must be *analysed*. The digital or analog record of a seismograph must be studied by a trained seismologist (or by a computer that has been taught to 'think' like a trained seismologist) according to certain rules and procedures which seismology has evolved over many years of experience. Data taken from the bookkeeping records of a nuclear reprocessing plant must be analysed according to certain standard statistical methods and put into a form useful for subsequent stages of the safeguards process.

Following analysis comes the problem of *identification*; is the observed event a violation or is it not? At this stage it is common for information from other sources to be brought to bear on the problem, since it is rare that a violation can be unambiguously identified from a single source. For example, if a satellite sensor detects what appears to be the light flash from a nuclear weapon test in the atmosphere, it is possible to study various meterorological, seismological and radiological data to attempt to gain confirmatory or contradictory evidence.

One excellent, but all too infrequently used, means of gaining additional information is to consult with the party responsible for the observed event and ask for additional evidence or explanations. Encouragement of such cooperative behaviour is the basis for the creation of consultative commissions in many recent agreements, for example the Standing Consultative Commission of the SALT Treaties.

Most often the result of the best efforts at identification of a suspicious event will be some probability that the event represents a violation. For example, if one of the two parties to the SALT II Treaty tests a modified intercontinental ballistic missile (ICBM), the question may arise as to whether the throw-weight of the missile exceeds that of the earlier version by more than 5 per cent, a change forbidden by the Treaty. It may well be that existing verification techniques are only capable of determining a 5 per cent change to something like a 50 per cent confidence level. In such a case an indication of a violation would have to be treated with the same caution as any other variable subject to uncertainties in measurement.

A particularly important concept which should be introduced at this stage is the *false alarm*. This can be defined as an event which triggers any of the processes from monitoring to identification in a manner similar to a violation, even though it originates from some innocuous or irrelevant source. False alarms can be prevented from occurring at any stage of the process, but only by raising the threshold of sensitivity at that stage to real violations. For example, the monitoring of communications is usually designed to recognize certain key words or certain sending−receiving combinations and to ignore the rest. The more specific and limited this set is made, the easier it will be to spot relevant messages against the background of irrelevant ones, that is, the *signal to noise ratio* will be greater. But in doing this one risks missing possibly vital information in the huge volume that is ignored.

An alternative is to keep the monitors highly sensitive and to use special processing techniques to filter out false alarms or to set both monitoring and processing thresholds at a low level and count on analytical procedures to separate real from false events. But the higher in the sequence false alarms are allowed to propagate before being detected, the more technically sophisticated and time-consuming the filtering process becomes.

There is an unavoidable trade-off in verification between the demands for thoroughness and depth of coverage and the need to keep the false alarm rate at an acceptable level. The designers of any verification system must attempt to balance the military and political consequences of possibly missing some important events against the difficulties of trying to pick the real events out of the noisy background of false ones, as well as the political consequences of possibly responding to false alarms as if they were real.[5]

Once a violation has been identified, or a pattern of ambiguous and worrisome events established, there must ensue a process of *evaluation*. Decision makers and representatives of relevant agencies and political constituencies must decide how important this possible violation or pattern of behaviour is in the overall problem of national security.

It will be noticed that throughout all of the earlier stages leading up to this one, the degrees of professional judgement and political sensitivity have increased steadily. At the evaluation stage these assume full importance, and the evaluation of a possible violation is very much a political process. It will generally be relatively easy for people to agree on what the evidence *says*, it will be far more difficult to get agreement on what it *means*.

The final stage of the process is *response*. Once a decision has been reached on the significance of a possible violation there are a wide variety of possible responses ranging from a decision to ignore the incident (possibly to protect intelligence sources) and hope it will not be repeated, or quiet diplomatic efforts to obtain a satisfactory explanation or a change of behaviour, to public accusations, the threat or actuality of retaliation, and even abrogation of the treaty. This decision on how to respond takes the process beyond what can accurately be called verification. It is better to use the term *compliance* to denote the full range of activities from monitoring to response. Since the problem of response will not be considered in any depth in this book, the term verification in the title is in fact the appropriate one.

The above description of the several steps of verification has emphasized the unilateral character of the process. National technical means are employed to monitor and process information; analysis and evaluation are carried out by national intelligence, military and foreign policy bureaucracies; and responses are determined by internal political processes. But verification is in fact an inherently *co-operative* process, and some elements of this co-operation have already been alluded to, for example the use of a consultative commission to resolve ambiguities and the agreement not to interfere with or impede NTM.

There are a number of other so-called *co-operative measures* which have been included in treaties or are under serious consideration for future treaties. These include arrangements for one party deploying monitoring devices or observation stations on the territory of another, for example seismographs in 'black boxes' which transmit data via satellite back to the state or international organization that controls them. Another increasingly common co-operative measure is the exchange of data by two or more states in order to establish an *agreed data base* for monitoring purposes. The creation of such a data base was an important achievement of the SALT II Treaty, and the failure to agree on such a base has for many years been a prominent obstacle to progress in the Mutual Force Reduction Talks in Vienna.

Another set of co-operative measures involves the prior notification by a party to a treaty of activities which might lead to misinterpretation or false alarms. For example, the Peaceful Nuclear Explosions Treaty requires prior notification of any planned peaceful nuclear explosion, and the Final Act of the 1975 Conference on Security and Co-operation in Europe (CSCE) requires prior notification of any military maneouvres in Europe involving more than 25000 troops.

This latter agreement is part of a group of provisions of the CSCE which have acquired the name *confidence-building measures* (CBMs), or, more recently, *confidence- and security-building measures* (CSBMs). It is worth dwelling on this name for a moment since the concept of a confidence-building measure has both a general and a particular meaning.[6] In its most general sense the term confidence-building measure should encompass verification, since the purpose of the latter is to build confidence between parties to a treaty by demonstrating compliance. But this is not the way in which the term CBM is generally used. Instead it almost always is used in connection with the particular measures which have been created by the CSCE process to reduce political tensions and fears of surprise attack in Europe, that is the CSBM. That is how the phrase will be used in this book as well.

The final class of co-operative measures involves a variety of forms of *on-site inspection*, an activity which obviously requires the co-operation of the state on whose territory the inspection occurs. In this class can be included the regular inspections carried out by the International Atomic Energy Agency at commercial and research nuclear facilities under its safeguards programme. Other treaties, such as those covering the Antarctic, outer space and the sea bed, include provisions for unlimited on-site inspection by any party, and while such inspections do take place under the Antarctic Treaty they are of very limited military or political significance.

On-site inspection has been highly controversial throughout the history of arms control negotiations. It is generally seen as an *intrusive* form of verification as opposed to the supposedly *non-intrusive* national technical means, such as satellites and seismographs. But this distinction between intrusive and non-intrusive measures is a strange one, which grew out of historical and political conditions rather than from a strict interpretation of the usual meanings of these words.

One analysis has stated the paradox as follows:

> In practice all kinds of verification require some degree of access to the national affairs or to the territory of the state being verified. Even a report or questionnaire answered by a state in connection with the implementation of a treaty constitutes some form of access to a state's internal affairs. In addition their territories are constantly being photographed from outer space by high resolution cameras; radio and other telecommunications are monitored from abroad; movements of weapons and personnel are watched; levels of production are measured; the construction of fresh installations is established and so forth. All such monitoring encroaches deeply into a state's affairs and the information gained by it is extremely detailed and comprehensive. However, because such activities are not covered by any specific rules of international law, they cannot be prohibited by the states which are subjected to them. What is remarkable is that this type of verification is often termed 'non-intrusive'. The only explanation for the term is that direct personal access to sovereign territory, waters, or airspace is not required.[7]

An analogy might be helpful in appreciating the contradictions implied in the concept of 'non-intrusive' methods. The owner of a house could under the above definition have his property periodically photographed from the air, his telephone and postal communications monitored, his visitors 'debriefed' at the end of their visits, his comings and goings closely watched and his financial transactions monitored. But as long as this was all achieved without physical encroachment on his property the process would be, according to customary verification usage, non-intrusive.

One study has recognized the fact that all forms of intelligence gathering are intrusive and has distinguished between *physical* intrusion and *cognitive* intrusion.[8] The former refers only to physical access by foreign inspectors to the territory of the state being monitored, while the latter encompasses all other measures by which foreigners acquire sensitive military or economic information. According to this study the distinction has some meaning because even though "cognitive intrusion usually implies some physical intrusion, it is possible to conceive of a system where no physical access is needed to acquire sensitive information".[9]

This distinction seems rather an academic one given the historical evolution of concepts of intrusion and the acceptance or rejection of the legitimacy of various forms of monitoring. This evolution is analysed in more detail in chapter 4, and here it is enough to say that intrusiveness has been and is likely to remain in the eye of the beholder. There is no monitoring technique, no matter how remote or purely 'cognitive' in nature, which cannot be interfered with or spoofed by a state unwilling to accept its legitimacy and willing to accept the costs and risks of such interference. States have agreed to accept or to tolerate certain forms of intrusion on their affairs for a variety of reasons, but this acceptance does not change the nature of the intrusion. For these reasons no attempt will be made in this study to distinguish instrusive from non-intrusive forms of verification, and the use of these words will be held to a minimum.

Overview

The basic organizing principle of this book is the treatment of verification as a complex and intimate interaction between technology and politics. In this sense it is similar to many modern problems in the fields of energy, health care, mass communications, information processing and so forth. Each of these problems has a technological dimension characterized by continual innovation, the demand for efficiency and an apparently endlessly expanding frontier of possible applications. Each problem also has a political dimension characterized by internal popular and bureaucratic conflicts, and external demands for international equity and co-operation, in conflict with national sovereignty and self-interest.

Verification displays all of these features, and much of the history and possible future evolution of this field can be analysed in terms of the interactions between these two aspects. It therefore seems appropriate to organize the analysis in the following way. Chapter 2 surveys the technological developments which have so dramatically expanded the potential for effective verification over the years since the end of World War II. The descriptions focus on basic principles and, because they are intended to be understood by the general reader, excessive detail and technical jargon are avoided. The objective is to provide a simple, yet not over-simple, summary of the capabilities and limitations of these systems and the ways in which they can and might contribute to verification.

Chapter 3 considers the politics of verification both from an international and a domestic point of view. Because the international arms control arena has been effectively dominated by the United States and the Soviet Union, their political interaction with respect to verification issues is given primary attention. However, the political concerns of other states are also dealt with to demonstrate the growing pressures for internationalization of this field. Internal politics is divided into popular political concerns and bureaucratic dynamics. Here the focus is very much on the United States where verification plays a significant domestic political role and where far more information is available on the internal bureaucratic struggles on this issue.

Chapter 4 then combines technology and politics and focuses on four problems for which the interaction of these factors seems highly significant. These problems are the legitimacy of verification measures, the diagnosis and treatment of non-compliance, the role of co-operative measures and on-site inspection and the problems faced by efforts to make verification more international, both in scope and in control.

Finally, chapter 5 presents conclusions and propositions supported by the evidence and analysis of the preceding chapters. No attempt is made to deal systematically with the verification issues raised by particular treaties or negotiations. Instead, the treaties and negotiations are treated here as a data base from which to draw examples to illustrate particular propositions or generalizations. It is felt that these will be more useful to the general reader who needs some context in which to understand the almost overwhelming flood of information, whether relevant or irrelevant, accurate or inaccurate, sincere or disingenuous, which characterizes the present public discussion of verification.

References

1. ACDA, *Verification: The Critical Element of Arms Control*, US ACDA Publication No. 85 (US Arms Control and Disarmament Agency, Washington, DC, March 1976).
2. Issraelyan, V., quoted in Final Report of the 119th meeting of the Committee on Disarmament, Committee on Disarmament document CD/PV.119, Geneva, 31 March 1981, p. 17.
3. There have been three minor agreements signed since the SALT II Treaty in 1979. These are an agreement governing activities on the Moon, one on the physical protection of nuclear material, and one on the use of inhumane conventional

weapons (see Goldblat, J., *Agreements for Arms Control: A Critical Survey* (Taylor & Francis, London, 1982), pp. 286-302 [a SIPRI book]). However none of these agreements involves significant verification provisions and all are of very minor military and political significance. Their existence does not affect any of the analysis based on table 1.

4. Velocci, T., 'Strategic reconnaissance/surveillance', *Military Technology*, October 1983, p. 38.
5. Meyer, S.M., 'Verification and risk in arms control', *International Security*, Vol. 8, No. 4, Spring 1984, pp. 115-17.
6. Freedman, L., 'Assured detection: needs and dysfunctions of verification', in Nerlich, U. (ed.), *Soviet Power and Western Negotiating Policies*, Vol. 2 (Ballinger, Cambridge, MA, 1983), p. 249.
7. SIPRI, *Strategic Disarmament, Verification and National Security* (Taylor & Francis, London, 1977), pp. 22-23.
8. 'A conceptual working paper on arms control verification', Arms Control and Disarmament Division, Department of External Affairs, Department of National Defence, Ottawa, June 1981, pp. 30-33.
9. 'A conceptual working paper on arms control verification', (note 8), pp. 30-31.

Chapter 2. The technology of verification

I. Introduction

The instruments and techniques used for arms control verification are exactly the same as those used for the gathering of military and political intelligence. The great importance of getting as clear and accurate a picture as possible of an adversary's military capabilities and political intentions has meant that enormous resources of money, time and creative talent have been devoted to the task of creating sensitive, precise, reliable and thorough monitoring devices as well as the processing and analytical techniques needed to interpret the data they produce.

Arms control verification, as the junior partner of military intelligence, has been the mostly inadvertent beneficiary of this remarkable technical effort. Very few of the devices described in this chapter were developed primarily for verification purposes, yet now that they exist they have the potential to create the technological base for significant progress towards genuine disarmament. Whether or not they will realize this potential is another matter and this is discussed in later chapters.

The current military intelligence function of the technologies described here, as well as the importance of some level of secrecy and uncertainty to effective verification, require that many of the most interesting technical details of these devices remain classified. Therefore, any attempt to describe their capabilities and limitations must be preceded by the warning that all estimates are tentative and subject to error. No classified data or information have been used in making these descriptions, and the open literature can be contradictory and misleading since it is often based on hearsay or politically inspired leaks.

The best approach in such a situation is to stick as close as possible to the basic physical principles on which each monitoring technology is based and on generally accepted estimates of the state of the technological art, often obtainable from examination of civilian technology. The key assumption in this approach is that where sufficient motivation exists technical capabilities will generally approach theoretical limits reasonably quickly. There can be no doubt that the desire of states, in particular the two leading nuclear powers, to learn as much as possible about the military capabilities of rival states has provided ample motivation, and that the gap between practical and theoretical performance is now quite narrow for many of the monitoring devices used to gather intelligence. Examples of this narrow gap are to be found in seismological detection, satellite photography and communications monitoring. In other areas such as synthetic aperture radar, thermal infra-red imaging, information processing and artificial intelligence the actual capabilities may still be relatively far from their potential, but progress is clearly rapid and can be expected to continue.

In reading the technical descriptions below it may be useful for the reader to visualize the general process of monitoring as made up of a number of components. First, there is an appropriate instrument (a satellite camera, a seismometer, a human inspector); second, there is an appropriate target (a deployed missile, an underground nuclear explosion, an inventory of plutonium); third, there is a means of processing the data (photo interpretation, seismic data analysis, statistical analysis); fourth, there is a set of limitations to accuracy or transparency (clouds or atmospheric turbulence, high seismic noise levels, flow measurement uncertainties or bookkeeping errors); and fifth, there exists a set of evasion or deception techniques capable of spoofing the instrument (camouflage, decoupling, record falsification). The brief descriptions that follow do not allow for detailed examinations of each of these features for every technology, but the interested reader can explore any of them in more detail using the references, which provide a good sample of the important technical literature in each area.

II. Visible light photography

Certainly the most significant technological development in the field of arms control verification has been the photographic reconnaissance satellite. The potential for using satellites to observe the activities of other states was recognized from the earliest days of the effort to launch artificial Earth satellites; it was a natural extension of the already commonplace use of aerial reconnaissance to photograph enemy teritory in wartime. By the early 1950s, well before the capability existed to put objects into orbit, the potential for peace-time aerial and ultimately space reconnaissance over the Soviet Union was being evaluated at the highest levels in the Truman Administration.[1] Current US photographic satellites are direct descendents of the U-2 aircraft and Discoverer satellite programmes of the 1950s.

By 1961 "The ability to carry out satellite observation of large areas of the Soviet Union with sufficient photographic resolution to spot missile silos was available..."[2] The ensuing 24 years have seen a steady and substantial improvement in the technical capabilities of photographic satellites by both the USA and the Soviet Union, as well as several other states. Photography from space has proven useful for many purposes besides military intelligence and arms control, and a number of states have launched satellites for purposes of weather prediction, resource mapping and ocean surveillance.

The key requirements for useful satellite photography are the same as those for good photography on Earth, that is, good light and object contrast, clear air, precise and stable camera optics, and high-quality, high-resolution image recording, whether on film or directly to electrical signals for electronic processing.

Photographic reconnaissance satellites are placed in orbits which bring them as close to the Earth's surface as is consistent with the desired lifetime in orbit. The Earth's atmosphere grows less dense at high altitudes, decreasing roughly by a factor of one-half for each 5 kilometres above the surface.[3] For example, at an altitude of 20 km the atmosphere already has only about one-sixteenth of its density at the surface. However, because of the very high speed of a satellite in orbit (about 7.5 km per second) even this small amount of atmosphere would be sufficient to heat a normal satellite to incandescence. In fact most photo-reconnaissance satellites have been put into orbits in which their point of *closest* approach to the Earth's surface (the 'perigee' of the orbit) is at least 130–140 km.[4]

It is at or near the perigee of the orbit that photographs are taken, since the ground detail (or target detail) of the image is better if the camera is closer to the region being photographed. Even at 150 km altitude there is sufficient atmospheric drag on the satellite to cause it to lose energy rather rapidly and begin to fall towards the Earth. This effect can be reduced by giving the satellite an elliptical orbit which takes it well outside the atmosphere (say to maximum heights—'apogees'—of 300–400 km) when it is not taking pictures. A mission can also be extended by giving the satellite a booster engine which can compensate for the energy losses caused by atmospheric drag. Figure 1 shows the effects of such a booster on the orbit of a photographic satellite.[5]

When satellites are referred to as 'space vehicles' there is a tendency to visualize them as being far away from the Earth. But on the scale of the Earth itself a photographic satellite at an altitude of 200 km is in fact very close to the Earth's surface. Figure 2 illustrates the relationship of a satellite at this altitude to the surface and shows the width of a strip (2 750 km) which is within the line-of-sight of the satellite. The actual width of such a strip is in fact larger (3 200 km) because of the bending of light as it passes through the variable density of the atmosphere. It would of course be foolish to attempt to photograph this entire strip. Not only are the edges about 10 times as far away as the centre, but the light from the edges must pass through much more atmosphere, suffering much greater absorption, scattering and distortion than the light from directly below. A good example of these effects can be seen by observing the very different appearance of the Sun or Moon as it is rising or setting from that when it is nearly overhead.

The actual strip photographed by such a satellite is more likely to have a

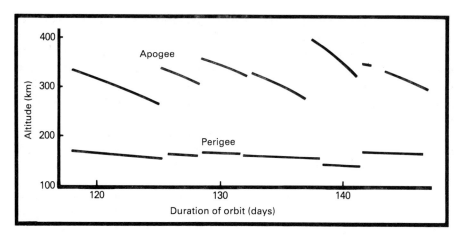

Figure 1. Effects of air resistance on satellite orbit
The graph shows the variations in apogee (upper curves) and perigee (lower curves) heights (in km) during the flight of Cosmos 1097. Note the decrease in each parameter as air resistance causes the satellite to lose energy and the sharp increases which result from firings of the booster engine.

Source: Jasani, B. (ed.), *Outer Space—A New Dimension of the Arms Race* (Taylor & Francis, London, 1982), p. 142 [a SIPRI book].

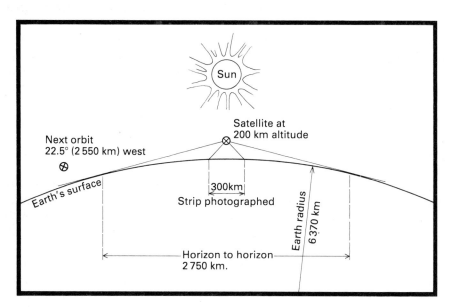

Figure 2. The spatial relationship between a photo-reconnaissance satellite and the Earth's surface
The diagram shows the relationship between the height of the satellite, the Earth's radius and the width of a typical strip photograph. The Sun is pictured at local noon as the photographs are being taken.

width of a few hundred kilometres at most, and considerably less if very high resolution is desired. For example, a camera with the high resolution capability of the Space Telescope (see below) at a height of 200 km could photograph an area only 800 m wide on a 23 cm wide piece of film. Such 'close-look' pictures are only taken when there is some reason to believe that they might produce important information. To attempt to survey vast areas at such high resolution is clearly impractical.

Another important technique is to produce overlapping photographs of the same area from different angles. This allows the creation of stereoscopic (three-dimensional) images, which can often be extremely helpful in interpretation.[6]

As it takes its pictures the satellite is moving with a velocity of roughly 7.5 km/s relative to the ground. This means that the camera must be designed to focus on objects for at least as long as the shutter stays open. If the exposure time is assumed to be about 0.1 second, then the satellite will move a distance of 750 metres relative to an object on the ground during the exposure. This means that the camera must rotate through an angle of about ¼ degree (15 minutes) in order to stay pointed at the object. This same relative motion could also be achieved by moving the film during the exposure or by the use of rotating elements inside the camera itself. Even if the photograph is somewhat blurred by motion effects it can be improved by image restoration techniques as long as the elements of interest on the target are not smeared together (see below).

After taking its strip photograph the satellite proceeds on its orbit while the Earth rotates from west to east under it. The polar orbits used by most photographic satellites are very nearly stationary in space. In fact, if the orbit is designed carefully it can be made 'Sun-synchronous', which means that the satellite always passes over the light side of the Earth at a given time of day. The time is picked to obtain the best combination of light and shadow length to produce good definition of objects in the photograph. This implies that photographs taken at low latitudes should be taken either in the morning or in the afternoon, while high-latitude pictures are taken near local noon.[7]

Just as local noon moves westwards with the rotation of the Earth, so will the ground track of the satellite's orbit. If the orbit has a period of 90 minutes, each time the satellite reaches its perigee it will be over a point 22.5 degrees west of the previous point. For example, if the first picture strip was taken over Kiev or New York, then the next would be over Frankfurt or Kansas City. If the period were exactly 90 minutes, then after every 16 orbits the satellite would repeat the same pattern of observations. Since this would leave large areas unphotographed, it is generally desirable to have the period differ by some small amount from 90 minutes. In this way the satellite can be made to photograph adjacent strips and, over a period of several days, achieve virtually total coverage of any desired area.

The process can be speeded up if the satellite camera is capable of photographing a wider strip. This can be accomplished by having it pass at a higher altitude, as long as the optical properties of the camera are sufficient to provide adequate resolution at such a distance. The observed gradual increase of perigee heights in both US and Soviet photo-reconnaissance satellites is good evidence of the improvements that have been made in these optical properties. For example, whereas early US 'close-look' satellites had perigees of 140–150 km, the current KH-11 (Keyhole) satellites combine both close-look and area-survey (wide-angle) cameras in the same satellite, whose perigee is now typically at or above 250 km.[8] It is interesting to note that the perigees of even the earliest Soviet photo-reconnaissance satellites were, with few exceptions, very close to 200 km, but that these began to come down to around 175 km for close-look satellites in the early 1970s. The 35 Soviet photo-reconnaissance satellites launched during 1982 had perigees ranging from 170 km all the way to 358 km. These higher altitudes should permit longer orbital lifetimes, but it still seems to be Soviet practice to bring down satellites after two weeks to a month in orbit. This may indicate either a preference or the necessity for carrying and processing smaller quantities of film that is typical for US satellites.

In the early days of satellite photography it was necessary to return exposed film capsules to Earth for developing and processing. More modern photographic satellites develop the film on-board and use optical-electronic scanning devices to convert the image to a digital code and transmit it back to Earth. Image processing can then be done directly on this coded information. The newest satellites, for example the KH-11, reportedly possess the capability for so-called 'real-time' photography and image processing. Images are coded and transmitted instantly to Earth via a geosynchronous relay satellite, enabling photo interpreters and intelligence analysts to monitor crisis situations as they develop.[9]

Camera optics for satellite photography

The next major consideration in achieving high-resolution pictures is that of the camera optics. These are illustrated in very simplified form in figure 3. The essential element in any satellite camera is a focusing mirror which reflects rays of light coming from an object on the ground to create an image of that object at a focus near the mirror.[10] An example of the truly remarkable quality now achievable in such mirrors is the one being installed in the US Space Telescope scheduled to be launched into orbit in 1985 aboard the space shuttle (see figure 4).[11] There is no reason to doubt that the optical components used in military spacecraft are at least as carefully designed and crafted as this example.

Figure 3 illustrates in a highly schematic way the basic parameters for evaluating the optical properties of a focusing mirror. A distant object of length L reflects light towards the mirror. If the object is hundreds of kilometres away the light reaching the mirror can be described as a bundle of rays parallel

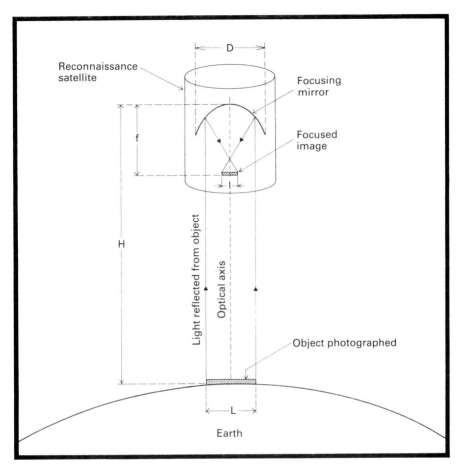

Figure 3. Camera optics for satellite photography
A high-resolution satellite camera at altitude H utilizes a large diameter (D) mirror which produces at a distance f from the mirror a real image of an object on the ground. A characteristic dimension of the object is labelled L and the corresponding image size is 1. Note that the camera is shown pointing straight down for ease of representation. Actual satellite cameras can be oriented at oblique angles if necessary. (The photograph in figure 6 was taken at an oblique angle.)

to the axis of the mirror. This bundle of rays is reflected and brought to a focus at a distance from the mirror known as the focal length (f). By changing the shape of the mirror and by introducing other mirrors into the path of the beam the focal length can be made quite long. For example the Space Telescope mirror has been ground to a concave hyperboloid shape, and it will be combined with another much smaller convex mirror (see figure 5) to produce a focal length of 57.6 m in a telescope whose overall length is only 12.8 m. This technique of packing a long focal length into a much shorter distance is called 'folding' the optics.

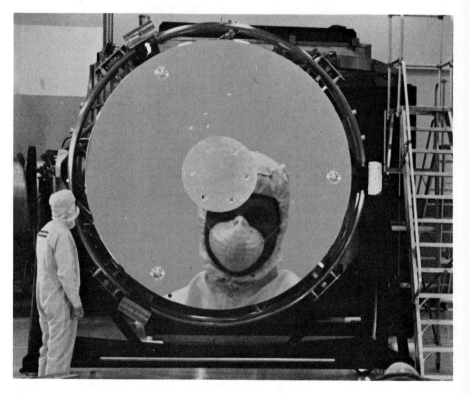

Figure 4. Primary mirror for the US Space Telescope
The primary mirror for the Space Telescope was photographed at the Wilton, CT, plant of the Perkin-Elmer Corporation just after its front surface had been coated with a reflective film of aluminium 0.076 μm thick, followed by a protective layer of magnesium fluoride 0.025 μm thick. The mirror, which is made of fused silica glass with an extremely low coefficient of thermal expansion, is 2.4 m in diameter and weighs about 818 kg. It consists of a lightweight cellular core approximately 25.4 cm thick sandwiched between two endplates, each about 2.5 cm thick. Some 91 kg of material were removed from the front plate in the course of the 28 months of grinding and polishing required to give the surface its proper figure, which is that of a concave hyperboloid. The masked man seen enlarged in reflection is standing next to the photographer some 18.3 m from the mirror. Another man, also wearing a mask and a special suit to maintain the cleanliness of the mirror's surface, is at the left. A metal plate temporarily covers the hole in the centre of the mirror through which light from the telescope's secondary mirror will pass.

Source: Photo courtesy of the Perkin-Elmer Corp., Norwalk, CT, USA.

Even when the optical path is folded, there is a simple proportional relationship connecting the sizes and positions of the object and image. If the object has length L and is a distance H from the mirror, and if focal length is f and the image length l, then the relationship is as follows:

$$\frac{l}{L} = \frac{f}{H} \tag{1}$$

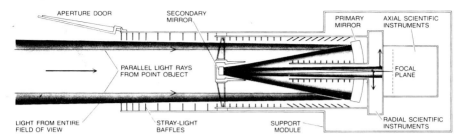

Figure 5. The optical path in the Space Telescope
The optical path in the Space Telescope is said to be folded: light from the concave primary mirror is reflected from the convex secondary mirror and passes through a hole in the centre of the primary before coming to a focus at the image plane in the instrument section several feet behind the primary. Technically the telescope is described as a Ritchey-Chrétien type of Cassegrain optical system.

Some representative dimensions are the diameter of the primary mirror (2.4 m), the diameter of the secondary mirror (0.3 m), and the distance behind the primary mirror of the focal plane (1.52 m).[12]

Source: Bahcall J. N. and Spitzer, L., Jr, 'The Space Telescope', *Scientific American*, Vol. 247, No. 1, July 1982, p. 39. Copyright 1982 by Scientific American, Inc. All rights reserved.

The ratio l/L is called the magnification, and the formula shows that the longer the focal length the greater the magnification of an object at a given distance. Since the focal length is always much smaller than the altitude of the camera, the 'magnification' is really a small fractional number, and the image is a tiny replica of the object.

A simple application of the above formula would be to imagine taking a picture with a typical personal camera from a satellite 200 km above the Earth. Such a camera has a focal length of about 5 cm which implies a magnification of $0.05/2 \times 10^5$ or 1 : 4 000 000. In order to appear 1 mm long on the film a feature on the Earth's surface would have to be 4 km long. But this same 1 millimetre of film when exposed in the 57.6 metre focal length Space Telescope would record an object only 3.5 m long, roughly the length of an average motor car.

If the capabilities of the film are now taken into account it is possible to calculate how much detail could be recorded within this millimetre of film. The resolving power of photographic film is usually expressed in terms of lines per millimetre, that is, the number of distinguishable parallel line pairs that can be squeezed into 1 millimetre of film. Typical resolutions for commercial film are around 100 lines/mm, but for films used in military surveillance activities resolutions of up to 900 lines/mm have been reported.[13]

Using such a film in the Space Telescope would result in a resolution on the ground of one nine-hundredth of 3.5 metres, or 4 millimetres. Such a photograph would certainly enable one to read the licence number of a motor car from an altitude of 200 km—indeed, one could probably recognize the driver!

It may be calculations such as these that lead some writers on verification to assert that satellite cameras can read car licence numbers.[14] But in practice the use of such high-resolution film is almost never warranted. In the first place high resolution demands excessively long exposure times or very good lighting, neither of which may be available in satellite photography. Second, there are a group of other resolution-degrading effects which render such high-resolution film superfluous. These effects are vibrations and instabilities in the camera itself, diffraction effects, and the presence of turbulence and density variations in the atmosphere, even on the clearest of days.

Vibrations and instabilities

Even though the satellite is in almost empty space and is therefore not buffeted by winds or air drag, it still contains moving parts such as film drives, pointing motors, rotating or oscillating mirrors, and so on. It also passes periodically in and out of direct sunlight, which means that its temperature will fluctuate. These effects produce vibrations and distortions which must be stablilized to a very high degree. That this is feasible is shown again by the capabilities of the Space Telescope which can hold its optical axis steady to within 0.01 arc seconds for as long as 10 hours.[15] A deviation of 0.01 arc seconds at 200 km altitude corresponds to a pointing error on the ground of 1 cm. This can be taken as a reasonable estimate of the optical stability of a sophisticated reconnaissance satellite.

Diffraction

This phenomenon results from the fact that the camera mirror has a finite diameter and can therefore capture only a fraction of the light reflected by the object. The result of this limitation is that the image of a geometrical point (that is, a point with diameter equal to zero) on the ground is spread out into a spot on the film whose diameter gets larger for smaller diameters of the light-gathering mirror. The angular width of the diffracted light beam is given by

$$\Delta = \frac{w}{D} \tag{2}$$

where w is the wavelength of the light being focused, and D is the diameter of the telescope mirror (see figure 3). The diameter of the spot on the film is then computed by multiplying Δ by the focal length

$$d = \Delta f \tag{3}$$

Wavelengths of visible light vary from 400 nanometres (nm) for violet to 700 nm for red, with the brightest part of the spectrum in the yellow-green at about 500 nm. If this last value is taken for w, D is taken to be 2.4 m and f is 57.6 m, it can be shown that a pure geometrical point on the ground will be recorded as a spot on the film with diameter 0.013 mm. But the previous formula shows that 0.013 mm on the film corresponds to a distance of 4.6 cm on the ground. Therefore two point sources of light separated by only 4.6 cm on the ground would produce heavily overlapping spots on the film and be indistinguishable as individual sources. This is the so-called 'diffraction limit' on ground resolution. One authoritative forecast of technological developments predicts that by 1990 available telescope diameters will be 3 m, with 3.5 m a possibility.[16] Such diameters would reduce the diffraction limit on resolution from a height of 200 km to 3.3 cm, or possibly 2.8 cm.

Atmospheric turbulence

Light on its way from an object on the ground to a camera in space must pass through air whose density varies from place to place and fluctuates in time. There is first of all the overall variation of density with altitude which causes light rays to bend. Then there are local and essentially random fluctuations caused by winds and temperature variations. These latter density variations cause slight random bending of the light rays as they pass through the atmosphere, and the result at the camera is an image which tends to wander and flicker over a small region of the focal plane. This effect is the precise analogue of the 'twinkling' of stars on a clear night.[17] There is no easy method of estimating the effect on resolution of this twinkling, but various attempts have produced values between 5 and 10 cm.

Taking together the uncertainties from pointing error, diffraction and atmospheric turbulence it can be estimated that if the Space Telescope were directed at the Earth's surface from an altitude of 200 km (there is, of course, no intention of actually doing this; the Space Telescope is designed for astronomical research and will be pointed *away* from the Earth) a ground resolution of something like 10–15 cm could be achieved on clear, cloudless days. (Some techniques which might enable these limits to be improved by manipulating the developed photographic image or by computerized operations on electronic data from the focal plane sensors are discussed in section V on image processing, pp. 51–54.) There is good reason to assume that this also gives a reasonable estimate of the capabilities of existing military reconnaissance satellites. For example, the Big Bird satellite is reported to be about 14 m long and 3 m in diameter.[18] This compares quite well with the 12.8 m length and 4.3 m diameter of the Space Telescope.[19] It would also not be surprising to learn that much of the technical know-how needed to construct and operate the Space Telescope was first developed in the military space programme.

In conclusion, while it may not be possible to read motor car licence plates from an altitude of 200 km it is probably possible to distinguish different makes of car.[20] Or as William Colby, former Director of the US Central Intelligence Agency, has put it

> You can see the tanks, you see the artillery, but you may not quite see the insignia on the fellow's uniform.[21]

A more systematic assessment of the capabilities of photographic satellites can be made by referring to table 2.[22] For example, from the entries for 'Missile sites (SSM/SAM)' it can be seen that the resolution required for 'detection' of such a site is 3 m (Soviet ICBM silos are 5–6 m in diameter),

Table 2. Resolution (in metres) required for interpretation tasks

Target	Detection[a]	General identification[b]	Precise identification[c]	Description[d]	Analysis
Bridges	6	4.6	1.5	0.9	0.3
Communications					
Radar	3	0.9	0.3	0.15	0.04
Radio	3	1.5	0.3	0.15	0.15
Supply dump	1.5	0.6	0.3	0.03	0.03
Troop units	6	2	1.2	0.3	0.08
Airfield facilities	6	4.6	3	0.3	0.15
Rockets and artillery	0.9	0.6	0.15	0.05	0.01
Aircraft	4.6	1.5	0.9	0.15	0.03
Command and control headquarters	3	1.5	0.9	0.15	0.03
Missile sites (SSM/SAM)[e]	3	1.5	0.6	0.3	0.08
Surface ships	7.6	4.6	0.6	0.3	0.08
Nuclear weapon components	2.4	1.5	0.3	0.03	0.01
Vehicles	1.5	0.6	0.3	0.05	0.03
Land minefields	9	6	0.9	0.03	–
Ports and harbours	30.5	15	6	3	0.3
Coasts and landing beaches	30.5	4.6	3	1.5	0.08
Railway yards and shops	30.5	15	6	1.5	0.6
Roads	9	6	1.8	0.6	0.15
Urban areas	61	30.5	3	3	0.3
Terrain	–	91	4.6	1.5	0.15
Surfaced submarines	30.5	6	1.5	0.9	0.03

[a] Requires location of a class of units, object or activity of military interest.
[b] Requires determination of general target type.
[c] Requires discrimination within target types of known types.
[d] Requires size/dimension, configuration/layout, components construction, count of equipment, etc.
[e] SSM and SAM refer to surface-to-surface missiles (i.e., intercontinental or intermediate range missiles) and surface-to-air (i.e., anti-aircraft) missiles respectively.

Source: Reconnaissance Handy Book (McDonnell Douglas Corp., USA, p. 125.

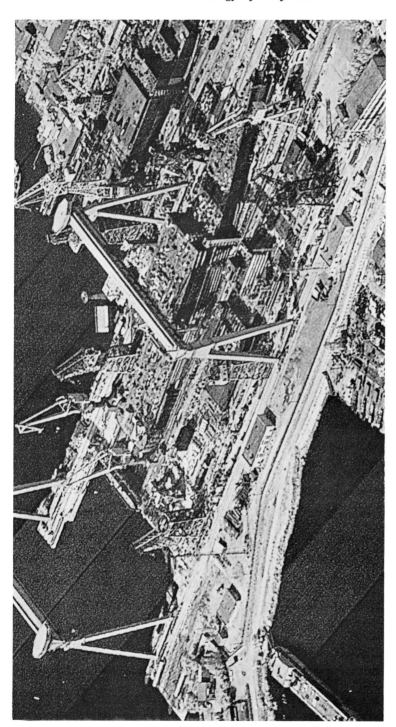

Figure 6. Computer-enhanced satellite photograph

A Soviet aircraft-carrier under construction at the Nikolaiev shipyard on the Black Sea as photographed by a US photo-reconnaissance satellite. The resolution of this photograph appears to be somewhat better than 1 m, probably not the best that can be achieved with current technology.

Source: Jane's Defence Weekly.

with 1.5 m resolution required for 'general identification'. Presumably this was the range of resolution available to the first US photographic satellites which in 1961 were able to 'spot' Soviet missile silos. [23]

In 1974, during the SALT II negotiations, it was pointed out that it would be possible to verify the proposed limitation on changes in silo diameter to a maximum of 10–15 per cent. [24] This implies that a ground resolution of at least 0.5–0.75 m was available in 1974.

Current resolution capabilities of about 0.1 m could detect even smaller changes in silo design as well as a great many other details of missile site layout; equipment such as radars, communications facilities, vehicles, storage buildings, and so on, can now also be seen and described in considerable detail.

Figure 6 shows a Soviet aircraft carrier under construction at a shipyard on the Black Sea. [25] The photo was taken from a US satellite and processed by one or more of the computerized techniques described below in the image processing section. Its resolution appears to be in the neighbourhood of 1 m, suggesting that even sharper satellite photographs are possible.

A brief study of table 2 will show that current satellite ground resolutions are sufficient to allow 'precise identification' of every item listed as well as 'description' of all but five. This adds up to a very impressive list of capabilities for satellite photo-reconnaissance.

While these capabilities are impressive and extremely valuable for verification purposes, it must be kept in mind that they represent the upper limits of achievable resolution. Such high-quality photography depends on good light, which in some important areas at high latitudes is not available for substantial portions of the year. Other areas suffer from unusually frequent cloud cover, making it impossible to photograph them for long periods of time. This limitation can be mitigated somewhat by manoeuvring the satellite to take advantage of fortuitous breaks in cloud cover. There has been a considerable effort applied over many years to accumulate accurate cloud cover statistics to be used in optimizing satellite orbits. [26] Objects which are underground, inside buildings, camouflaged or underwater cannot be photographed with visible light. However, as will be shown below, there are other techniques which can compensate to some degree for these limitations.

III. Infra-red detection and imaging

The cameras described in the previous section use *visible* light to produce their images. Visible light has wavelengths in the interval between 0.4 and 0.7 micrometres (μm), the same interval within which the Sun emits light with the greatest intensity. It is of course no coincidence that the human eye has evolved to take full advantage of the light emitted by the Sun.

Every object emits radiation with a spectrum of wavelength characteristic of its temperature. There are two important general laws which govern this phenomenon: one (called the Stefan-Boltzmann law) states that the total amount of radiation emitted by an object is proportional to the fourth power of its absolute temperature. The second law (called the Wien displacement law) states that the wavelength at which maximum intensity is emitted is inversely proportional to the absolute temperature.

Table 3 illustrates these laws by showing the relative brightnesses and dominant wavelengths of the same object at a number of different temperatures. Notice how strongly the brightness of an object depends on its temperature. An object at 84°C (still below the temperature of boiling water) is already emitting twice as much infra-red radiation as a body at room temperature, and by the time the object becomes just barely visible in a dark room (500°C) it is emitting 48 times the room temperature value. The same object raised to the surface temperature of the Sun would be 165 000 times brighter.

As the brightness of the object increases rapidly the dominant wavelength of the emitted radiation falls more slowly. The light from a room-temperature object is centred near 10 μm while the light from the Sun is centred near 0.5 μm, close to the centre of the visible portion of the electromagnetic spectrum.

The wavelength spectrum of any object extends well out on both sides of the maximum, although the extension to longer wavelengths is considerably greater. So, for example, the Sun emits considerable amounts of light in both the ultraviolet (less than 0.4 μm) and infra-red (greater than 0.7 μm) portions of the spectrum. Although most of the ultraviolet light is filtered out by the ozone layer, most of the solar infra-red light reaches the Earth's surface. A number of constituents of the atmosphere, especially water vapour and carbon dioxide, strongly absorb certain wavelengths of infra-red light, so the atmosphere is transparent only in certain ranges of wavelengths, called infra-red windows. The most important of these windows for reconnaissance purposes are from 0.7 to 1.0 μm (just above the visible spectrum), from 3 to 5 μm and from 8 to 14 μm.[27]

Table 3. Relative brightness and dominant wavelength of an object at different temperatures

| | Temperature | | Relative brightness | Dominant wavelength (μm) |
	(°C)	(K)		
Room temperature	20	293	1	9.87 ⎫
Sauna	84	357	2	8.13 ⎬ far infra-red
Just visible	500	773	48	3.75 ⎭
ICBM plume[a]	1 727	2 000	2 170	1.45 near infra-red
Sun surface	5 630	5 903	165 000	0.49 visible light
Nuclear fireball	10^7	10^7	1.4×10^{18}	2.9×10^{-4} X-rays

[a] See Hudson, R. D. and Hudson, J. W., 'The military applications of remote sensing by infra-red', *Proceedings of the IEEE*, Vol. 63, No. 1, January 1975, p. 123.

Photographic infra-red

Infra-red light with wavelengths between 0.7 and 1.0 μm is generally called photographic infra-red because it interacts with certain photographic films in exactly the same way as visible light, making it possible to take photographs using a broader spectrum of wavelengths. This has a number of advantages. First, at longer wavelengths the radiation is less scattered by small haze particles, so infra-red photographs taken on a hazy day will show distant objects with more clarity and contrast than visible-light photographs.[28] Other advantages derive from the high infra-red reflectance of vegetation and the greater contrast in reflectance between land and water. These can improve photographic contrasts and, most importantly, can often detect attempts at camouflage. While green paint, dying vegetation and living vegetation all look the same on an ordinary photograph, they look very different on an infra-red photograph.[29]

Film sensitive in the infra-red can be used in combination with other film to produce so-called 'false colour' images of areas on the Earth's surface.[30] The resolution of such photographs can be comparable to that of good quality black and white photographs using visible light, and 'multi-spectral' cameras are generally assumed to be part of the equipment of modern reconnaissance satellites.[31]

The use of photographic infra-red light faces problems similar to the use of visible light. Because the technique relies on reflected sunlight it is only usable in the daytime on relatively clear days. While the use of infra-red has some haze-penetrating capabilities this should not be overstated, and fog and cloud cover remain serious obstacles to satellite photography.[32]

Thermal infra-red

The two atmospheric windows at longer wavelengths are used to observe infra-red light emitted (as opposed to reflected) from hot or warm objects. These windows lie in what is called the thermal infra-red region, generally taken to range between 3 and 14 μm in wavelength.[33]

Photographic film cannot be used to detect light at these longer wavelengths since film sensitivity falls sharply beyond 1.1 μm. But there are many other materials which are sensitive to infra-red light at longer wavelengths. Semiconductor compounds such as silicon, lead sulphide, indium antimonide and lead tin telluride can absorb infra-red light and convert the energy into a detectable voltage or current. By this principle photoelectric cells can convert solar radiation directly into electricity.

Infra-red detectors can be made both extremely small and highly sensitive. They also have some important advantages over film in that they have a linear response and a much broader dynamic range. 'Linear response' means that the electrical output signal is directly proportional to the intensity of the light that falls on the detector. Film does not respond linearly. A large dynamic range allows for much greater sensitivity to contrast variations.

On the other hand thermal infra-red imagery cannot approach photographic imagery in resolution because of two important limitations. First, the much longer wavelength of thermal infra-red radiation leads to much larger diffraction effects (see above, equation 2). In order to achieve the same 3–4 cm diffraction limit on ground resolution obtained with visible light (see above, p. 25), an infra-red telescope would have to have a diameter about 20 times as large as the Space Telescope, that is, about 50 m. Second, there are limits to the density with which infra-red sensors can be packed in an array. Each individual sensor produces an electrical signal, and a single image might consist of more than one million such signals (see below, p. 36). Any attempt to further increase resolution causes an even more rapid increase in the rate at which information must be transmitted to produce images, and any attempt to use an array of detectors with the same density as the tiny silver halide grains on photographic film would require astronomically high data transmission rates.

As a result of these two limitations the best thermal infra-red imagery will generally have resolutions about 100 times poorer than the best visible light photographs,[34] that is, at best 10 m from an altitude of 200 km. In 1972 a US Air Force meteorological satellite was reported to have a ground resolution of 600 m from an orbital height of 830 km,[35] which becomes a resolution of 150 m at 200 m altitude. By 1982 it was reported that an infra-red telescope carried by the US space shuttle would provide better than 0.1 milliradian angular resolution, which corresponds to a 20 m ground resolution from an altitude of 200 km.[36] This particular telescope is not designed for ground surveillance, but it suggests that technological developments in optics, sensor arrays and information processing may be bringing thermal infra-red imaging close to its theoretical limits.

Resolutions of 20 m or so will never produce sharp pictures of warm objects on the ground but are useful for locating and measuring the temperatures of such objects. For example, a sensor with a 20 m resolution could easily locate nuclear power or other industrial facilities that generate heat. It could also make thermal maps of areas to display subtle temperature variations which might be created by underground objects or an underground nuclear test. Such thermal mapping would also be useful in monitoring an agreement to shut down plutonium production facilities, which require either cooling towers or a river to carry away waste heat. The thermal plume from the Savannah River plutonium reactors in the USA would be readily visible from a satellite.[37]

Sensitivities of thermal infra-red detectors to temperature differences are very great, so even a slight warming or cooling of the Earth in a localized region can be detected. For example, it was claimed as long ago as 1967 that airborne infra-red sensors designed to search for submarines could, under optimum conditions, detect temperature differences of only 0.005°C.[38] This would allow the detection of submarines at depths substantially greater than 40 m, the depth at which a submarine raises surface temperatures by 10–100 times this amount. If it were in fact possible to detect and track submarines at depths of a few hundred metres this would have serious implications for the vulnerability of nuclear missile submarines, which depend for their survival on an ability to hide in deep water.

Thermal infra-red images are generally taken at night to avoid interference from reflected solar infra-red light and the elevated temperature of the illuminated background. Night photography using thermal infra-red is an excellent reconnaissance and surveillance technique and could serve many functions in verification, for example in aerial monitoring of a military disengagement zone for illegal activities. Figure 7 shows a night infra-red image taken from an aircraft at an altitude of 300 m. Clearly visible on the image are a camp-fire near a road junction (careful examination of the image shows people near the camp-fire), vehicles whose engines are still warm from recent running, and a set of aluminium foil 'resolution targets'. The very low emissivity of the aluminium makes the strips appear black, and for contrast each one has been placed next to a small pit containing three or four hot charcoal briquets, the bright spot adjacent to the black strip.

Imaging systems

Infra-red imaging devices come in two varieties: those that operate in a *scanning* mode and those that employ a *staring* mode. In the scanning mode a single detector (or if multi-spectral detection is desired a few detectors with appropriate filters) is used in conjunction with a rotating or oscillating mirror to scan an area (see figure 8). In this way the radiation from adjacent patches of the area is focused sequentially on the detector and the current or voltage produced is monitored electronically and either stored on tape or transmitted directly to receivers on Earth, where the signal can be transformed back into an image of the scene. The image will show variations in temperature, with warmer areas appearing brighter than cooler ones. Such scanning imagers are

---

Figure 7. Night infra-red image
This image was produced from the digitized record of a thermal infra-red scanner in an aircraft at an altitude of 300 m. The large white spot at the upper left is an open campfire around which can be seen several people, recorded as small white spots. The bright spots adjacent to black strips just above right centre are vehicles whose engines had been warmed up and then turned off shortly before the image was recorded. The bright segment is the part of the vehicle which contains the engine, while the dark segment reveals a cold metal surface. The V-shaped set of images at the lower centre is a resolution target consisting of strips of aluminium foil (dark) placed next to small, 10 cm deep pits containing three or four hot charcoal briquets (bright). Notice the very different infra-red brightness of various types of vegetation and surface features (e.g., roads).

Source: Image courtesy of Daedalus Enterprises, Inc., Ann Arbor, MI, USA.

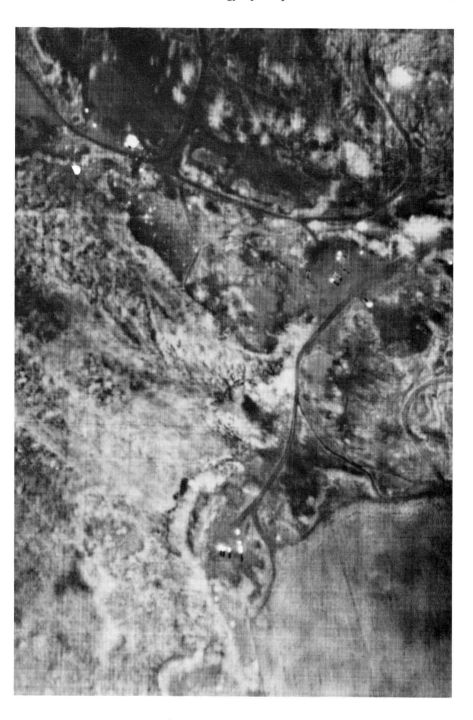

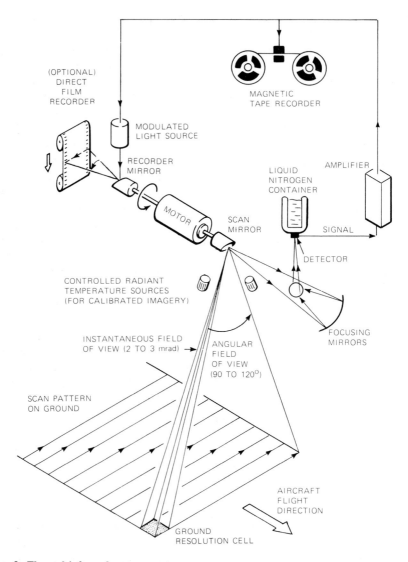

Figure 8. Thermal infra-red scanner system
As the scan mirror rotates it reflects infra-red radiation from a strip on the ground to a focusing mirror and then to a cooled detector. The signal from the detector is amplified and recorded. The recorded signal can then be used, either immediately or at some later time, to produce a photographic image by modulating a beam of light directed at photographic film. The calibration sources are used to provide brightness standards so that the temperatures of objects on the ground can be determined from the brightness of their images. Note that an instantaneous field of view of 2–3 mrad corresponds to a ground resolution of 400–600 m from a satellite at an altitude of 200 km or 60–90 cm from an aircraft at 300 m.

Source: Sabins, F. F., Jr, *Remote Sensing: Principles and Interpretation* (W. H. Freeman, San Francisco, 1978), p. 131, figure 5.9.

the most commonly used for thermal mapping and night surveillance and reconnaissance missions.

This ideal picture is greatly complicated in practical infra-red imagery by interference from other infra-red emitters. Radiation at certain wavelengths may come from objects of interest on the ground, but at other wavelengths it can be coming from some layer of the atmosphere. At still other wavelengths the atmosphere both absorbs radiation from objects on the ground and emits some of its own radiation, partially obscuring the object of interest.[39]

The radiation from an object depends not only on its temperature, but also on the nature of its emitting surface. The total radiation emitted at a given temperature depends directly on the size (i.e., surface area) of the object as well as on the radiation efficiency (emissivity) of the surface. Emissivity varies for different wavelengths, and different materials and surface textures have different emissivity functions. Therefore, if several infra-red frequencies are observed it is often possible to distinguish one type of hot object from another by comparing the infra-red 'signatures' of the two objects. For example, such signatures are associated with missile re-entry vehicles as they pass through the Earth's atmosphere. Friction with the air causes them to become very hot and to radiate intensely in the infra-red. Detection and spectral analysis of this radiation provides information on the size and shape of re-entry vehicles.[40] This technique was, of course, not created for the purpose of arms control verification, but for research and development on anti-ballistic missile systems. Nevertheless it has applications to verification, since measurements on re-entering warheads can help determine the throw-weight of a MIRVed ICBM, a parameter controlled by the SALT II Treaty.

The other form of infra-red imager is the staring type, which consists of a mosaic, or two-dimensional array, of small detectors placed in the focal plane of a telescope. Instead of scanning the field of view the imager 'stares' at it, just as an ordinary camera would do, except that the staring is continuous for the infra-red imager and not controlled by a shutter as in a camera. Such imagers can be made extremely sensitive, as illustrated by the ability of early-warning satellites stationed in geosynchronous orbits (36 000 km above the Earth's surface) to detect the exhaust plumes of missiles launched from the ground. These detectors are more than 100 times as far from their target as are the visible light cameras described in the previous section, yet geosynchronous satellites equipped with staring infra-red imagers can detect any launch of an intermediate or long-range ballistic missile anywhere within their field of view which, because of their long distance from the Earth, encompasses virtually an entire hemisphere.

While it is useful to detect objects like missile plumes and jet aircraft exhausts, it is even more useful to be able to track such objects. By tracking the exhaust plume of an ICBM during the powered segment of its flight an accurate prediction of the impact point of the warhead can be made. As usual such a capability has both military and arms control applications, and the military applications have apparently been important enough to provide the incentive to develop this capability to a high level of sophistication. US early-warning satellites can both detect and track Soviet ICBMs using infra-red radiation from the exhaust and can predict the impact point within one minute of the initial detection.[41] This precise tracking ability is useful in verifying restrictions on launch and throw-weights, but in doing so it also provides militarily important collateral data from which the accuracy of the missile can be estimated.

The exhaust plume of a missile is made up almost entirely of the products of fuel combustion, mainly carbon dioxide and water vapour. The molecules of these substances radiate energy strongly in the same spectral region as they absorb energy, at a wavelength of about 2.7 μm. Generally the detectors used to detect missile launches are designed to be most sensitive at this wavelength, which means that they cannot see the exhaust plume until it rises above any clouds, which, because they are saturated with water vapour, are opaque at 2.7 μm. However, even with this limitation the satellite is capable of tracking the missile through most of its powered flight. Another problem arises in tracking missiles launched at sea. Reflections from ocean waves cause a flickering noise background called 'ocean glitter' which is difficult to filter out of the signal received by the imager.[42]

Recent progress in micro-electronics has allowed the construction of three-dimensional mosaics in which the imaging sensors are deposited on top of sophisticated signal processing chips which convert the image directly into digital data for real-time transmission and display. Such a mosaic might consist of more than one million individual detector elements packed at a density of about 150 per square millimetre, equivalent to a resolution of 12 lines per millimetre.[43] When light falls on a detector it creates a small 'bunch' of electrons, whose size is proportional to the intensity of the light. The electrons then pass directly into a so-called 'charge-coupled device' which is capable of converting the array of one million individual electron bunches into a stream of digitized data ready for transmission to Earth.[44] Modern microprocessors allow extremely rapid and elaborate signal processing techniques to be applied to these data permitting, for example, the discrimination of the desired target from background clutter.[45] Mosaic arrays of this type can also track several objects simultaneously and, if they are made from detectors sensitive to longer wavelengths, can even be used to track relatively 'cold' objects such as satellites or re-entry vehicles in space.[46]

An example of the use of such mosaic staring detectors is the so-called 'Teal Ruby' system being prepared for the US Air Force (see figure 9).[47] This device is supposed to detect and track flying aircraft from an orbital height of 650 km. Its sensor uses 'thousands' of detector chips and is operated at a very low temperature (probably liquid helium temperature—about 4 K) to increase its sensitivity to long-wavelength infra-red radiation (up to about 16 μm).

The necessity for keeping an infra-red detector at a temperature much lower

Figure 9. Teal Ruby mosaic staring detector system
The focal plane of the sensor is visible at the centre of the dark, circular structure, which interfaces with sensor optics. Electronic components for the infra-red detectors in the focal plane are located in the cylindrical structure.

Source: Photo courtesy of US Air Force.

than that of the object it is looking at can be understood when it is recognized that the detector itself is a source of infra-red radiation whose spectrum and intensity depends on its own temperature. Attempting to detect an object at 20°C with an infra-red sensor at the same temperature would be equivalent to attempting to take a photograph using film that gave off its own light. The need for long-lasting, reliable cooling of infra-red sensors adds considerably to their cost.

The Teal Ruby system has encountered a number of developmental delays and cost overrun problems[48] suggesting that it is pushing at the current technological limits. If it is successful it will demonstrate the capability of monitoring from space the flights of aircraft or cruise missiles, a capability which could be very important in verifying a ban on testing or deployment of such weapons.

IV. Radar

The photographic and sensor systems described so far detect radiation of short wavelength (0.4–14 μm) either reflected or emitted by objects. These systems are generally referred to as 'passive' since they depend on radiation from other sources for their detection capability. In contrast an 'active' surveillance system generates its own radiation and then detects it after reflection from objects of interest. A common example of such an active system is a camera with a flash attachment.

Radar is an active system which employs electromagnetic radiation of much longer wavelengths than light—generally in the range 3–50 cm. A typical radar consists of a signal generator which produces a pulse of electromagnetic radiation; an antenna which sends this pulse off in a well-defined direction and then remains quiet in order to detect the return ('echo') from objects which reflect the radiation; a collection of electronic devices which process the return signal; and some form of visual display or recording device to enable the radar operator to 'see' the detected objects.

Radar surveillance has both advantages and disadvantages when compared with optical or infra-red techniques. First, because radar wavelengths are so much longer than those of light, radar waves do not interact strongly with small particles such as water droplets or suspended dust or aerosols. This means that radar has no trouble in penetrating any thickness of fog, cloud or other material opaque to short wavelength radiation. Second, because radar is an active system it can be used at any time of day or night. It has been called an "all-time, all weather sensor... not limited by any environmental factor".[49]

The disadvantages of radar have to do with its need for an accompanying power source, its relatively long wavelength, which means that small objects cannot be resolved and identified, and some peculiarities of image formation which make the job of image processing and interpretation more difficult. The latter will be discussed further in the section on image processing.

Despite their need for a power source radars can be quite portable. They are widely used on ships, aircraft and, more recently, on satellites, as well as at permanent ground stations. Three types of radar are most relevant to the issue of verification: large ground- or ship-based phased-array radars (PARs), used for early warning of attack, missile test monitoring, and space object tracking; over-the-horizon (OTH) radars, used to observe distant objects which are hidden from line-of-sight radars by the Earth's curvature; and synthetic aperture radars (SARs), used to produce high-resolution images of objects on the ground either from aircraft or satellites.

Phased-array radars

The purpose of large phased-array radars is to detect and track with high accuracy a large number of objects moving at high speeds, for example the many re-entry vehicles which would be approaching a country during a massive nuclear attack. Both the United States and the Soviet Union have a number of such radars, with the US versions having such exotic names as Cobra Dane (figure 10) and Pave Paws (figure 11).[50]

In order to resolve closely spaced objects at long distances the radar beam must have a very narrow spread in angle—it must have high angular resolution. The spreading of the beam is caused by the same diffraction effect discussed above in connection with an optical camera (see pp. 24–25) and the angular spread of the beam is given by the ratio of the wavelength of the radiation to the width of the antenna. For example, the Cobra Dane radar beam has a wavelength of 24 cm (called 'L-Band') and its aperture has a diameter of 29 m. This gives an angular spread of just about 0.01 radian or 0.57 degrees. Such a beam would be able to resolve two objects 10 km apart at a distance of 1 000 km.

Figure 10. The Cobra Dane radar
This phased-array radar based on Shemya Island in the Aleutians has a diameter of 29 m and consists of 34 769 individual elements of which 15 360 are active and 19 409 are 'dummy' elements. The latter could be activated at some future time if greater sensitivity were desired.

Source: Brookner, E., 'A review of array radars', *Microwave Journal*, Vol. 24, No. 10, October 1981, p. 25. Photo courtesy of Eli Brookner, Raytheon Co.

Figure 11. The Pave Paws radar
This radar is 22 m in diameter and uses 1 792 active elements and 885 dummy elements, a total of 2677.

Source: Brookner, E., 'A review of array radars', *Microwave Journal*, Vol. 24, No. 10, October 1981, p. 26. Photo courtesy of Raytheon Co.

The range resolution of a radar is defined as its ability to resolve two objects at different distances within the same beam angle. The distance to an object is determined by the time it takes the radar pulse travelling at the speed of light to go out to the object and return to the antenna. A second object slightly further away would be seen as a reflected pulse returning slightly after the first one. In order to separate these two pulses the duration in time of the pulse itself must be shorter than the time between the returning pulses. For example, the Cobra Dane radar is said to be able to resolve two objects whose distance from the radar differs by only 75 cm.[51] The radar pulse from the farther object must travel an extra 150 cm in its round trip, and since radar waves move at 3×10^8 m/s this adds only 5 nanoseconds (5×10^{-9} s) to the total travel time. Therefore the pulse duration transmitted by the radar must be shorter than 5 nanoseconds. (The actual radiated pulse has a longer duration than this in order to allow sufficient energy to be put into it. But by a process called 'pulse compression', which involves frequency or phase modulation, the effective duration of the pulse can be shortened to the required value.[52])

In addition to being able to locate an object in distance and angle a radar can also determine its velocity towards or away from the radar. When the pulse is reflected off the object, the frequency of the reflected radiation is changed in proportion to the speed of the moving reflector. This is called the Doppler effect, and radars can be designed to detect these 'Doppler shifts' and indicate the rate at which the distance to the object is increasing or decreasing. Velocity in the cross-beam direction cannot be measured this way and must be determined by 'tracking' the object with the beam.

In most common radars the beam is 'steered' by rotating the antenna. But this mechanical motion is too slow to allow the tracking of fast-moving objects, so in a phased-array radar the beam is steered electronically. The antenna is constructed as an array of many thousands of identical small antennas, each of which can be driven independently (see figure 12).[53] The resultant radar beam is the sum of all the individual beams, and by electronically varying the timing (phase) relationships among the many sub-beams, the full beam can be steered very rapidly. Rotations through large angles can be accomplished in millionths of a second.[54]

Figure 12. Individual phased-array elements
A close-up of the Pave Paws radar of figure 11. Each active element is a radiator of radar waves and a detector as well. Each element occupies an area of 0.14 m^2, which corresponds to a square with sides of about 38 cm. The elements themselves appear to be about 50 cm high.

Source: Photo courtesy of Eli Brookner, Raytheon Co.

This feature permits the Cobra Dane radar to track as many as 100 re-entry vehicles simultaneously at a distance of 2 000 km and make accurate measurements of their speed and trajectories.[55] Located on Shemya Island in the Aleutians, and accompanied by a smaller but similar ship-borne PAR called Cobra Judy, the Cobra Dane is well placed to monitor Soviet intercontinental ballistic missile tests. A number of qualitative features of Soviet ICBMs, such as throw-weight and accuracy, can be determined in this way.[56]

Phased-array radars are essential to any attempt to create an effective anti-ballistic missile (ABM) system, an application recently highlighted by the US discovery of such a radar under construction by the Soviet Union at Krasnoyarsk in Siberia. The USA has accused the Soviet Union of a violation of the ABM Treaty on the basis of this discovery. In reply the Soviet Union has made similar charges against the Shemya Island Cobra Dane radar. Such problems of interpretation are not surprising since phased-array radars can serve a wide variety of functions in which the simultaneous tracking of a number of flying objects is necessary. While the design of a given radar may be optimized for a specific purpose, for example to monitor tests of ICBMs, the performance characteristics are virtually indistinguishable from those needed to support an ABM system. A phased-array radar can therefore be at the same time a national technical means of verification and an apparent violation of a treaty. Such ambiguities are extremely difficult to resolve in a technical way. They are the stuff of political compromise.

Over-the-horizon radar

Normal radars are limited in useful range because the beam they produce travels in a straight line, while the Earth's surface is curved. This means that a beam emitted parallel to the Earth's surface at one point will pass other points on the surface at progressively higher altitudes, making it impossible to detect low flying aircraft at large distances, even though the beam still has sufficient power. For example, an aircraft flying at an altitude of 5 000 m cannot be seen by ground-based, line-of-sight radar at distances greater than 250 km.

The possibility of using radar at considerably greater distances arises from the reflection of radar waves by the Earth's ionosphere, a layer of electrically charged gases at an altitude of from 80 to a few hundred kilometres. When they encounter the free electrical charges which constitute the ionosphere, radar waves are partially reflected and can return towards the Earth's surface at distances of from 1 000 to 3 000 km from their point of origin (see figure 13).[57] If they are reflected from an object during this downward portion of their path, the waves can return along roughly the same path and be detected near the original antenna location.

It is not surprising to learn that an OTH radar antenna must be both large and powerful if it is to accomplish such a task. One such radar under develop-

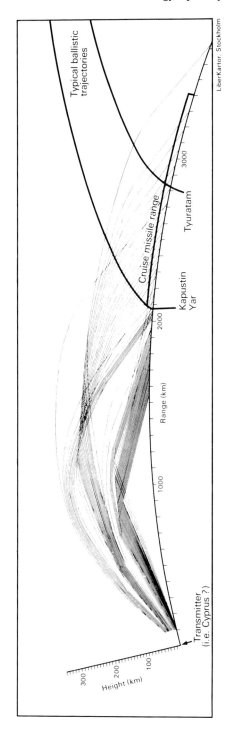

Figure 13. Backscatter over-the-horizon (OTH) radar

Radio beams from the transmitter are reflected back down to Earth by the ionosphere. Scattered radio energy is reflected back to the transmitter along the same paths. Objects such as missiles reflect a signal detectable at the transmitter site. The figure shows trajectories of missiles from Kapustin Yar and Tyuratam superimposed on the ray paths of a typical OTH radar.

Source: SIPRI, *World Armaments and Disarmament, SIPRI Yearbook 1980* (Taylor & Francis, London, 1980), p. 298.

ment by the US Air Force and the General Electric Corporation consists of an antenna which is 690 m long located on the eastern coast of Maine in the USA (see figure 14).[58] Plans are eventually to expand this antenna to a length of 1 100 m and to have it employ a variety of wavelengths between 11 and 60 m. At the 11 m wavelength the beam should have an angular width of 0.01 radian, giving it a target resolution of 20 km at a distance of 2 000 km (see equation 2, p. 24). The beam can be steered electronically to track moving objects in a manner similar to that of a phased-array radar.[59] Such a broad beam would not be able to resolve and identify aircraft by their size or shape, but it could detect and track objects, such as ballistic or cruise missiles, which would be difficult to observe reliably in any other way. The greatest advantage of a stationary OTH radar over satellite-based sensors is its ability to maintain more-or-less continuous surveillance of relatively small areas, such as missile test ranges.

Figure 14. OTH transmitting antenna array
This experimental OTH transmitting antenna was located near Moscow/Caratunk, Maine in the USA and had a length of 690 m. The receiving and signal processing site is near Columbia Falls, Maine about 175 km to the south-east. The transmitting antennas are the diagonal elements in front of the 30 m high towers. The antennas were driven by twelve 100 kW transmitters powerful enough to detect and track aircraft at ranges of 3 000 km.[58] The experimental system has been dismantled and is in the process of being upgraded to an operational system.

Source: US Air Force.

There are some serious difficulties which restrict rather severely the applicability of such radars to verification. The radar must be located so that the major portion of the beam path is over water, and this naturally restricts the number of areas that can be monitored in this way.[60] There has been speculation, but no firm evidence, that the USA has such a radar deployed in Cyprus, an ideal location for observing flight tests of missiles or aircraft at the Soviet testing centres of Kapustin Yar and Tyuratam.[61] If such a radar exists it may be possible for the USA to monitor the boost phase of Soviet rocket tests and use these data along with information gathered by other sensors to verify SALT limitations on launch weight and throw-weight.

It is interesting to note that given the size and power of such a radar, it would be impossible to keep its existence and capabilities secret from a state like the Soviet Union, which possesses sophisticated satellite and electronic reconnaissance systems. Therefore, if such an installation does exist, there is no military justification for keeping it a secret. However, such secrecy does have political motivations and these are examined in chapter 4.

Synthetic aperture radar

One feature held in common by all radars which resolve small objects at large distances is the enormous size of their antennas. The OTH radar just described is nearly 700 m long, and the Cobra Dane and Pave Paws radars have diameters of 29 m and 22 m respectively.[62] The areas of the two PARs are 660 m^2 and 384 m^2, and each must be constructed from thousands or tens of thousands of individual radiating and detecting elements.

The requirement for large antenna size is dictated in part by the need to put large amounts of energy into the beam in order to be able to detect small, distant objects. But it is also required if a beam with a narrow angular spread is to be achieved, that is, if the diffraction spreading phenomenon is to be minimized. As was shown above, even the 29 m diameter of Cobra Dane is capable of only about a 10 km resolution at a distance of 1 000 km. So even if such a large antenna could be carried on a satellite, its ability to resolve small objects on the ground would be quite limited. For example, to achieve a 10 m resolution from an altitude of 200 km would require an angular beam spread of only 50 microradians, 200 times narrower than the Cobra Dane beam. Producing such a narrow beam of radiation with a wavelength of 24 cm would require a circular antenna 200 times the size of Cobra Dane—almost 6 km in diameter. Obviously some other method must be used to obtain high-resolution radar images from satellites.

This method is called 'synthetic aperture' radar. It uses a relatively small antenna but takes advantage of the motion of the antenna relative to the ground to create the same effect as that of a very large antenna. Figure 15 illustrates how this works.[63] A satellite or aircraft passing over some region of interest emits radar pulses which are directed downward and to either side

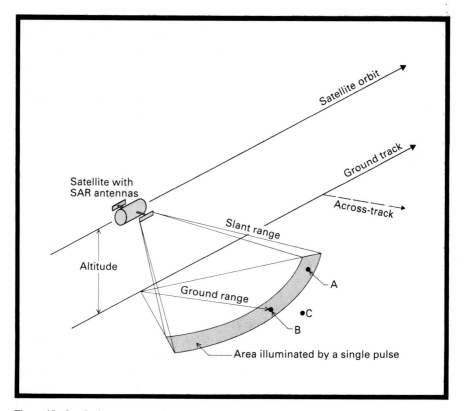

Figure 15. Synthetic aperture radar
Pulses of radiation emitted by the satellite antenna are reflected from objects on the ground and
received by the same antenna. The shaded area on the ground shows the width of a strip defined
by the duration of a single pulse. Two objects within that area (A and B) cannot be distinguished
by a single pulse from the radar. However, if all the pulses which reflect off both A and B while
the satellite is passing overhead are stored in the satellite and processed, these objects can be
resolved.

of the ground track. Reflections of these pulses from objects on the ground
return to the satellite where they are detected and recorded. The ground resolution problem can be described in terms of three objects on the ground denoted
by A, B, and C. Objects A and C are at different distances from the satellite,
so their resolution in range is accomplished in the normal way. The pulse is
made of very short duration so that the return pulses from two objects very
close together can be distinguished. For example, if C is 1.5 m further from
the antenna than A, then the pulse to and from C must travel 3 extra metres
at the speed of light, a delay of 10 nanoseconds (10^{-8} s). This requires only
that the radar pulse be less than 10 nanoseconds long, a goal already seen to
be achievable in ground-based radars (see above). Therefore, resolutions in
range of the order of 1 m should be achievable from satellite or airborne
SARs.

Resolution in angle is another matter, and figure 15 shows the objects A and B to be equal distances from the satellite and both within the angular spread of the beam from the relatively small antenna carried by the satellite. The width of this beam can be estimated if it is assumed that the radar wavelength is 10 cm and the antenna is 5 m long. Such a beam would have an angular spread of 0.02 radians (see equation 2, p. 24) which means that a swath 10 km wide would be illuminated at a slant range of 500 km. Even if A and B were as much as 10 km apart, the return pulses from them would be indistinguishable and they would not be resolved.

The solution to this problem lies in the fact that A and B will stay within the beam for many pulses, and that during this time their spatial relationships to the satellite will change continuously in different ways. As an example suppose that A and B lie at a distance of 400 km from the satellite ground track, and that the satellite is at an altitude of 300 kilometres. The radar pulses to A and B must then travel a round trip of 1 000 km (this example assumes that the Earth is flat; a more accurate treatment would change the numbers somewhat but not the essential features of the example), which takes 3.3 milliseconds, during which time the radar must be in the receiving mode. Once the echo is received from the objects of interest another pulse can be emitted, so if A and B are at the outer boundaries of the region being surveyed the radar can emit pulses at the rate of 300 per second. Since the satellite is moving at the rate of 7.5 km/s and the width of the beam is 10 km (see above) an object such as A will stay within the beam for 1.33 seconds, during which time it will reflect 400 pulses back to the satellite, each from a slightly different location relative to the satellite. If the entire history of 400 pulses from each object could be analysed then enough information would exist to distinguish A from B and in fact distinguish objects even much closer together in the direction parallel to the ground track.

This process of combining the information of many pulses from a moving antenna is exactly equivalent to what can be done using a single pulse from a very long antenna. So the resolution obtainable parallel to the ground track is the same as could be obtained using 24 cm waves from an antenna with a length of 20 km or about 10^{-5} radians. At 500 km range this represents a ground resolution of only 5 m, comparable to the size of the antenna. A more rigorous mathematical treatment of this problem shows that the theoretical limit of resolution is one-half the length of the antenna.[64] So in principle this satellite could achieve resolutions of 1.5 m in the cross-track dimension and 2.5 m parallel to the ground track in a swath 800 km wide. Such resolution is about 10 times poorer than that obtainable from optical infra-red photographs, but this sacrifice in resolution is compensated for by the ability of synthetic aperture radars to obtain their pictures through the heaviest cloud cover and at any time of night or day. It is also very important to note that the ground resolution of an SAR, unlike all other imaging techniques discussed so far, does not depend on the distance between the antenna and the

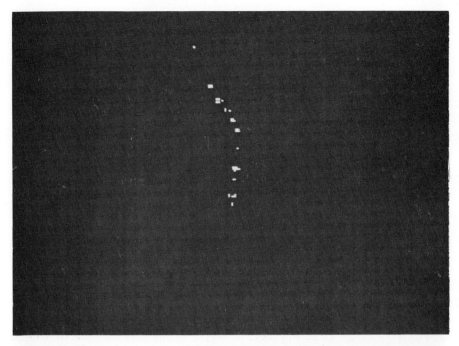

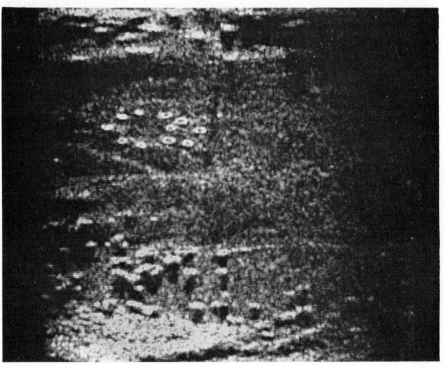

target.[65] This means that SAR images from satellites can have just as high resolutions as those taken from aircraft at less then one-hundredth the altitude. It also means that SAR satellites can be placed in higher, longer-lasting orbits as long as sufficient power is provided to make up for the additional wave-propagation distance.

The problem of supplying the electrical power for an SAR is a serious one. Existing space-based SARs require at least 20 times as much power as optical photographic systems, and if this is to be supplied by arrays of photovoltaic solar cells these arrays must be very large and expensive. Such concerns have led to serious discussion of using nuclear power sources for military SAR systems, and such power sources are under active development.[66]

Reference to table 2 (p. 26) will show that if SAR resolutions of 1–2 m are achievable, they will be very useful in many monitoring tasks, especially if SAR is used in conjunction with other, higher resolution forms of imagery. As to when such resolutions may be available, one forecast predicts 1 m resolutions from space-based radars by the year 2000 and states that "Radar component capabilities and available power sources are such that progress in achievable resolution is mainly paced by available data-handling rates".[67] Meanwhile, SARs mounted on aircraft such as the US RC-135, TR-1, or SR-71 recon-naissance aircraft probably already have at least such resolutions. One source attributes to such airborne SARs a range of 300 nautical miles (560 km) "enabling the TR-1 to 'see' at least into Eastern Poland [from FR Germany] and probably beyond. On surveillance missions the TR-1 can cover 131,800 sq nm [450 000 km²] per hour".[68] Figure 16 shows images of tank formations obtained with one such radar which is produced and advertised by the General Electric Company.

The major difficulty which remains to be solved for satellite-based SAR is the rapid processing of vast amounts of data, and this problem is discussed further in the next section. As this obstacle is overcome much more extensive use of SARs can be expected for a wide variety of Earth survey, military intelligence and arms control verification tasks.

V. Image processing

The information obtained from optical and infra-red photography and radar is in the form of images. These can be photographs, readings from sensors,

---

Figure 16. SAR images of tank formations
Two SAR images, one of a tank/truck column (top) and the other an assembled tank formation, (bottom) were made by an airborne radar system called Multimode Surveillance Radar (MSR) manufactured by the General Electric Corp.

Source: Photos courtesy of General Electric Aerospace Electronic Systems, Utica, NY, USA.

or detected radar signals which have been recorded on film, magnetic tape, or in the memory of a computer. These images must now be put into a form in which they can be examined and analysed by skilled interpreters. It is conceivable that some day this process of recognition and interpretation of images might be almost totally automated, and this particular aspect of "artificial intelligence" research is receiving considerable attention.[69] But at present, and for the foreseeable future, the involvement of a skilled and experienced human intelligence is essential for the interpretation of photographic images. Considering that ground resolutions of 10 cm are now possible, and comparing this with the vast areas that are routinely photographed (not all at such high resolutions, of course), it is clear that the number of images being routinely scanned and interpreted by intelligence analysts must be enormous.[70] There are simply not enough analysts to handle the flow of military and commercial information. For example, probably 90 per cent of the data gathered to date by the US Earth Resources Satellite programme has not yet been analysed, and there exists a genuine danger of the intelligence system being swamped by unmanageable amounts of data. A similar flood of data has inundated the US Infrared Astronomy Satellite (IRAS) programme.[71] If such quantities of data are to be effectively utilized, automated analytical methods will have to be devised to reduce the load on human interpreters by filtering and pre-analysing images.[72]

The images received from modern satellites are almost never analysed in their raw form. They are first processed to make the job of interpretation easier. Image processing is a general term which includes two sub-classes of operation: *restoration* and *enhancement*.[73] Image *restoration* is the process of correcting certain image defects caused by transmission through a less than perfectly transparent medium, distortions and limitations of optics, relative motion of camera and target, incorrect exposure times, and so on. Such restoration is generally based on some mathematical model of the processes which have degraded the image. Its object is to produce the highest possible fidelity of the image to the object it represents.

The purpose of image *enhancement* is to alter the image in ways which clarify or accentuate objects of interest and suppress unwanted background or redundant information. While enhancement can also employ mathematical models,[74] the range of possible techniques is far broader, more flexible and more subjective than formal models would permit. Image enhancement has perhaps more appropriately been called a "bag of tricks"[75] whose objective is to produce optimal image "quality", a concept for which no mathematical criterion exists. Such techniques include manipulations of contrast and colour and the sharpening of edges to highlight objects of interest.[76] In such manipulations the skill and imagination of the human interpreter are an essential ingredient, and since different interpreters have different levels of skill and imagination; "an image which causes one analyst to conclude that no enhancement is possible may be treated with great success by another analyst. For images with great significance, such as those which might be used in weapons verification monitoring, it is disturbing to think of the consequences of an analyst failing to produce the optimum visual quality from a given image".[77]

Virtually all image processing is now carried out on digital computers, and the first step is therefore to convert the image into digital form. The only major exception to this generalization is the photographic technique of displaying synthetic aperture radar pictures (see below). Images from sensors which convert light directly into electrical signals can easily be converted into digital form for direct transmission back to Earth. Images recorded on photographic film are digitized by developing the film and scanning the image with a light-sensitive sensor. The digitized electrical signals from this sensor are stored on magnetic tape or in a computer memory for further processing.

The typical digital format for image processing is to have each picture element, called a 'pixel', represented by a binary number of 8−12 bits.[78] An 8-bit number would produce a 'dynamic range' of brightness values from 0 for total black to 255 for full white. There is in fact a wide variation in the dynamic-range capabilities of different sensors. Photographic film or a television screen can cover a dynamic range of only about 100, while modern charge-coupled device sensors can have dynamic ranges of 5 000, that is, they can distinguish 5 000 different levels of brightness.[79] Such discrimination is obviously helpful in situations where subtle differences of brightness are important, but it also adds to the information processing demands, since a dynamic range of 5 000 requires that each pixel be represented by 13 binary digits instead of 8. In practice this would involve the use of chips with 16-bit word lengths, since such chips are relatively cheap and available.

Some idea of the amount of information contained in a single high-resolution photograph can be obtained by imagining a 15 cm × 15 cm photograph with a film resolution of 50 lines per mm. A single pixel on such a photograph would measure only 20 μm^2 and the entire picture would contain 56 million pixels. A digitized record of such a photograph would therefore contain 56 million 8-bit binary numbers. High-resolution aerial or satellite photographs can contain more than 100 times as much information as this.[80]

Once an image has been digitized there are a wide variety of operations that can be carried out under the general rubric of image restoration or enhancement. A few of these can be mentioned briefly here, and more details can be found in the references.

Image restoration

Two examples of image restoration are noise suppression and corrections for lens or mirror distortions. 'Noise' is a familiar phenomenon in all signal processing. A television viewer attempting to watch a programme coming from a distant transmitter will see 'snow' on the screen as random noise signals compete with the weak programme signal. The hiss or static on a weak radio station is another example.

Noise is an essentially random phenomenon, so it is amenable to analysis by mathematical techniques which exploit this randomness. Since an information-carrying signal (say a photograph) has a high degree of coherence, it is possible to devise computer routines (called noise-cleaning masks) which accentuate this coherence and suppress random noise signals.[81] Figure 17 illustrates an example of the effects of one such noise-cleaning operation.

All optical systems introduce some distortion into the images they create, although this can be minimized by careful design and construction. The remaining distortion can be analysed mathematically, both from basic optical principles and by empirical measurements on the actual optical system. This analysis can then be translated into a computer program which can be applied to any image produced by the system to remove the distortions. Such routines can also be used to produce a sharp focus in slightly out-of-focus image or to correct for blurring caused by the relative motion of camera and subject (see figure 18). In principle, and almost certainly in practice, any degradation or distortion of an image which can be expressed in an empirical or analytical algorithm can be corrected for in this way. Even diffraction effects can be reduced by such algorithms, although there is no way to obtain information

 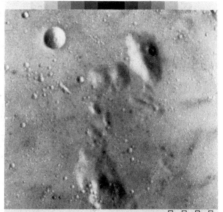

Figure 17. Noise cleaning
Image noise caused by sensor or signal errors usually produces random pixels which are very different from their neighbours (see image on left). These noise pixels can be removed by a simple computerized algorithm which computes for each pixel the difference between its brightness value and the average brightness of the eight nearest neighbours. If this difference exceeds some chosen threshold (49 in the images above) the deviant pixel is replaced by the average of the neighbours. The image on the right is the result of the noise cleaning algorithm.

Source: Photos courtesy of Vicom Systems, San José, CA, USA.

Figure 18. Motion de-blurring
The photograph on the left was blurred by intentionally moving the camera during the exposure. A computer program determined the direction and the extent of the camera's motion from the digitized photograph (left) and then produced the restored image (right).

Source: Photos courtesy of Michael Cannon, Los Alamos National Laboratory, Los Alamos, NM, USA.

beyond the fundamental limit described above (see pp. 24–25).[82] Still, if the diffraction limit is 5 cm, objects with dimensions of 10–20 cm will be significantly distorted by diffraction effects, and their resolution could be greatly improved with a diffraction-correcting algorithm.

Image enhancement

The single most important application of image enhancement is in the manipulation of contrast to increase the visibility of objects in shadow, obscured by haze, or photographed with too much or too little exposure. Contrast enhancement can be done in several ways, only two of which will be mentioned here: histogram equalization and adaptive filtering.

Histogram equalization[83] begins with the construction of a histogram, that is, a frequency distribution of brightness in the picture. This is done by counting the number of pixels having each brightness level and plotting these numbers on a bar graph.[84] An underexposed or low-contrast picture will utilize only a small portion of the available dynamic range of film, and contrast can therefore be enhanced by expanding the histogram to take up the full range. By redistributing some brightness values the histogram can also be levelled. The two processes greatly enhance the contrast in the picture, as illustrated in figure 19.

A somewhat more complex technique that achieves similar results is called adaptive filtering and is illustrated in figure 20.[85] The thin cloud cover almost totally obscures the image in two ways: first, it partially obstructs the transmission of light from the ground to the camera; and second, it reflects considerable amounts of light directly back to the camera causing overexposure of the haze relative to that of the ground. The adaptive filtering process first computes the average brightness and the local contrast values for all regions of the picture and then reduces the average brightness and increases the variations in such a way that contrast is greatly enhanced.

One of the most important purposes of image enhancement is the detection of objects, some of which may be so small that their images comprise only a few pixels. Such small, indistinct images are extremely difficult to pick out with the unaided eye, so a number of techniques have been developed to make object detection more reliable and efficient. One such technique is optical image subtraction in which two images of the same scene taken at different times are optically combined in such a way that the earlier image is 'subtracted' from the later one.[86] The result is an image which records only the *changes* in the scene in the interval between the two images, thereby highlighting objects which have been moved into or out of the area.

A second object detection technique uses an intensity prediction algorithm somewhat analogous to the noise cleaning masks described above,[87] but now the purpose is to enhance anomalies instead of eliminating them. In this process the expected intensity of each pixel is predicted from the intensity

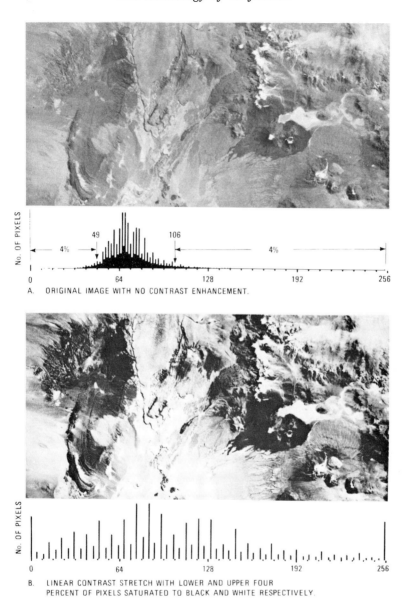

A.   ORIGINAL IMAGE WITH NO CONTRAST ENHANCEMENT.

B.   LINEAR CONTRAST STRETCH WITH LOWER AND UPPER FOUR
     PERCENT OF PIXELS SATURATED TO BLACK AND WHITE RESPECTIVELY.

Figure 19. Histogram equalization
The top picture shows a low-contrast satellite photograph of a region on the Chilean–Bolivian border. Beneath the photograph is the histogram of pixel intensity values, and the narrowness of this histogram is directly related to the lack of contrast in the photograph. The lower picture is the result of the histogram equalization process which makes use of the full dynamic range of the display medium to enhance contrast and emphasize details which are obscure on the unprocessed image.

Source: Sabins, F. F., 'Thermal infrared imagery and its application to structural mapping in Southern California', *Geological Society of America Bulletin*, Vol. 80, 1969, pp. 397–404, figure 2.

Figure 20. Adaptive filtering
The photograph on the left is of an airport runway almost totally obscured by haze. The image on the right is the result of applying the adaptive filtering contrast enhancement process mentioned in the text. The diagonal lines on the enhanced image are called 'digital line-artifacts' and can be removed by yet another restoration procedure.

Source: Peli, T. and Verly, J. G., 'Digital line-artifact removal', *Optical Engineering*, Vol. 22, No. 4 July/August 1983, pp. 479–484, figures 12 and 14.

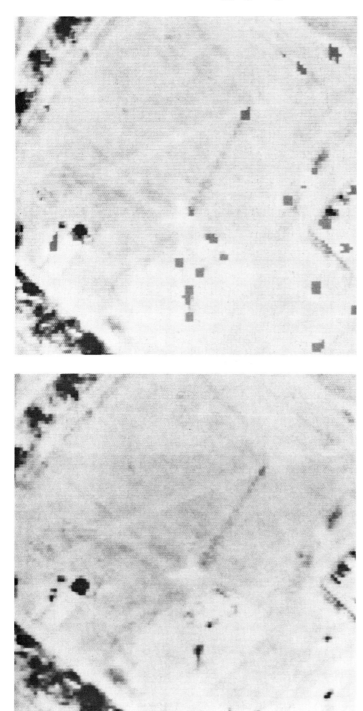

Figure 21. Object detection

The image on the right is the result of applying the object detection algorithm to the low-resolution image on the left. The 'objects' are the rectangular dark grey spots which are made up of at most a few pixels and are therefore not identifiable. While it is possible that very small 'objects' are in fact noise pixels, the algorithm is designed to make the number of false alarms small. Therefore it is highly probable that most of the objects detected are in fact real objects which might be identified by a higher resolution image acquired at some future time.

Source: Photos courtesy of Thomas F. Quatieri, Lincoln Laboratories, MIT, Lexington, MA, USA.

values of a large number of pixels in its neighbourhood. A statistical test is then applied to determine if the pixel intensity differs significantly from the predicted value, in which case it is classified as an anomaly, that is, an object (see figure 21). An object detection process such as this would be very useful in examining low-resolution images to determine if there is sufficient interest to warrant the taking of higher resolution photographs to better identify the detected objects.

These are only a sample of the image enhancer's 'bag of tricks', and many more exist.[88] Generally an interpreter working with an important picture will use several such techniques, and it has now become possible to build special computers capable of applying these techniques so rapidly that an interpreter can experiment with various restoration and enhancement techniques sitting at a computer console and observing the changes in the image in real time.[89] Even relatively complex operations such as image subtraction can be accomplished in real time.[90]

Figure 22. VLSIC chip
This very large-scale integrated circuit combines two types of memory and a central processing unit on a chip that measures about 6 mm square. It can execute five million instructions per second, about 100 times faster than conventional microcomputers, making it very useful in image processing applications.

Source: Photo courtesy of Texas Instruments Inc.

It is clear from just the small sample of techniques described here that remarkable improvements can be made in satellite photographs as long as sufficient computer capacity and ample numbers of skilled interpreters are available. Given the rapid reductions in size and increases in speed of present-day and projected computers, the problem of sufficient capacity would seem to be soluble. For example, it has been estimated that a contrast enhancement of a single image requires between 100 million and 1 000 million individual computer operations.[91] But one forecast of computing capabilities predicted image processing speeds of 10^{12} bits per second by the mid-1980s.[92] Such a computer could perform hundreds of contrast enhancements per second, enabling the kind of real-time interactive interpretation described above. The situation is expected to continue to improve as the development of microelectronic technology continues. Improvements have in some cases proven to be even more rapid than expected, producing memory chips which can store one million bits of information on a 50 mm^2 chip.[93] Other chips designed for very high-speed processing have achieved rates of 100 million multiplication operations per second.[94] Figure 22 shows a so-called 'very large-scale integrated circuit' (VLSIC) which combines both memory and processing functions on a single chip. Individual feature sizes on such a chip are as small as 5 μm.[95]

Radar image processing

A radar image is created from radiation which has been reflected off distant objects and returned to a detector. The return signal is in the form of a fluctuating voltage, which must be processed electronically to convert it into a bright spot on a screen calibrated to show the distance and direction to the object. Such radar images are the stock in trade of air traffic controllers, fighter pilots, reconnaissance aircraft, ship navigators and many others. A similar image is obtained from the large phased-array radars, although with these the display must be more sophisticated and the amount of electronic processing much greater.

For synthetic aperture radar the signal processing problem is truly gigantic. As was shown above, the location of a single object with good resolution will require the information contained in many hundreds of complex voltage pulses. Each pulse reflected from the object also contains information on the many other objects encountered by that same pulse, and the creation of a detailed image requires an enormous number of elementary mathematical computations.

A example of the magnitude of the problem is the SAR imagery obtained from Seasat, a US ocean surveillance satellite which was placed in orbit in 1978.[96] Seasat images had 25 m resolution and the satellite could transmit the raw data for a 40×40 km image (2.56 million pixels) in 2.5 seconds. The digital processing of these data into a visible image requires the equivalent of

10 billion (10^{10}) multiplication and addition operations. As recently as 1979 this process required 25 hours of computer time for each 40×40 km image.

Such computational problems explain why digital methods have not been used extensively for SAR image processing until very recently. The traditional method has been to use the returning radar signal to modulate a beam of light which in turn exposes photographic film.[97] The returns from a single radar pulse then appear as a thin vertical strip of varying brightness on the film. The film is moved so that subsequent pulses will produce adjacent strips until an entire piece of film is exposed. The image produced on the film is a 'hologram' of the scene, that is, an image which is related to the scene by a complex mathematical transformation.[98] The transformation can be performed optically by shining a laser beam on the hologram and manipulating the transmitted light with lenses. In this way the hologram can be converted into a high-resolution 'photograph' in a single operation.

The optical process requires no digitizing or computing (it is called an 'analog' process), but it does require the use of film with all of the accompanying inconvenience of chemical development. This has made it awkward to use in satellites, and unsuitable for the production of images in real time. Nevertheless, some very high-quality images have been obtained in this way and in January 1982 the optical process was still six times faster in producing images than the best digital processor available at that time.[99]

However, the rapid increase in speed and compactness of digital computers promises that high-quality, real-time SAR images will be available in the very near future.[100] One system under test is designed for use in fighter aircraft. It will achieve resolutions of 2.5 m and process the images with a computer capable of performing 45 million complex operations per second and storing 3 million bits of information (300 000–400 000 pixels). The computer itself weighs only 32 kg, uses 375 watts of power and occupies a volume of only 0.05 m^3 (roughly the size of an office typewriter).[101] It should be emphasized that such computational capabilities are required for real-time imaging, and most monitoring tasks in arms control verification do not require such rapid image analysis. The real-time capability has been mentioned here only to show that existing and projected capabilities are already more than adequate for many verification tasks.

Even when a good radar image is obtained it still requires skilled interpretation. Radar waves reflect differently from many surfaces than do light waves, and a given object can look very different on a radar image if its orientation changes with respect to the radar beam or if it is in motion. One peculiar property of synthetic aperture radar images is that a moving object appears on the image as stationary but in a different location, depending on its velocity relative to the aircraft or satellite taking the picture. Interpreting such images may be very tricky, and considerable effort is being put into classifying various kinds of radar image for more routine interpretation. One technique that promises vast improvements in object identification capability is to merge SAR images with visible and infra-red images of the same scene. Radar images are principally responsive to surface shapes and contours, while visible/infra-red images are more sensitive to surface chemistry. Combining the three types of image provides much more information than can be obtained from any single one, a good example of the synergism between different systems.[102]

Since radar signals are subject to several forms of attenuation and distortion there is also a need for image restoration and enhancement techniques similar to those used in visual photography. Such techniques exist already and are also well on their way to being digitized and automated.

All of these capabilities lead to the unmistakable conclusion that satellite cameras, sensors and radars will permit observation of objects and activities on the surface of the Earth in remarkable detail from altitudes of several hundred kilometres. The major limitation on all of this will remain the number of experienced, talented and reliable human monitors and interpreters. Such people will require training to a high standard of integrity and professionalism, and much of the success of any verification regime will depend on their alertness, skill and integrity. It is safe to assume that there already exists a large number of such people in the intelligence agencies of the USA, the USSR and other countries. The acquisition and retention of such people would be one of the highest priorities for any international satellite monitoring agency (see chapter 4).

VI. Seismology

There is no technical area of verification which can even approach seismology for the volume of detailed analytical studies available in the open literature. Since the early 1950s there has been an active interest in detecting underground nuclear explosions for both intelligence and arms control reasons, and many states have sponsored active research programmes in this area. The United States alone has spent over $600 million on research and instrumentation related to verification of a nuclear test ban agreement[103] and, because of the high degree of international co-operation required for seismological research, most of the knowledge gained from this intensive programme is in the public domain.

A brief review such as this cannot hope to do justice to this interesting and still very active field. Only the basic concepts are introduced here along with an outline of the capabilities and limitations of current technology. For more detailed studies the reader is referred to any of a number of excellent recent reviews.[104]

There are a great many analogies between the basic principles of seismology and those of electromagnetic radiation which have been considered in previous sections. In both cases the fundamental phenomenon is a form of radiation which propagates for long distances in the form of waves. The radiation is emitted from a source, scattered or reflected off of objects in its path, absorbed or dispersed in transmission through a medium and detected by instruments which can record arrival times, frequency spectra, amplitudes and polarizations. In the case of seismology the source is some short-lived release of energy, such as an explosion or an earthquake; the medium of transmission is the interior or surface of the Earth; and the detectors are seismometers, instruments which respond to extremely small displacements of the Earth at their

Figure 23. Portable short-period seismometer
The uncased instrument to the right shows the suspension of the oscillating mass by springs. This is one of the most widely used instruments for recording the short-period P-waves from earthquakes or underground explosions. Its maximum response is in the neighbourhood of 1 Hz, that is, a period of 1 second.

Source: Photo courtesy of Teledyne Geotech, Garland, TX, USA.

point of location. Seismometers can be in the form of individual instruments (analogous to a single infra-red sensor element or radar antenna) or arrays of instruments co-ordinated by electronic processors (analogous to phased-array radars). [105]

The basic design of a seismometer is very simple. A mass is hung from springs which are attached to a frame rigidly fixed to the Earth—preferably on or in solid rock. When the Earth moves the mass is set into movement by the springs and this movement is converted to an electrical signal by a magnet surrounding the mass (see figure 23). The sensitivity of modern seismometers is remarkable. The motion of the Earth in all but the most violent seismic disturbances is imperceptible to human beings, but useful information can be extracted from motions with amplitudes as small as or even smaller than one nanometre (10^{-9} m), comparable to the diameter of a single atom. However, even this is not good enough for the detection of very small events at long distances, so new instruments are being designed capable of faithfully recording displacements 10 000 times smaller than this, that is, between 10^{-14} and 10^{-13} m.[106] Such instruments must be located where seismic 'noise' (the random disturbances caused by winds, waves, human activity, etc.) is at very low levels. There is a continuing search for such areas, with a major focus in the United States on placing sensitive seismometers in deep 'bore-holes' in the ocean floor. [107]

While there are many similarities between electromagnetic and seismic waves there are also some very importance differences. One of the most fundamental results from the different mechanisms by which the waves are excited and the various media through which they propagate. While electromagnetic waves come in many 'colours' (i.e., frequencies) there is really only one basic wave type involved. Seismic waves on the other hand come in many forms as well as in a wide range of frequencies. There are two types of 'body' wave (i.e., those which pass through the body of the Earth), one which involves compressional motion (P waves) and the other transverse or 'shearing' motion (S waves). Then there are two other waves, which travel only over the surface of the Earth, called Rayleigh waves and Love waves. These are distinguished by the differing motions (vertical and horizontal respectively) of elements of the Earth's surface as the wave passes by (see figures 24 and 25).

Different seismic waves travel on different paths, at different speeds, have different characteristic frequencies and wavelengths, and are absorbed and scattered with different strengths. This means that the signal that reaches a detector at some distance from a source is extremely complex, consisting of several 'phases' which correspond to the arrivals of different types of wave (see figure 26). The nature of these phases depends strongly on the distance between the source and the detector, and seismologists consider the problems of observation and analysis to be quite different at 'regional' (i.e., less than 2 000 km) and 'teleseismic' (i.e., greater than 2 000 km) distances (see figure 24). Most of the research effort in seismological identification since 1960 has been carried out at teleseismic ranges in order to develop 'national technical means' of verification of underground nuclear weapon testing limitations. However, in recent years a number of proposals for extensive seismological networks have revived interest in using regional data, and research at these distances is now quite active.[108] Most seismologists agree that some reliance on regional data would greatly enhance the ability to monitor a comprehensive nuclear test ban, but there are differences of opinion as to how much is needed.[109]

The capabilities needed in a seismological monitoring system depend on the nature of the treaty which must be verified. First, the system must be capable of distinguishing between earthquakes and explosions above some specified level of energy release (i.e., yield). If the treaty is a threshold type, which prohibits explosions only above a certain maximum yield, then the monitoring network must be capable of effective location and discrimination at or above this level as well as able to provide reliable estimates of explosion yields. If the treaty is a comprehensive one prohibiting *all* nuclear explosions, then the system must be able to locate and identify nuclear explosions at such low yields that any explosions smaller than this limit are agreed by all parties to be militarily and politically insignificant.

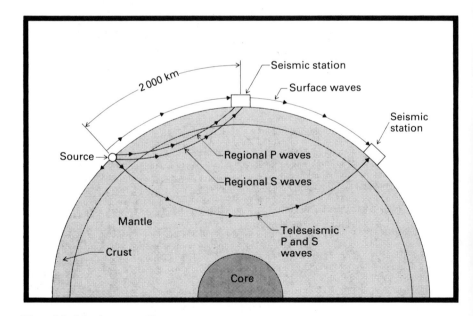

Figure 24. Seismic wave paths
The figure indicates the paths of both body and surface waves at regional and teleseismic distances. The bending of the body waves is a result of the variations in density with depth in the Earth's mantle. This effect is analogous to the bending of light rays as they pass through a medium of varying density. Note that the distances and sizes on the drawing are not to proper scale.

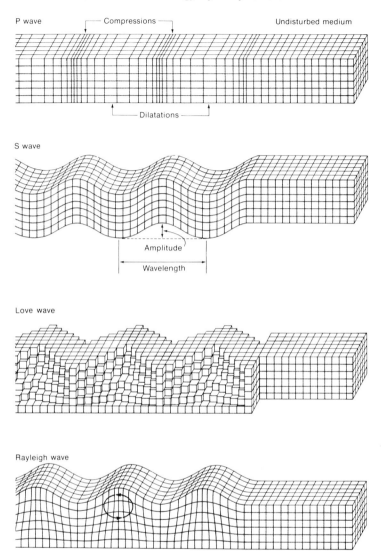

Figure 25. Seismic wave types
Seismic waves are differentiated by the medium through which they propagate (P and S waves through the body of the Earth and Love and Rayleigh waves over the surface) and by the relationship between particle motion and wave propagation direction (longitudinal: P waves; transverse: S and Love waves; and vertical/longitudinal: Rayleigh waves). A seismic station capable of detecting all of these waves must have six individual instruments: three short- and three long-period seismometers, with each set oriented in three perpendicular directions.

Source: Bolt, B. A., *Nuclear Explosions and Earthquakes. The Parted Veil* (W. H. Freeman, San Francisco, 1976), p. 49, figure 3.5. W. H. Freeman and Company, Copyright 1976.

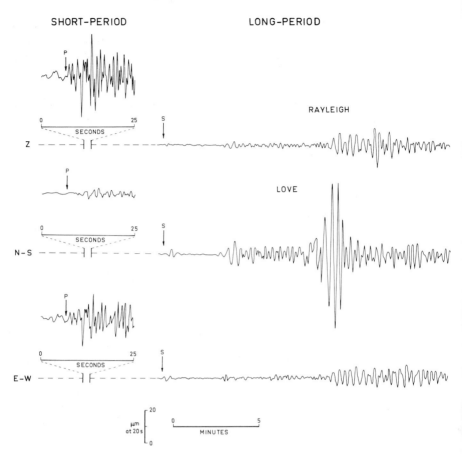

Figure 26. A typical seismic record
The three records display Earth motion in three different dimensions. The top record (labelled Z) shows vertical motion and therefore consists almost entirely of the P-wave (short-period) and Rayleigh-wave (long-period) phases. Note the approximately 1-second period of the P-wave phase shown with an expanded time-scale. The horizontal motion records (N–S and E–W) show smaller P-wave and larger S-wave amplitudes as well as the Love-wave phase. Note that the average period of the Love wave is roughly 15–20 seconds and its maximum peak-to-peak amplitude is about 90 μm.

Source: Dahlman, O. and Israelson, H., *Monitoring Underground Nuclear Explosions* (Elsevier, Amsterdam, 1977), p. 60, figure 4.8. Reproduced by permission of Elsevier Science Publishers, Amsterdam.

Detection and identification

There are two particular phases which are most often used in detecting and identifying nuclear explosions. At teleseismic distances the important phases are the initial P phase which travels through the Earth at a speed of from 8–12 km/s and has frequencies in the neighbourhood of 1 Hz (a period of 1 second), and a Rayleigh-type surface wave which travels at a speed of 3–4 km/s and has frequencies around 0.05 Hz (a period of 20 seconds). [110] The two frequencies mentioned here are the ones for which most seismometers are optimized, because seismic noise levels are significantly lower at these frequencies than at intermediate ones. [111]

Using two phases at different frequencies to discriminate between different kinds of seismic event is analogous to using multi-spectral information in photography to distinguish different objects which all look the same if no frequency separations are made (see p. 30). This is, in essence, the fundamental principle underlying the most successful and most commonly employed earthquake-explosion 'discriminant': the $m_b : M_s$ criterion.

The symbols m_b and M_s refers to the 'magnitudes' of the body-wave and surface-wave phases respectively. Each magnitude is a measure of the local velocity of Earth movements and is determined by first dividing the amplitude of the motion by the period, then taking the logarithm and finally applying corrections for the distance between the detector and the source as well as any biases associated with the equipment used or the location of the seismometer. [112] The magnitude of a particular phase is closely related to the amount of seismic energy in that phase, so to compare the body- and surface-wave magnitudes is equivalent to comparing the relative amounts of energy put into these different forms of ground motion by the source.

Explosions and earthquakes are very different phenomena. An explosion takes place in a very short time in a relatively small region and imparts a strong outward compressional impulse to the Earth in all directions simultaneously. On the other hand an earthquake is a more slowly developing phenomenon which usually involves the release of seismic stresses over a large volume of the Earth and which has a highly directional, that is unsymmetrical, pattern of seismic radiation (see figure 27). While an explosion will produce almost exclusively compressional waves, an earthquake will produce both compressional and shear waves. The latter when they reach the Earth's surface are much more effective in producing surface waves, so the fraction of an earthquake's energy which ends up in surface waves is generally quite a bit larger than for an explosion.

The time during which an event takes place determines the frequency spectrum of the radiation from the event, with short events creating higher frequency radiation than long ones. Since P waves have much higher frequencies than Rayleigh waves, more P waves can be expected from explosions and a much greater generation of low-frequency Rayleigh waves can be expected from earthquakes. The combination of the above effects leads in most cases to clearly distinguishable seismograms for explosions and earthquakes (see figure 28).

The standard procedure for determining whether a given signal came from an earthquake or an explosion is to compute the magnitudes m_b and M_s of the short-period (P) and long-period (Rayleigh) phases respectively and then to display the relationship between the two magnitudes on a graph (see figure 29).

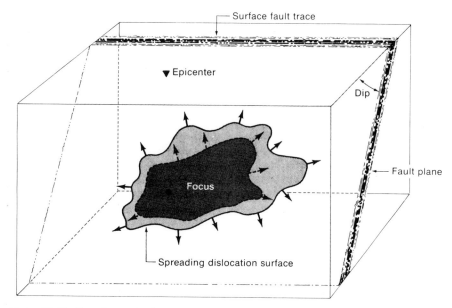

Figure 27. Earthquake mechanism
A three-dimensional section of the Earth's crust showing a rupture spreading out from the focus of the earthquake along the fault plane. The release of seismic energy is produced by the relative slippage of the two sides of the fault plane, a slippage which begins with the release of strain at the focus and spreads rapidly outwards. Note the highly non-symmetrical nature of the disturbance.

Source: Bolt, B. A., *Nuclear Explosions and Earthquakes. The Parted Veil* (W. H. Freeman, San Francisco, 1976), p. 68, figure 4.3. W. H. Freeman and Company, Copyright 1976.

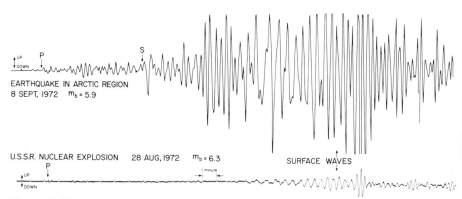

Figure 28. Earthquake and explosion seismograms
Note that the P-wave magnitudes of the two events are roughly similar but that the surface-wave magnitude of the earthquake is dramatically larger than that of the explosion. In general, shallow earthquakes couple energy far more strongly into surface waves than do explosions.

Source: Courtesy of Lynn R. Sykes, Lamont Doherty Geological Observatory, Columbia University, NY, USA.

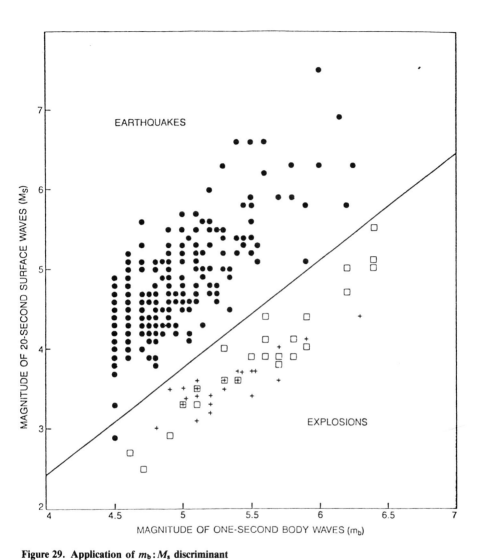

Figure 29. Application of $m_b:M_s$ discriminant
The black dots represent a population of 383 earthquakes with focal depths less than 30 km recorded world-wide over a six-month interval. (There are not 383 dots because many events had the same magnitudes). The squares designate explosions in the USA and the crosses explosions in the USSR. The one earthquake which falls on the explosion side of the line was a very weak event which occurred in a region of the south-west Pacific Ocean poorly covered by the existing network of seismological stations.

Source: Sykes, L. R. and Evernden, J. F., 'The verification of a comprehensive nuclear test ban', *Scientific American*, Vol. 247, No. 4, October 1982, p. 35. Copyright 1982 by Scientific American, Inc. All rights reserved.

It has been found from many studies that an event can be identified with high confidence by its location on this graph.

The $m_b : M_s$ discriminant is the most effective one yet devised for use at teleseismic distances, and there is a similar discriminant which employs analogous but different phases at regional distances and appears promising.[113] But these discriminants are by no means perfect, and it is highly unlikely that any single discriminant will be found which can distinguish earthquakes from explosions with 100 per cent confidence. The geological medium through which seismic waves travel is far too complex to allow for such hopes.

The answer to this problem is to use several analytical techniques and discriminants to reduce the uncertainty in ambiguous events. For example, some earthquakes have produced $m_b : M_s$ values which made them look like explosions because of unusually clear transmission of P waves from the source to the detector.[114] But when the depth of the sources of these waves was measured from other characteristics of the signal,[115] they were found to be at least 20 km deep, putting them well below the depth at which nuclear explosives can be placed. In fact the deepest known nuclear explosion was conducted at a depth of 2 km,[116] and the limits of modern drilling technology are about 12 km.[117] So any source located with high confidence at a depth below 10 km can be safely identified as an earthquake. This criterion alone can rule out a substantial fraction of 'false alarms'.[118]

Another useful discriminant is the location of the source. With good data from a few seismological stations a source can be located to an accuracy of about 10–20 km.[119] If the location is found to be under the ocean, then the possibility of it being an explosion can be effectively ruled out, since any attempt to conduct a nuclear test under the ocean would be easily detectable by a number of other means. Since over 90 per cent of all earthquakes occur under oceans and/or at depths greater than 30 km only a relatively small number of earthquakes remain to produce false alarms.[120]

The combination of location, depth and the $m_b : M_s$ discriminant is a powerful method for distinguishing earthquakes from explosions. Having applied this method to a very large data sample, one group of analysts summarized their results as follows: "We know of no Eurasian earthquake with 1 second P-wave magnitude of 4 or more of the past 20 years whose waves are classified as those of an explosion . . . Furthermore, to our knowledge not one of several hundred underground nuclear explosions set off in the same period radiated seismic waves that could be mistaken for those of an earthquake."[121]

Yield estimates

It is quite a bit easier to determine whether or not an explosion has taken place than it is to get a reliable estimate of its yield. There is an enormous variability in the magnitude values recorded at different seismic stations for a single explosion (see figure 30).[122] The variability can be illustrated by computing

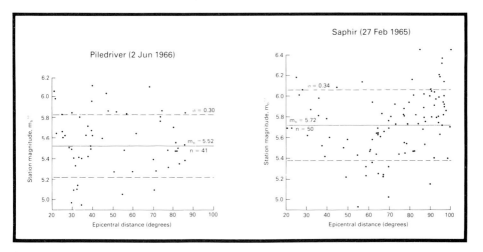

Figure 30. Variation in body-wave magnitudes
The m_b values recorded at a large number of seismological stations (41 and 50 respectively) for two test explosions are shown plotted against the distance of the station from the test site. Note that the distance is measured in degrees as is customary in seismology (10 degrees represents a distance of about 1 100 km on the Earth's surface). The average magnitudes for the two explosions are 5.52 and 5.72 and both show standard deviations of at least 0.3, implying an uncertainty in yield estimate of at least a factor of 2 (see text).

Source: Based on Bache, T. C., 'Estimating the yield of underground nuclear explosions', *Bulletin of the Seismological Society of America*, Vol. 72, No. 6, Part B, December 1982, p. S113, figure 1.

the difference in yield estimates which would result from using the lowest and highest recorded magnitudes for the Saphir explosion in figure 30. Using a standard average formula relating yield Y, in kilotons, to body-wave magnitude [123]

$$m_b = 3.8 + 0.75 \log_{10} Y$$

and the two extreme magnitudes of 5.1 and 6.4 gives a range of yield estimates from 54 to 2 900 kilotons. The correct value was 120 kt. The same formula can be used to show that an error of only 0.1 in the value of m_b corresponds to an error of 30 per cent in the yield estimate. The sensitivity to small errors illustrates the great danger in using magnitude estimates from only one or a few stations to estimate yields as well as the need for large amounts of data to get yield values which are correct even within error limits of 100 per cent, that is, a magnitude estimate valid within ±0.3 or so.

The scatter in m_b data is only one of many problems facing the yield estimator. Explosions carried out in different geological media will generally be more or less 'decoupled' from the surrounding medium, that is, they will transfer a larger or smaller fraction of their released energy into seismic waves. [124] (The formula used above assumed a well-coupled explosion in hard rock.) For example, explosions in dry alluvium (a soft, porous sedimentary medium) can give magnitudes from 0.5 to 1.0 lower than for the same yield explosion in hard rock. An explosion carried out in a large underground cavity would be even more decoupled, leading to reductions in apparent yield by as much as a factor of 100 (e.g., from 100 kt to 1 kt). It is also known that the yield–magnitude relationship for a given test site is affected by the tectonic history of that site. Recent (on a geological time-scale) tectonic activity causes a site to produce lower magnitudes for a given yield than a site which has been free of such activity for hundreds of millions of years.[125] The US test site in Nevada is an example of the former type, while the Soviet eastern Kazakh test site is one of the latter. The different site properties produce a systematic bias in any attempt to apply Nevada test-site data to estimating the yields of Soviet test explosions. The assumed value of this bias is a crucial factor in evaluating the Reagan Administration charges that the Soviet Union has violated the Threshold Test Ban Treaty by testing weapons with yields over 150 kt (see chapter 4). One recent study of this problem employs surface-wave magnitudes which are subject to less variation in bias to establish that Soviet tests have in fact not exceeded the 150 kt limit.[126]

One more simple application of the average magnitude–yield formula shows that a value of m_b = 4.0 corresponds to a yield in hard rock of about 2 kt. On the basis of this value and the quotation on p. 70, a highly reliable existing capability to distinguish between earthquakes and any explosion with a yield greater than 2 kt in hard rock can be assumed. The many estimates of this limit in the literature range from 1 to 5 kt, with most tending towards the lower end of the range.

The possibility that explosions in this yield range or even larger might be concealed by conducting them in large cavities (see above) has for many years been the most commonly mentioned means by which a party to a ban on underground tests could evade detection.[127] It is true that the apparent yield of such a cavity-decoupled explosion is greatly reduced, possibly by a factor of 100 or more, when measured on the usual short-period seismometers optimized to record signals in the neighbourhood of 1 Hz. However, recent studies have shown that the decoupling effect is dramatically reduced at higher frequencies.[128] As has already been noted, explosions are far better generators of high frequencies than are earthquakes, and there is also mounting evidence that the higher frequency seismic waves propagate for much longer distances than had previously been believed. Finally, seismic noise is greatly reduced at frequencies of 30 Hz or higher, allowing for excellent signal-to-noise ratios for even relatively weak high-frequency signals.[129]

This new information has been used to compute the effectiveness of a network of high-frequency seismometers in detecting decoupled explosions. The conclusion of this analysis is that even fully decoupled explosions of fractional kiloton yields are identifiable and therefore "that all discussions of the feasibility and utility for evasion via large cavity decoupling are passé".[130]

Seismic image processing

Another similarity between seismological and optical or radar observations is worth examining in some detail: the need for image processing. A seismological 'image' consists of the recorded seismometer readings at all stations which received signals from the event. On most present seismographs these readings are still in analog form, that is they are recorded as complex waveforms drawn on paper by a chart recorder. (See for example figures 26 and 28). But rapid technological change, again led by advances in micro-elecronic and computer technology, is leading to more and more use of digital seismographs. These devices record the seismic signal directly on magnetic tape or into a computer memory in the form of binary numbers, exactly like photographic pixels.

Once the image is recorded, the problem facing the seismologist sounds remarkably similar to that facing the photo-interpreter: "complexities of the earth strongly affect the seismic signal, thus presenting us with a blurred and distorted observational image of the source. To improve this image we have to remove complicating wave propagation and recording effects".[131]

One of the major sources of image degradation is seismic noise. This can be minimized by placing seismometers deep in solid rock formations and by using electronic filters of various types. It can also be reduced by deploying an array of seismometers at a given location and combining the signals from all elements in the array (see figure 31). This technique was originally motivated by the expectation that seismic waves arriving from a source thousands of kilometres away would be coherent over distances of the order of 100 km at the location of the detector. 'Coherence' in this sense means that all of the detectors are excited in the same way, or in a way that is analytically predictable once the distance and direction to the source are known. On the other hand seismic noise is quite incoherent over distances of 1 km or more, so that noise signals from different elements of the array will have no predictable or constant relationship to each other. When the signals from many elements of an array are combined in the appropriate way (in some cases a simple sum might be sufficient) the true signal will be enhanced relative to the noise. Theoretically the enhancement should be proportional to the square root of the number of elements in the array, so a 25-element array should increase the signal-to-noise ratio by a factor of 5.

These considerations led the United States to build three very large arrays in Alaska (ALPA), Montana (LASA) and Norway (NORSAR) under the so-called Vela Uniform Programme.[132] These arrays had diameters of between 100 and 200 km and were made up of hundreds of individual seismometers, quite analogous to the phased-array radars discussed above. When they are accompanied by appropriate data transmission and processing capabilities, seismological arrays can be 'steered' very much in the manner of a phased-array radar in order to be optimally sensitive to seismic waves coming

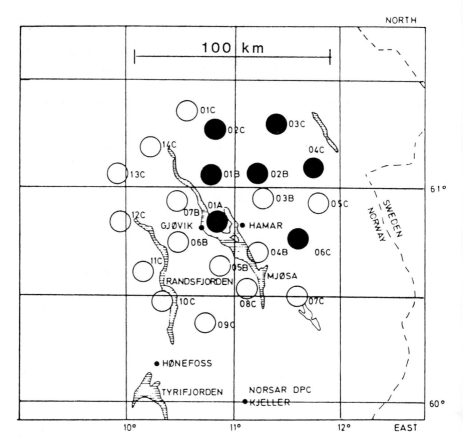

Figure 31. The NORSAR array
The original array was made up of 22 sub-stations arranged in a roughly circular pattern about
100 km in diameter. The current array uses only 7 sub-stations and has a diameter of about 60 km.
Note the similarity of this array of seismometers to the array of radiating elements in the radars
of figures 10 and 11. The principle of beam forming in a seismic array is precisely the same as
that for a phased-array radar.

Source: Courtesy of NORSAR.

from particular directions (called 'beam forming') or with particular velocities
(called 'velocity filtering'). These capabilities allow, at least in principle, for
seismic arrays to 'scan' the Earth, much as a phased-array radar scans the
skies. Naturally the seismological array does not move; the scanning is done
electronically by changing the time-delay relationships among the detectors.[133]

The actual performance of the three very large arrays turned out to be less
than was hoped for, largely because the distances over which teleseismic P
waves exhibit coherence turned out to be smaller than anticipated.[134] Both the
LASA and ALPA arrays have been shut down, while the NORSAR array has

been reduced in size from 22 subarrays to 7 (see figure 31). Such smaller arrays are still a considerable improvement on individual seismometers.

Distortions of the seismic image are also caused by absorption and scattering of seismic waves along the path from source to detector and by the specific response features of the seismometer. For example, waves with different frequencies are degraded at different rates as they move through the Earth, and seismometers respond differently to signals at different frequencies. Both of these effects can in principle be modelled mathematically, and these models can be used in an 'image restoration' process quite analogous to those used in photography to remove atmospheric and optical distortions. In seismology the process of applying these corrections to the signal is called 'deconvolving', and many useful features of a seismic signal can be revealed by successful deconvolution. The major difficulty in applying this method is the lack of precise models for seismic-wave propagation through the Earth. Much research remains to be done to improve such models, and it is evident that the Earth will never be as 'transparent' as the atmosphere.

There are many other image restoration techniques which are in various stages of development and application. The key to effective seismic-image processing is the same as for optical and radar images: more, faster and cheaper digital computers. The data processing demands on a world-wide network of seismometers in continuous operation will be at least as severe as for satellite photography. And, since the number of human interpreters will always be far too small to examine all these data, there must be a considerable amount of automatic processing, that is, artificial intelligence, which can make preliminary judgements about the significance of events and leave only the most important or ambiguous for human interpretation. While such capabilities are still far from realization, much progress is being made and much more is expected as the result of current research.[135]

VII. Nuclear explosion detectors

A nuclear explosion in the atmosphere or in outer space is an exceptionally violent event which provides ample evidence of its occurrence. The essence of the explosion is the sudden release of an enormous quantity of energy into a very small volume. For example, a 10 kt explosion will in the first millionth of a second or so release the energy equivalent of 10 000 tons of TNT into a volume no bigger than a grapefruit. This creates extremely high temperatures—at least 10 million degrees Celsius—and as a result of the Wien displacement law (see table 3, p. 29) the average wavelength of the radiation is extremely short, characteristic of X-rays, a form of electromagnetic radiation whose characteristic energies are from 1 000 to 100 000 times as large as those of visible light. These X-rays account for more than half of the total energy released by the explosion, with most of the rest being in the form of fast-moving fragments of the original bomb materials.[136] Nuclear explosions also produce large numbers of an even more energetic form of radiation, called 'gamma-rays'. These can have energies more than one million times as great as visible light. As column 4 of table 3 makes clear, the intensity of the X-rays emitted (that is, the relative 'brightness' of the fireball) is unimaginably large. No comparisons to such intensities exist in human experience, and even one of the most graphic attempts, *Brighter than a Thousand Suns*,[137] is still 10 orders of magnitude too small.

The detection of X- and gamma-rays requires a very different type of detector from the visible and infra-red sensors considered in sections II and III. However, such detectors have existed for many years and have been used to monitor nuclear explosions at least since the early 1960s when both the USA and the Soviet Union were confident that they could verify a ban on nuclear tests in the atmosphere and in space. This confidence led to the signing of the Partial Test Ban Treaty in August 1963.

The most common form of X-ray and gamma-ray detector (see figure 32) uses a material called a 'scintillator' which converts the energy of the incoming photon into a pulse of visible light. When an X- or gamma-photon enters the scintillating material it can cause one or more electrons to be ejected from atoms in the crystal. As these electrons recombine with the positively charged

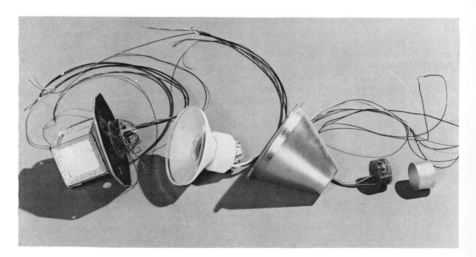

Figure 32. The M4 X-ray detector
X-rays enter the cubical box at the left of the detector and interact with the atoms of a caesium iodide (CsI) 'scintillator' producing flashes of light which are then converted to electrical signals by a photomultiplier tube at the base of the cube. The conical shaped scintillator and photomultiplier in the centre form a so-called 'guard' detector whose function is to identify and reject high-energy cosmic ray events which also trigger the main detector and could produce false alarms.

Source: Photo courtesy of Los Alamos National Laboratory.

ions from which they were detached, light is emitted. This light is captured by a 'photomultiplier' tube which converts the light energy into an electrical voltage pulse whose magnitude is proportional to the energy delivered by the original X- or gamma-ray photons. The voltage pulses from the photomultiplier can be digitized and stored for later transmission to Earth if the detector is in a satellite, or they can be stored on magnetic tape for computer processing or observed directly on a video screen if the instrument is based on Earth. Scintillation counters can be quite small, light and portable, and they require very little electrical power for their operation.

If the explosion takes place above the atmosphere in the near-perfect vacuum of space these X-rays move outward from the explosion in all directions at the speed of light. Because the total radiated energy is so large, the intensity of X-rays remains large even at great distances from the explosion. This enables a single satellite, such as the US Vela satellite, to detect the X-rays from nuclear explosions at distances comparable to the diameter of the Earth's orbit about the Sun, approximately 300 million kilometres.[138]

If the explosion occurs in the atmosphere, the X-rays are absorbed within a few metres of the centre of the explosion, causing rapid heating and com-

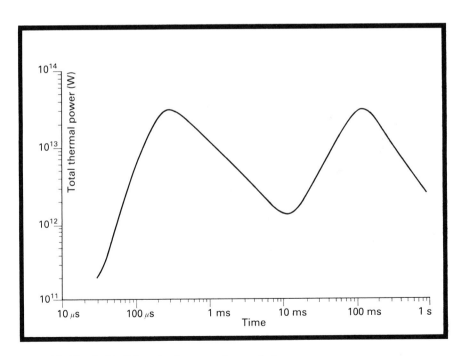

Figure 33. The double light pulse from a nuclear explosion
The general shape of this double pulse is the same for all nuclear explosions, and the yield of an explosion can be estimated quite accurately from measurements of the time intervals between the two maxima and the minimum.

Figure 34. The Launch 1 Vela spacecraft
The X-ray detectors are the cubes projecting from the corners of the triangular solar panels which provide the energy source for the detectors and data transmitters.

Source: Photo courtesy of Los Alamos National Laboratory.

pression of the surrounding air. The hot gases become incandescent and emit intense visible light. As the shock wave becomes more intense the air around the fireball becomes opaque for a brief period and then, as the shock wave expands, the air becomes transparent again, allowing the release of another burst of light. It is this unique double flash of light that is the most useful signal of a nuclear explosion in the atmosphere (see figure 33). The general shape of the double pulse is the same for all nuclear explosions, regardless of yield or detailed design features, and the times to the two maxima and the minimum are well-known functions of the yield of the weapon. [139]

The double light pulse can be detected from a satellite with a device called a 'bhangmeter', [140] a special kind of photometer which uses sensors similar to the visible and infra-red sensors described earlier. The bhangmeter is focused on the Earth from a circular orbit at an altitude of 115 000 km (roughly one-third of the distance from the Earth to the Moon). From this distance the Earth is a relatively small, but very bright, sphere. Because of its large size and high reflectivity the Earth has a total luminosity which can be several thousand times that of a small nuclear explosion. [141] So the bhangmeter must incorporate electronic circuits which can separate the rapid fluctuations of light intensity characteristic of a nuclear explosion from the nearly constant bright background of light reflected from the Earth.

Both bhangmeters and X- and gamma-ray detectors, along with a number of other detection devices, have been watching the Earth and outer space since the first Vela satellite was launched in 1963 [142] (see figure 34). Presumably similar devices are in use by the Soviet Union, and possibly other states as well. The last Vela satellite was launched in 1970, but nuclear detection equipment similar to that carried by Vela has been deployed on other types of satellite since then. The next generation of X- and gamma-ray detectors and bhangmeters will be part of the payload of the Navstar global positioning satellites (GPS), which will therefore also be nuclear detection satellites (NDS). The GPS/NDS satellites will be in operation by 1988 and will include "18 satellites deployed in 6 circular orbits of radius 26,600 kilometres, inclined at 60° to the equator and equally spaced in azimuth [longitude]" [143] (see figure 35). These satellites will serve the dual function of supplying navigational fixes for vehicles, ships and aircraft and watching for nuclear explosions in the atmosphere or in outer space. [144] The likelihood of any such explosion escaping detection by this system is extremely small.

VIII. Electronic reconnaissance

The monitoring of radio and radar signals is at once the easiest to explain of all the technologies so far described and the one about which the fewest specific details are known. No technical intelligence-gathering methods are as sensitive and closely guarded as the signals (SIGINT) and communications (COMINT) intelligence techniques and devices used by many countries to

Figure 35 a. A GPS/NDS satellite
The satellite shown under construction is one of 21 which will ultimately be deployed in space by
the USA. The wings of the satellite carry the solar power source, and the cylindrical structures
pointing to the right are the various communication antennas used to provide navigational fixes
for ships, aircraft, missiles and land vehicles. Not visible on the photograph are the bhangmeter
and X- and gamma-ray detectors which will enable the satellite to detect nuclear explosions in the
Earth's atmosphere or in outer space.

Source: Photo courtesy of US Air Force.

intercept the communications and radar signals of friends and enemies alike.
Because of this secrecy the available literature on the subject is skimpy on
details and riddled with speculations and contradictory assertions. In view of
this situation it is not possible to give a satisfactory picture of the capabilities
and limitations of electronic reconnaissance techniques, and one must be
satisfied with a few rather superficial comments.

The most widespread use of electronic intelligence is in the interception of
communications (COMINT). This ranges all the way from the tapping of
telephones to the monitoring by satellites of microwave transmissions from
Earth-based transmitters. Somewhere in this broad range lies the indistinct but
significant border between legitimate national technical means of verification
and illegitimate espionage. The precise location of this border is an issue which

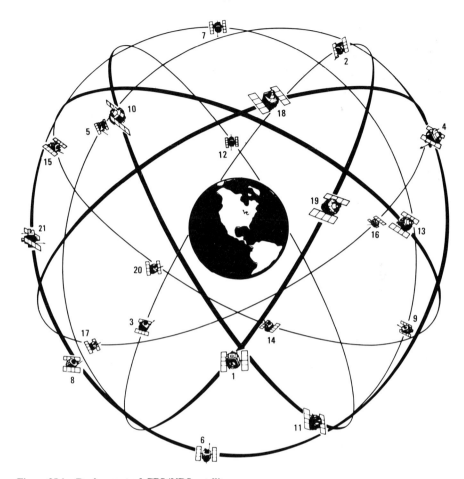

Figure 35 b. Deployment of GPS/NDS satellites
The GPS/NDS system, also called the Navstar system, will consist of 21 satellites deployed in 6 orbits as shown. The primary purpose of the system is to provide precise positioning information for a wide variety of applications, including such military uses as weapon delivery, rendezvous, precision mapping and point-to-point navigation. It is clear from the figure that the system will also provide a highly redundant capability for nuclear explosion detection.

Source: Courtesy of US Air Force.

no country seems anxious to discuss, and the phrase "national technical means of verification" has never been clearly defined, mainly to avoid any serious examination of these techniques.

It is remarkable that such a highly secret and sensitive activity is carried out on such an enormous scale. For example, the US National Security Agency (NSA) attempts to collect and preserve on magnetic tape ("more or less forever") *all* Soviet radio transmissions, including "the full daily broadcast of every conventional radio station in all the Soviet republics, every transmission to every Soviet embassy abroad, every broadcast to a ship at sea, every transmission by military units on maneuvers in Eastern Europe, the radio traffic of every control tower at Soviet airports".[145] To this must be added the substantial efforts applied to monitoring the communications of many other states as well.[146] Soviet SIGINT/COMINT activities are obviously also extensive, although almost nothing has been written about them in the open literature.

The collection, decoding (decrypting), monitoring and storing of this vast volume of radio traffic requires an enormous organization including tens-of-thousands of people and facilities distributed all around the Earth, on land, on sea, in the air and in space. The main NSA facility at Fort Meade, Maryland has a floor area of 180 000 square metres of which some 25 per cent (45 000 square metres), is devoted to computers used for code breaking, traffic and content analysis and record keeping.[147]

The vast majority of this information has little or nothing to do with the verification of arms control agreements, and is related to political, military and economic intelligence gathering. But it is important to understand that this capability to monitor virtually all of the communications of another state must act as a powerful inhibiting factor on any attempts by that state to carry out clandestine activities, especially activities which require the co-operation of several separate facilities and substantial numbers of people. Almost any significant violation of an arms control agreement would fit this definition and would therefore face serious risks of discovery unless highly elaborate and expensive precautions were taken, precautions which would not only reduce the efficiency of the clandestine activity, but which might in themselves arouse suspicion and increased attention. An interesting historical example was the realization in 1942 by Soviet scientists that the USA was working on an atomic bomb. The very secrecy of the project, which resulted in the disappearance of many prominent physicists and the sudden absence of articles on nuclear fission in physics journals, alerted Soviet researchers to the Manhattan Project.[148]

The aspects of SIGINT/COMINT which are most relevant to present arms control problems and which seem to have become accepted as legitimate national technical means are the monitoring of radar signals and the radio transmissions (telemetry) from missile test-flights. Radar signals must be monitored to verify that large phased-array radars are not being tested in an 'ABM mode' as forbidden in the SALT I Treaty, and the monitoring of telemetry is important, possibly essential, in verifying compliance with the highly detailed and complex prohibitions against 'new types' of ICBMs and limits on multiple warhead deployments included in the SALT II Treaty.

Radar signals

Radars emit pulses of electromagnetic energy with distinctive frequency and amplitude characteristics, which are reflected off objects and returned to receivers designed to interpret them. But these pulses can also be intercepted by antennas deployed on aircraft or satellites, and much can be learned in this way about the location, purpose and capabilities of the radar.

The shooting down of a Korean Airlines passenger aircraft by Soviet air defence forces in September 1983 called attention to the use of aircraft by intelligence agencies to monitor radar transmissions. Most commonly the aircraft stay just outside the airspace of the state being observed, but execute maneouvres designed to alert air defences. For example, "About seventy times each year big Soviet Tu-95 'Bear' reconnaissance aircraft veer inside the [US] Air Force's Aerospace Defence Indentification Zone (ADIZ), a buffer area surrounding US airspace, which ranges from 60 to 200 miles [96–320 km] wide ... The US intercepts more than 300 Soviet aircraft each year in the ADIZ".[149] More rare, but still surprisingly frequent, are the actual penetrations of national airspace by hostile reconnaissance aircraft.

Such activities clearly cross the boundary between legitimate and illegitimate national technical means, and a substantial number of aircraft have been shot down as a result of such activities.[150] Soviet officials publicly charged that the Korean airliner was being used for just such a mission, but no persuasive evidence has been produced to support this charge.

Satellites used for SIGINT are often called 'ferret' satellites.[151] They are usually placed in orbits slightly higher than those used for photographic satellites and are sometimes used in pairs with one satellite at relatively high altitude and the other at a low altitude (around 200 km).[152] Very little is publicly known about the configurations and capabilities of these satellites, and the literature abounds with contradictory and confusing statements. For example a recent generation of US satellites called 'Rhyolite' has been described by one source as designed primarily "to scan the Soviet Union with infra-red sensors to detect missile booster exhaust plumes"[153] and by another as "pure SIGINT".[154] Most likely the Rhyolite satellites carry out both missions, but in the absence of hard information on the real missions and capabilities of Rhyolite and other ferret satellites there is no way to resolve such contradictory statements. And the level of secrecy surrounding these satellites is increasing rather than decreasing. In June 1983 the US government stopped releasing even the launch-times and orbital parameters of its own military satellites.[155]

The use of ferret satellites and other SIGINT monitors to verify the ABM Treaty (SALT I) involves determining whether or not a given phased-array radar exceeds certain power and size limitations or is tested in an "ABM mode".[156] The power of a radar can be measured by determining the strength of the signal at a known distance from the radar if the radiation pattern emitted by it is known. This is a straightforward measurement which can be carried out by several types of monitor.

The question of whether or not a given radar is being tested in an ABM mode is far more complex. Attempts to clarify this notion in the SALT I negotiations were not successful, as evidenced by a "unilateral statement" attached to the Treaty by the United States in which the US definition of "tested in an ABM mode" is spelled out. No indication of Soviet agreement with this unilateral statement is given, and there is no alternative Soviet definition. Therefore the monitoring of compliance with Article II of the ABM Treaty, which defines an ABM radar as one which has been tested in an ABM mode, remains an ambiguous process.

The USA in 1973–74 gathered evidence which it believed revealed Soviet testing of a phased-array radar in an ABM mode and made a complaint in the Standing Consultative Commission.[157] However, it was very difficult to build such evidence into a case for a violation, as indicated by the need to observe and analyse 40 incidents of Soviet testing of radars before a pattern could be established to show that that radar was being tested in an ABM mode.

So while ferret satellites and other SIGINT 'platforms' are capable of very thorough and precise monitoring of radar emissions, there do remain limits to their application to monitoring arms control agreements, especially when what is important to know is not simply the characteristics of the radar itself but its interaction with other components in a complex weapon system.

Telemetry monitoring

In the context of arms control, telemetry generally refers to the radio data transmissions from missiles which are being flight-tested. In such a test it is important to monitor a great many components and sub-systems in the missile to see if they are functioning according to design and to locate malfunctions and design flaws. A missile under test contains all sorts of devices for measuring temperatures, voltages, currents, accelerations, vibrations, stresses, and so forth. Each one of these devices can be connected to a 'transducer' which converts its output into an electrical signal which is fed to a radio transmitter. The signal is then broadcast from one or more atennas mounted on the missile or its payload to receivers on land, on ships at sea, on aircraft or on satellites. An example of such a system for the monitoring of Trident I (C4) missile tests is shown in figure 36.[158]

The telemetry is radiated in many directions, so it can be received by anyone with an appropriate receiver in a line-of-sight from the missile. It has been shown by a group at the Kettering School in Great Britain that some very interesting and useful information can be obtained from satellite telemetry even with relatively inexpensive equipment and unsophisticated analytical techniques.[159]

A modern ballistic missile is a complex object, and in a test-flight of such a missile there are so many systems to be monitored that the data from several of them must be combined and transmitted together on a single channel. (A channel is characterized by a central frequency, called the 'carrier', and a

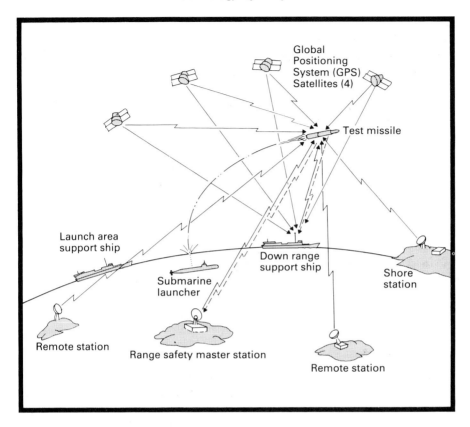

Figure 36. Trident missile test telemetry
The figure shows radio communications both to and from the missile being tested. Telemetry data from the missile is shown being received by the range safety master station and the down-range support ship. The transmissions to the missile from the GPS satellites and ground stations are tracking signals used to monitor the missile's precise position and velocity. If there is a malfunction and the missile begins to wander off course, a signal can be sent from a ground station to destroy it.

'bandwidth', that is, a certain spread of frequencies on either side of this central frequency. The bandwidth is related to the rate of transmission of information on the channel: the greater the information rate the greater the necessary bandwidth.) The mixing of several signals on a single channel is called 'multiplexing', and it makes intercepted telemetry signals very difficult to interpret.

There are a number of different modes for the transmission of telemetry. One, called pulse duration modulation (PDM), uses a signal of a fixed amplitude which can be turned on for varying fractions of a known time interval. The on-time can then be made proportional to some quantity of interest on the missile. The Soyuz satellite telemetry interpreted at the Kettering School was in PDM form, and the pulse durations appeared to be related to heart and respiration rates of the cosmonauts on board the satellite. [160]

An increasingly common mode of data transmission is called pulse code modulation (PCM). In PCM the data are first digitized, that is, put into the form of binary numbers (see section V, above), which are then transmitted on a channel made up of two separate carrier frequencies very close together. The ones are transmitted as pulses on one of these frequencies and the zeros as pulses on the other.

The Trident I tests use PCM on 192 channels, each of which is sampled 400 times per second by the multiplexer. The data stream consists of 76 800 numbers per second, each of which is in the form of an 8-bit digital 'word' (i.e., a number between 0 and 255), resulting in a data transmission rate of 614 400 bits per second. [161] Telemetry from Soviet missile tests has also moved increasingly to digital formats and PCM in recent years. One analyst has even speculated that reports of Soviet 'encoding' of telemetry were a result of this change from PDM to digital format. [162] It is true that converting data to digital form can be described as 'encoding' but this must be seen as different from 'encryption', which is a form of encoding whose sole purpose is to make the data incomprehensible to observers who are not supposed to receive them. It seems clear from the intensity of the controversy over the alleged encryption of missile test telemetry by the Soviet Union (see chapter 4, pp. 186–91) that the issue concerns more than the simple conversion from PDM to digital data formats.

While the analysis of missile telemetry is clearly a complex and difficult process, it is also clear that such analysis is conducted routinely and has been for many years. [163] The ability to intercept and analyse telemetry is an integral part of each side's national technical means of verification and is explicitly included in the SALT II Treaty. [164]

Telemetry is broadcast throughout the flight-test of an ICBM, starting with pre-launch preparations and ending with the impact of the warheads at their targets. Pre-launch and early boost-phase telemetry is important for an accurate determination of the launch-weight of the missile, a feature restricted by SALT II. But telemetry from low altitudes must be monitored from systems which are not too far away from the launching site, because the curvature of the Earth prevents reception of telemetry at great distances. This is no problem for Soviet intelligence, since both US launching sites are on coastlines, and Soviet 'trawlers' equipped with sophisticated receivers can, and do, approach these areas, as well as the target areas, quite closely. [165]

For the United States the problem is more difficult, since Soviet test sites are deep in the interior of Soviet territory. The USA uses ground stations in Norway, Turkey, China and other states bordering on the Soviet Union as well as aircraft patrolling border areas to monitor Soviet telemetry. [166] The loss of two ground stations in Iran in the revolution of 1979 dealt a severe blow to the hopes of ratification of SALT II in the US Senate, as a number of Senators argued that without the Iranian ground stations the Treaty could not be verified adequately.[167] Proponents of SALT II verification argued that the loss of these sites did not prevent adequate verification, but they were unable to make these arguments convincing, either because the loss of Iranian sites really *did* seriously degrade US monitoring capabilities, or because the alternative systems which could replace them were too secret to reveal in public. This problem of attempting to gain public confidence in verification while maintaining maximum secrecy about capabilities is analysed in chapter 3.

Once the missile rises above about 100 km its telemetry can be monitored by more distant stations and by aircraft and satellites. Telemetry from high altitudes carries information on the detailed manoeuvres of the MIRV 'bus', the vehicle that releases the individual re-entry vehicles. This telemetry is useful for monitoring the SALT limitations on numbers of warheads (fractionation), but it is also very useful in monitoring accuracy, a property not covered by arms control agreements.[168]

Most accounts of the US Rhyolite satellite assume that it has the capability to monitor Soviet missile telemetry, and one even suggests that it could monitor boost-phase telemetry.[169] Given the great height of the orbit (the Rhyolite is in geostationary orbit 37 300 km above the Earth) it can be shown that a very large antenna is necessary to achieve a satisfactory signal to noise ratio.[170] It is reported that the main Rhyolite antenna is a concave dish 21.3 m in diameter, and that the satellite carries other antennas as well as "a number of other appendages".[171]

Telemetry can more easily be monitored from the lower orbits used by ferret satellites. Again the open literature is confusing and sometimes contradictory on the capabilities of ferret satellites to monitor missile tests. A 1979 source predicted a new satellite with a 20 m antenna under development and scheduled for deployment in 1982,[172] while a 1982 source referred to a "new ferret satellite equipped with a long antenna tailored for telemetry interception" which was "reportedly under development".[173]

Given the secrecy surrounding the launching of military satellites it may be that such a ferret has already been deployed, or, if the deployment of the satellite was dependent on the use of the US space shuttle, the deployment may have been delayed until January 1985. On 24 January a highly secret satellite with the orbital characteristics of a new type of ferret satellite[174] was placed into orbit as part of a space shuttle mission.

Whatever the current capabilities of US systems (and even less is known about Soviet SIGINT systems) it is clear that the interception and interpretation of missile-test telemetry is a high priority mission for US and Soviet national intelligence services, a mission deemed worthy of large expenditures of money and talent. Apparently the benefits to be gained from unrestricted access to such telemetry are substantial. This would explain the intense reaction generated in the US intelligence community to the alleged encryption by the Soviet Union of some portions of its telemetry. Given the importance of this issue in the arms control debate it is worth giving a short introduction to the techniques of encryption and decryption.

Data encryption

The first point that must be made is that even when there is no intent to encrypt digital telemetry data, its interpretation can be very difficult. A given channel will carry multiplexed information from many instruments, some of which may be continuously monitored while others are only sampled at longer intervals. In addition, the relationship between the binary number transmitted for a given quantity and the actual value of that quantity may be very obscure. For example, a temperature at some location in the missile may vary under normal conditions over a range of 10 degrees, but if it is necessary to detect small variations in this temperature, then the 10-degree range can be divided into 256 intervals and the temperature value transmitted as an 8-bit binary number. To transform this number back into a temperature it is necessary to know both the nominal range and the temperature value assigned to the lower end. If, for example, the temperature being measured is known to be in the range $50°$ to $60°$, and the binary number 00110010 (50) is received, then the temperature can be read as 50/256 of 10 degrees over the base of 50 degrees, that is, 51.95 degrees. Unless an unauthorized listener knows the nominal base value and range the number 50 is of no value.

The only way in which one side can interpret another's telemetry is if certain standard channels and parameters are used repeatedly and it is possible to observe many tests and look for patterns in the data. Once patterns are found it is often possible to infer what quantities are being measured as did the Kettering group in the case of Soyuz telemetry.

There are considerable advantages in adopting standard procedures for telemetry broadcasts. Hardware can be standardized and computer analysis of received data simplified. It is reasonable to infer that both the USA and the Soviet Union have used such standard procedures for many years and that each is capable of interpreting significant amounts, if not all, of the other's telemetry.

But with advances in digital computer technology the ease with which telemetry can be encrypted has been greatly increased. To encrypt digital telemetry it is necessary only to put the digitized data through a process in which a secret binary 'key' number is added to the correct number.[175] The key can be an extremely long string of 1s and 0s or a shorter string repeated over and over again. When the key has been added the data become totally obscured and can be deciphered only by subtracting the identical key.

There are many routine uses of codes (for example in the transmission of financial records or diplomatic messages) in which the same key is used repeatedly.[176] Such codes can often be broken if the code-breaker has access to a large computer which can generate thousands of keys per second until the correct one is found. Such 'brute force' techniques are used routinely by the US National Security Agency which possesses an enormous computer capability. For certain other types of commercial code, clever mathematical techniques (algorithms) have been devised to break supposedly unbreakable codes with surprising speed. [177]

However, for relatively infrequent events such as missile tests there is no need to use the same key repeatedly, and the key can be changed for each test (presumably even *during* a test). Such 'one-time keys' are to all intents and purposes unbreakable, especially when the data being sent are not in the form of text but are already only strings of numbers. Therefore any state that wishes to withhold test data from unauthorized listeners can certainly do so with little risk that the data can be decrypted. In older encryption methods there was always the possibility that a spy might communicate the keys to the other side. But in modern computerized encryption a one-time key can be generated entirely within the computer, and there is nothing for a spy to communicate.

This ability to encrypt telemetry casts considerable doubt on the ability to monitor some of the more detailed restrictions embodied in existing arms control agreements. One solution to this problem would be to agree that telemetry encryption itself be banned, but both sides have shown resistance to such an agreement (see chapter 4). In the absence of a total ban on encryption the only solution is for the interested parties to negotiate detailed rules governing such encryption, but such negotiations would encounter deep resistance from the intelligence community who would want to prevent any discussion with the other side of existing SIGINT/COMINT capabilities.

IX. Safeguards

The final set of verification technologies to be discussed depends far less on sophisticated hardware than those so far described and much more on an elaborate set of record-keeping and administrative techniques. These are the so-called 'safeguards' administered by the International Atomic Energy Agency (IAEA) in Vienna, an operation which began on a very small scale in 1957 and which by February 1984 had negotiated safeguards agreements with 84 states. [178] These agreements and the monitoring activities carried out under them constitute an unprecedented international co-operation to attempt to prevent the proliferation of nuclear weapons.

Objectives

The objectives of the IAEA safeguards are: "the timely detection of diversion of significant quantities of *nuclear material* from peaceful nuclear activities to the manufacture of nuclear weapons or of other nuclear explosive devices or for purposes unknown, and deterrence of such diversion by the risk of early detection".[179] This statement has been carefully drafted not only to specify the Agency's responsibility but also to make clear the very significant limits on its responsibility. An understanding of these limits is crucial to an appreciation of the role that the safeguards system plays in current arms control verification and of how it might be extended or adapted to other arms control situations.

According to the statement of purpose, safeguards apply only to 'peaceful nuclear activities', that is, to nuclear facilities and materials devoted to non-military functions such as electric power generation or research. This means that the military nuclear facilities of the so-called 'nuclear weapon states' (USA, USSR, UK, France and China) are not subjected to safeguards, even for the three states (USA, USSR, UK) that have signed the Non-Proliferation Treaty. Nor are the civilian nuclear facilities of these states required to be under safeguards. It has only been in the past several years that the USA, UK and USSR have agreed to place some of their non-military nuclear activities under IAEA safeguards.

The clear separation of military and civilian applications of nuclear energy implied by the statement of objectives has been questioned by many people ever since the earliest days of the nuclear age. In fact, the original study on which the US Baruch Plan for international control of atomic energy was based (the Acheson–Lilienthal Report) denied the practicality of making this separation, emphasizing that "*safe* [i.e. non-explosive] *operations are possible only because dangerous ones are being carried out concurrently*".[180]

A second limitation of safeguards is that they are intended to deter diversions of sensitive materials, not prevent them. Actual prevention of diversion requires the authority of a sovereign state and falls under the concept of 'physical protection' of such materials, not safeguards.[181] Because the IAEA is an international organization it does not have the authority to use force or other coercive measures to modify the behaviour of nuclear facility operators or states. It can only serve as a deterrent by threatening exposure of an attempt to divert nuclear materials from non-military to military purposes. Just how effective this deterrence function is cannot be assessed accurately, since it depends not only on the probability of detection but on the potential benefits a state might see in cheating successfully as compared with the costs of being exposed prematurely as a violator.

The next set of limitations on safeguards derives from the definitions of the phrases 'timely detection' and 'significant quantities of nuclear materials'. A significant quantity (SQ) of a nuclear material is defined as the approximate amount needed to produce a nuclear weapon after account is taken for whatever processing must be done to put the nuclear material into usable form as an explosive.[182] Values for 'significant quantities' of nuclear explosive materials can be inferred from the data in table 4. For example, a total amount of 92.9 tonnes of plutonium in irradiated fuel represents 11 600 SQs, implying that 1 SQ = 8.0 kg for plutonium in this form.

'Timely detection' has turned out to be much more difficult to define. This

Table 4. Approximate quantities of material subject to IAEA safeguards except that covered by voluntary-offer agreements with nuclear weapon states at the end of 1983

Type of material	Quantity of material (t) in NNWS	in NWS[a]	Quantity in SQ
Nuclear material			
Plutonium[b] contained in irradiated fuel	85.8	7.1	11 600
Separated plutonium	5.3	1.5	850
HEU (equal to or greater than 20% uranium-235)	11.0	0	260
LEU (less than 20% uranium-235)	17 600	990	5 820
Source material[c] (natural or depleted uranium and thorium)	28 000	0	2 270
Total significant quantity			20 800
Non-nuclear material[d]			
Heavy water	1 307	0	–[e]

[a] Material in facilities in nuclear weapon states subject to safeguards under safeguards transfer agreements.

[b] The quantity includes an estimated 39.7 t (4 970 SQ) of plutonium in irradiated fuel, which is not reported to the Agency under the reporting procedures agreed to (the non-reported plutonium is contained in irradiated fuel assemblies to which item accountancy and containment and surveillance measures are applied).

[c] This table does not include material within the terms of sub-paragraphs 34(*a*) and (*b*) of INFCIRC/153 (Corrected)—in essence, yellowcake.

[d] Non-nuclear material subject to Agency safeguards under INFCIRC/66/Rev.2-type agreements.

[e] "Quantity in SQ" does not apply to non-nuclear material.

Source: IAEA Annual Report for 1983 (IAEA, Vienna, 1984), p. 68.

is not so much a technical problem as a political and adminstrative one, since the timeliness criterion is used to set the frequency of on-site inspections, and facility operators have a strong interest in keeping these to a minimum.[183] The compromise solution arrived at by the IAEA has been to define the necessary detection time to have the same 'order of magnitude' as the 'conversion time',[184] which in turn is defined as the time required to convert a given material into the 'metallic components of a nuclear explosive device'.[185] The official conversion times for various materials are listed in table 5.

Most of the conversion times are reasonable and have led to arrangements for relatively frequent inspection visits. In fact, the IAEA has decided that diversion possibilities are so great at facilities that process plutonium that the continuous presence of inspectors is necessary.[186] However, one conversion time, the one year allowed for conversion of low-enriched uranium to highly enriched nuclear explosive, is quite unrealistic given the capabilities of modern ultra-centrifuge enrichment facilities. Using a small clandestine centrifuge plant a state could produce enough very pure uranium-235 for a bomb in less

Table 5. Estimated material conversion times

Material classification	Beginning material form	End process form	Estimated conversion time
1	Pu, HEU[a], or ^{233}U metal	Finished plutonium or uranium metal components	Order of days (7–10)
2	PuO$_2$, Pu(NO$_3$)$_4$ or other pure compounds; HEU or ^{233}U oxide or other pure compounds; MOX or other non-irradiated pure mixtures of Pu or U [(^{233}U + ^{235}U) > 20%]; Pu, HEU and/or ^{233}U in scrap or other miscellaneous impure compounds	Finished plutonium or uranium metal components	Order of weeks[b] (1–3)
3	Pu, HEU or ^{233}U in irradiated fuels[c]	Finished plutonium or uranium metal components	Order of months (1–3)
4	U containing <20% ^{235}U and ^{233}U; thorium		Order of one year

[a] Uranium enriched to 20 per cent or more in the isotope ^{235}U.
[b] While no single factor is completely responsible for the indicated range of 1–3 weeks for conversion of these plutonium and uranium compounds, the pure compounds will tend to be at the lower end of the range and the mixtures and scrap at the higher end.
[c] Irradiation level is chosen on a case-by-case basis.

Source: IAEA Bulletin, Vol. 22, No. 3/4, August 1980, p. 6.

than three weeks using an amount of low-enriched or natural uranium whose diversion from a large bulk-handling facility would be very difficult to detect.[187] Unfortunately, the process of changing such a number once it is set is extremely difficult in an agency as large and politically diverse as the IAEA. This kind of inflexibility is an important disadvantage of international approaches to verification (see chapter 4).

Materials accounting

The major technique employed by the IAEA in carrying out its verification responsibilities is 'nuclear materials accountancy'.[188] It begins with a detailed agreement between the IAEA and the state in which the facility to be safeguarded is located. The IAEA is first given design information on the facility, which is used to designate a number of 'material balance areas' (MBAs) and 'key measurement points' (KMPs). An MBA is an area where nuclear materials are stored, for example the spent fuel pool of a nuclear power reactor or the product storage area of an enrichment plant. A KMP is generally a point of transition at which nuclear materials move from one MBA to another or into or out of the facility, for example a pipe carrying waste out of a reprocessing facility or a loading dock at a fuel fabrication plant.

Also part of the IAEA-state agreement is the creation by the state of its own system of accounting for nuclear materials at the facility.[189] The state agrees to maintain accurate data on inventories in MBAs and flow or transport through KMPs. The IAEA keeps its own set of records based on the initial inventories established at the opening of a safeguarded facility and the subsequent reports of material flows and inventories submitted by the operators. The records kept by the operators are periodically verified by independent on-site measurements made by IAEA inspectors. In a typical site visit the inspectors will audit the records of the facility and make their own measurements of inventories in MBAs and flow rates through KMPs as well as sample measurements to verify the declared compositions of materials in the facility. Some of these composition measurements can be made on-site by so-called 'non-destructive assay' (NDA), while others must be made by taking samples which are sent for chemical, spectroscopic or radiometric analysis to the IAEA's own laboratory in Siebersdorf, Austria. This laboratory is capable of processing about 2 000 samples per year.[190]

Because such remote analysis is costly in both time and money it is desirable to make as many on-site non-destructive measurements as possible. Most of these are intended to measure the percentage composition of uranium and plutonium isotopes contained in fuel rods, casks, tanks and so on. The most commonly used devices for these measurements rely on gamma-ray counters similar to the X-ray detectors described in section VII.[191]

Every radioactive isotope has a unique 'signature' which is carried by the radiation it emits. Sensitive detectors can read this signature at considerable distances even if the material being monitored is shielded by barriers. For example, it was with a simple, portable gamma-ray detector that Swedish researchers were able to detect the presence of uranium—and therefore possibly a nuclear weapon—aboard a Soviet submarine which ran aground near Karlskrona in October 1981. The monitoring was carried out from a small boat next to the submarine, and enough radiation passed through the hull to allow positive identification of the presence of 10 kg of uranium-238 and the reasonable inference that this was part of a nuclear weapon carried in the submarine's torpedo room.[192]

The total on-site inspection effort of the IAEA in 1983 consisted of about 1 840 inspections carried out at 520 nuclear installations in 53 states. Non-destructive assays were conducted as part of 26 per cent of these inspections and more than 1 150 analyses of plutonium and uranium samples were performed at the Siebersdorf Laboratory.[193] The impressive scope of application of AEA safeguards can be seen in tables 4 and 6 which show the amounts of

Table 6. Installations in non-nuclear weapon states under safeguards or containing safeguarded material at the end of 1983

Installation category	Number of installations		
	INFCIRC/153^a	INFCIRC/66/Rev.2	Total^b
A. Power reactors	121	26	147 (143)
B. Research reactors and critical assemblies	151	26	177 (177)
C. Conversion plants	5	2	7 (6)
D. Fuel fabrication plants	32	8	40 (39)
E. Reprocessing plants	4	2	6 (6)
F. Enrichment plants	4	0	4 (4)
G. Separate storage facilities	26	2	28 (23)
H. Other facilities	45	1	46 (42)
I. Other locations	398	27	425 (404)
J. Non-nuclear installations	0	1	1 (0)
Totals	**786**	**95**	**881 (844)**

^{a} Covering safeguards agreements pursuant to NPT and/or Tlatelolco Treaty.
^{b} Numbers for 1982 are indicated in parentheses for comparison.

Source: IAEA Annual Report for 1983 (IAEA, Vienna, 1984), p. 69.

nuclear materials and the numbers and types of facilities under safeguards at the end of 1983.[194]

The end result of all of this measuring and accounting is a set of values for 'material unaccounted for' (MUF) at each MBA. The MUF value is the discrepancy between the 'book inventory' derived from accounting records and the 'physical inventory' as measured at the end of each 'material balance period'.[195] Every value of MUF must be accompanied by an estimate of the expected range of error so that standard statistical tests can be applied to determine whether or not the MUF is significant. A significant value of MUF is called an 'anomaly', and unless it is satisfactorily resolved by further investigation such an anomaly can lead to the conclusion that a diversion of nuclear materials has occurred and initiate the IAEA sanctions procedures.[196] The IAEA's Annual Report notes that 420 such anomalies were found during 1983 and that all but one had been satisfactorily explained at the time of publication of the report.[197]

Containment and surveillance

The total number of facilities under IAEA safeguards at the end of 1983 was 881 (see table 6), and as non-military facilities in the USA and USSR are added the number will rise appreciably. At the same time the IAEA is constrained in its ability to add new inspectors by budgetary restraints and the difficulty of recruiting and retaining qualified personnel.[198] It is not surprising, therefore, that the IAEA has placed increasing emphasis on containment and surveillance technology to limit the demand for human inspectors.

Containment is the process of restricting the movement of nuclear materials by the use of various kinds of physical barriers, such as walls, transport flasks, containers and so on.[199] The primary technology for containment purposes is a simple seal which is designed to reveal any attempt to break or tamper with it. As of December 1981, IAEA inspectors were applying over 3 000 such seals per year, and the computerized history of more than 10 000 seals had already been accumulated at IAEA headquarters.[200] One disadvantage of these seals is that they must be sent back to the laboratory to check for tampering or replacement. This has led to an effort to develop fibre optic (see figure 37) or electronic seals which could be checked either on-site or by remote control.[201] However, development of these new devices has been slow, and the Agency still relies almost entirely on the traditional seals. In 1983, 6 600 were used, more than double the number in 1981, illustrating both the expansion of the Agency's responsibilities and its increasing emphasis on containment measures.[202]

Figure 37. COBRA prototype fibre-optic seal and verifier
In a fibre-optic seal the seal wire is replaced by a multi-strand plastic fibre-optic loop, the ends of which are enclosed in a seal in such a way that a unique random pattern of fibres is formed. This can be verified by shining a light into the ends of the loop and observing the magnified pattern of the fibre ends, either visually or photographically; development is also being directed towards television recording of images.

Source: IAEA, *IAEA Safeguards, Safeguards Techniques and Equipment,* IAEA/SG/INF/5 (IAEA, Vienna, 1984), p. 29, figure 18.

The word 'surveillance' has much the same meaning when applied to safeguards as it has for more general intelligence activities. It is the collection of information through the use of monitoring devices (or on-site inspectors) in order to detect undeclared movements of nuclear material or tampering with safeguards devices.[203] For many years the most commonly used surveillance device was a dual super-8 motion picture camera which could take single-frame photographs every 20 minutes for 100 days before film reloading (7 200 frames).[204] A new generation of surveillance systems uses a closed circuit television monitor and magnetic tape recording (see figure 38), which not only eliminates the need for film developing but also permits remote monitoring.[205] Such television monitors can also be equipped with their own infra-red light source to allow surveillance at all light levels.

The concept of remote monitoring of containment and surveillance devices is a very attractive one and has been embodied in a project called RECOVER (remote continuous verification). In this system all electronic seals and television monitors would be connected via international telephone lines or relay satellites to IAEA headquarters, where their performance and status could be checked periodically by simply dialling a phone number.[206] The present RECOVER concept does not involve the actual transmission of data, but there

Figure 38. Closed circuit television monitor

Source: Photo courtesy of IAEA.

is no doubt that the system could be designed to do this, much in the same manner as the international seismic data exchange discussed in chapter 4. The RECOVER system has already been tested using encrypted digital data transmitted over secure communication lines.[207]

The RECOVER programme began in the USA during the Carter Administration with the original research contract going to the TRW Corporation.[208] Unfortunately, the programme has received very little support from the Reagan Administration, and the only serious research currently being done on it is in Japan, where it is being studied for possible adaptation to the Japanese national safeguards programme.[209]

Developments in modern containment and surveillance technology, along with remote monitoring concepts like RECOVER, have led to suggestions that the IAEA safeguards system might be extended to include the verification of a total ban on production of nuclear explosives or bans on chemical, biological or radiological weapons.[210] From the purely technical point of view there do seem to be some interesting possibilities for the adaptation of IAEA surveillance and containment concepts to, for example, the monitoring of certain chemical or nuclear production facilities which are shut down and moth-balled under an agreement.

One idea which has already been studied in some detail is the remote monitoring of a chemical weapon destruction facility.[211] Given the high toxicity of the materials being processed, such a facility would have to be highly automated, and the monitoring systems would have to be automated as well. However, the instruments for monitoring chemical substances must be very different from those used to monitor radioactive nuclear substances. Where the latter can often be assayed with non-destructive techniques this will usually not be possible with chemicals. So instead of the fuel bundle counter and gamma-ray spectrometer which could verify the input stream to a nuclear reprocessing plant, a chemical weapon destruction plant would need flow meters and gas chromatographs, instruments which are generally less precise and less convenient to use. However, this may not be a serious problem, since precision in measuring quantities is less important for chemicals than for nuclear materials. Adding a RECOVER system to allow remote monitoring of several facilities from a central location would certainly be feasible as well.[212]

This example shows that opportunities do exist to apply IAEA safeguards experience in new fields of arms control, but at the same time the prospects for such applications should not be exaggerated. Quite aside from the political and administrative problems which are analysed in chapter 4, there are also technical obstacles which will limit the use of on-site inspection, containment and surveillance, as well as remote monitoring in verifying bans on chemical or biological weapons. In contrast to the world nuclear industry, which involves fewer than one thousand facilities, the chemical industry comprises many thousands of facilities of all types and sizes. To attempt to inspect and monitor all of these would create data management problems at least on the scale of those faced by international satellite photography or an international seismic network. It is appropriate to ask whether the danger of chemical weapons is serious enough or the monitoring of declared facilities comprehensive enough to warrant the great expense and complexity such a system would entail.

X. The importance of synergism

The variety and sophistication of the monitoring systems just surveyed must be viewed as contributing to a powerful, integrated intelligence-gathering capability for any state which possesses them. There are many detailed discussions of individual systems such as photographic satellites or seismic networks in the literature on verification, but much less common are studies which point out the many interactions among these various systems in making the whole considerably greater than the sum of its parts.

It is relatively rare that a single piece of evidence gathered by a single monitoring system can be the basis for a charge of violation. Much more often the individual bits of evidence are ambiguous when taken separately and only acquire significance when assembled together in a pattern with other ambiguous bits of evidence. The art of intelligence is the ability to assemble such patterns, and this same art is necessary in analysing the vast quantities of data produced by so many different monitoring systems. A few simple examples will be considered here.

The verification of a comprehensive nuclear test ban would certainly involve a world-wide network of seismic detectors, but even such a network will inevitably have some threshold explosive yield below which the identification of a seismic event as an explosion or an earthquake becomes highly ambiguous. This ambiguity will lead to a certain rate of 'suspicious' events, and the usual remedy suggested for this problem is on-site inspection. Since this remedy may be considered by some to be either technically unfeasible or politically undesirable, or both, it is important to reduce the number of suspicious events by other means in order to keep the demands for on-site inspection to a minimum.

Such other means exist in the form of photographic satellites which can often detect the preparations for nuclear tests. Such a detection was made by both US and Soviet reconnaissance satellites when what appeared to be preparations for a nuclear test were discovered in South Africa in 1977.[213] Preparations for such a test involve drilling a deep hole, placing instruments around the test site and delivering and arming the device. Such activity inevitably takes at least several days, possibly much more, and is difficult to conceal from the prying eyes of photo-reconnaissance satellites.[214] In addition, an underground nuclear explosion often leaves a 'subsidence crater' as the Earth's surface above the explosion collapses into the newly created cavity (see figure 39).[215] Such craters are easily observed from satellites and may be

Figure 39. Subsidence craters at the Nevada Test Site
An underground nuclear explosion creates a large cavity into which the rock above the explosion can fall. This creates a 'chimney' which can reach all the way to the surface, causing a visible crater. In order to prevent such craters with high confidence, explosions must be set off at sufficiently great depths and in the proper geological environment.

Source: Courtesy of Lawrence Livermore National Laboratory, CA.

difficult to prevent with confidence in an untested geological area. Next there is the added risk that radioactive materials will be released into the atmosphere by the explosion and be detected downwind of the test site. Such releases are not uncommon even for underground tests, and the monitoring of ambient radioactivity is now carried on as a routine aspect of weather and air-quality monitoring in many states around the world. Finally, a space-based thermal infra-red sensor could possibly notice the increase in temperature of the test area after the explosion. Therefore, photographic satellites and radiation detectors can add considerably to the effectiveness and acceptability of a seismic network by reducing the number of ambiguous events and consequently the number of demands for on-site inspection.

A second example of synergistic interactions among a number of systems is the monitoring of ICBM tests. Such tests are observed by infra-red sensors from geostationary satellites, by ground- and sea-based radars and by the interception of communications and telemetry. All these systems interact to produce a much more detailed and complete picture of the test than any of the systems could provide by itself. In addition, it is possible to measure or observe the same feature with more than one of the systems and compare the results. Such cross-checks can greatly increase confidence that the measured values are accurate and can make far more difficult any attempt to disguise or hide the data. Another useful synergism, the superposition of radar, visual and infra-red images to aid in object detection and camouflage penetration, has already been mentioned in section V.

A third example is the monitoring of troop or weapon restrictions in certain zones, such as in Central Europe. Here again, photographic and infra-red satellites can play an important role along with ground-, air- and space-based radars and signals and communications intelligence. While clever camouflage might hide certain things from satellites, the challenge of hiding militarily significant activities from the combined vigilance of all of these systems is far more difficult and risky.

Many other examples of the advantages of synergism could be listed, and there is no doubt that taken together the technologies described here constitute a highly reliable mechanism for monitoring arms control agreements. Yet even this vast array of techniques is not perfect. For example, Argentina was able to construct a uranium enrichment facility in total secrecy over a period of several years.[216] The plant is based on the gaseous diffusion process and is said to be only the first module of a small commercial facility, which can explain why it was not recognized by satellites. A completed gaseous diffusion plant, even of relatively low capacity, would be extremely difficult to conceal. But if the gas-centrifuge process had been chosen instead of gaseous diffusion, it is quite possible that the existence of a militarily significant facility could have been kept a secret even longer.

Incidents such as this do not call into question the great value of verification in support of arms control agreements. They do, however, serve as useful reminders that no system will ever be perfect and that to demand perfection is, as it always has been, to make the best the enemy of the good.

XI. The technological dimension of verification

This chapter has described a remarkable range of monitoring technologies whose sophistication and comprehensiveness have been steadily increasing for many years and can be expected to continue to increase for many more. The impressive capabilities of individual systems combined with the synergistic effects of their interactions with each other give an encouraging picture of the existing and potential prospects for effectively monitoring many kinds of arms control or disarmament agreements.

However, this encouragement must be tempered by the realization that technological progress in the weapons to be monitored is proceeding at least as rapidly as is that of the monitoring systems. One cannot escape the intimate connection between arms control monitoring and military intelligence gathering, and as long as efforts continue to frustrate the latter process the former process will inevitably be made more difficult. There is in fact a qualitative arms race going on between "hiders and finders",[217] and it is not at all clear who the ultimate winners of this race will be.

A review of the monitoring devices and techniques just described will show that the easiest objects or events to monitor are those of large size, fixed location, substantial energy release, high temperature and distinctive appearance or signature. Fortunately this includes a considerable range of weapons and military preparations such as fixed-site ICBMs, nuclear missile submarines, nuclear weapon tests (both above and below the surface of the Earth), missile launches (whether for testing the missiles themselves or for experimenting with anti-satellite or ballistic missile defence systems), large phased-array radars, and most nuclear facilities. All of these objects are extremely difficult to hide from regular monitoring by the remote-sensing devices described here, and efforts to cheat on an agreement involving such weapons or activities would involve a very high risk of detection.

This positive view of verification must be balanced by some very important negative factors. First, there is the problem of political context in which evidence acquired by technical means is evaluated. History has shown that even the kinds of evidence just described as highly reliable can lead to intense political controversy as a result of differing attitudes towards arms control and military doctrine as well as differing assessment of the capabilities, motivations and intentions of rival states. This problem is important enough to deserve an entire chapter of its own, and it is the subject of chapter 3.

A second problem, also largely political, is the great expense and technical sophistication of most of these monitoring technologies. This means that they can be developed and deployed by only the richest and most technically advanced states, while less developed states, with security concerns which are at least as great of those of the major powers, must live in far greater uncertainty and/or become dependent on one or the other of the great powers for information vital to their national security. Such uncertainty and dependence are a source of increasing international concern and also require a separate discussion (see chapter 4).

The third problem is purely technical and involves the growing gap between the capabilities of monitoring systems and the qualitative features of newer generations of weapon. Probably the most important example of this trend is in land-based nuclear missiles where the same features of large size and stationary location which lead to easy monitoring also lead to high vulnerability to pre-emptive attack. As nuclear missiles have become more accurate this problem of vulnerability, and its accompanying sense of crisis instability, has become more acute. It has been suggested that the rational solution to this problem is to eliminate land-based ICBMs (either bilaterally or unilaterally) and rely on less vulnerable submarine-based systems for deterrence of nuclear attack.[218] However, the actual course taken by both the USA and USSR has been to develop smaller, more mobile and more flexible nuclear missiles such as the US cruise missiles, the Soviet SS-20 and SS-X-25, and the proposed US 'Midgetman' missile, which will be much smaller and more mobile than the present generation of Minuteman and MX ICBMs.

In this connection it has been revealed that actual deployment of US nuclear-armed cruise missiles on submarines has begun.[219] The presence of such missiles on submarines is simply impossible to verify by any means short of physical inspection, and even this method would not provide a high degree of reassurance. There is an inherent difficulty in attempting to use on-site inspections to verify the presence or absence of highly portable objects.

Another important trend is towards so-called 'dual-capable' weapons, that is, weapons which can be armed with either nuclear or conventional warheads. An example of such a system is the cruise missile, whose relatively low cost and potentially high accuracy and flexibility make it suitable for delivery of conventional explosives as well as nuclear warheads. An agreement which attempted to ban only nuclear warheads on cruise missiles while permitting conventional ones would present more serious technical verification problems. It has even been suggested that the Minuteman missiles displaced by the new MX missiles could be redeployed to bases in the United Kingdom and armed with conventional warheads instead of their current nuclear payload. While the US Defence Department spokesman who announced this proposal was confident that "we can solve verification issues,"[220] a certain amount of scepticism on this question is probably warranted.

At the same time these increased difficulties should not be exaggerated. Arming cruise or Minuteman missiles with nuclear warheads requires more elaborate and distinctive storage and support facilities which are vulnerable to detection.[221] In addition, this, like all efforts to cheat, faces the risk of exposure by leaks, spies or defectors. Clandestinely deploying nuclear warheads would inevitably involve many people, and the difficulty of keeping secrets increases rapidly with the number of people involved.

Efforts to develop anti-satellite (ASAT) weapons illustrate another technical problem in verification. The United States is currently developing a so-called 'direct-ascent' ASAT system which uses a small missile launched from an ordinary fighter aircraft. The testing of such a weapon is observable by Soviet national technical means, so a ban on the testing of such devices would be relatively easy to verify. [222] But once the weapon is developed and deployed its small size and non-distinctive deployment mode would make verification of a limit or ban on its deployment impossible. Such problems of timing are extremely important in verification, a lesson that has already been learned in the experience with multiple independently targetable re-entry vehicles (MIRVs). An agreement to ban the testing of multiple warhead missiles when they were under development in the 1960s would have been easily verifiable. Now that they are developed and deployed the problem of verifying limits on their numbers and qualitative capabilities is far more difficult.

To these examples of the tendency for qualitative weapon developments to outrun monitoring capabilities must be added the important class of weapon for which national technical means of verification have always had, and are certain to continue to have, extremely limited application. In this class fall chemical and biological weapons as well as the production or diversion of small quantities of nuclear explosives such as plutonium or highly enriched uranium. None of these activities is characterized by the kinds of distinctive and visible signatures associated with large missiles, submarines, aircraft or radars. Any attempt to monitor the production or stockpiling of such weapons or materials must inevitably involve more intrusive and politically sensitive measures than those associated with satellites or seismographs. While some technical measures can aid in the process and are certainly worthy of further study, the search for a purely technical solution to the problem of control of dangerous chemical, biological or nuclear materials is doomed to failure.

There is one area in which the capabilities of monitoring technology have developed faster than techniques for evasion: the monitoring of nuclear explosions. Seismological instruments, data analysis and information processing allow very reliable detection of nuclear explosions, and all the currently discussed schemes for clandestine testing seem highly implausible, especially when the synergistic effects of other monitoring processes are taken into account. A comprehensive nuclear test ban does seem to be verifiable down to very low yield tests (fractions of a kiloton) with a high degree of reliability. Therefore, no serious technical barriers remain to the verification of a comprehensive test ban. [223]

In summary, from a purely technical perspective it can be said with confidence that limits or bans on a substantial number of highly significant weapon systems could be verified with a high degree of reliability. If technical concerns about verifiability were the only obstacle to such agreements, there would be no reason not to have negotiated and signed them already and, in fact, a number of such agreements have been signed. The limited and threshold nuclear test bans, SALT I and II, and other treaties have been negotiated largely because of the existence of these national technical means.

Unfortunately, technological trends seem to be moving in a direction away from such agreements. One analysis of future developments in the 1980s concluded that "the ... direction of weapons technology is ... away from, not toward, greater certainty in surveillance".[224] These trends have caused the beginnings of a re-evaluation of the concept of arms control in the United States, not only among those who have traditionally been critical of it, but by those who were previously identified with efforts to achieve agreements. Former officials of both the Nixon and Carter Administrations have recently questioned the usefulness of the SALT approach largely on their assessment of the technological trends referred to above.[225] It is now being suggested that 'informal' restraints be agreed to under which each side would rely on purely unilateral verification measures and decide unilaterally how to deal with ambiguous or incriminating evidence.

Such a reversion to unilateralism would represent a serious setback to what had been painfully slow but still significant progress towards greater co-operation among states in arms control, both bilaterally between the USA and USSR and internationally through the Conference on Disarmament. Such a drastic step does not seem to be warranted on purely technical grounds, since the limitations of technical surveillance measures are only one, and probably not the most important, of the factors determining the likelihood of non-compliance with arms control agreements.[226] While technological trends certainly provide grounds for serious concern about a number of weapon systems, the notion that "we have come to the end of the road with traditional arms control agreements"[227] cannot be sustained on technical grounds. Such pessimism has its roots much more in political than technological developments, and these are the subject of the next chapter.

Notes and references

1. York, H.A., 'US air and space reconnaissance programmes', in SIPRI, *World Armaments and Disarmament, SIPRI Yearbook 1977* (Almqvist & Wiksell, Stockholm, 1977), Appendix 5A, p. 180.
2. Scoville, H., Jr, 'A leap forward in verification', in Willrich, M. and Rhinelander, J.B. (eds), *SALT—The Moscow Agreements and Beyond* (Free Press, New York, 1974), p. 162.
3. Evvard, J.C., *Limits on Observational Capabilities of Aerospacecraft*, NASA-TN-D-2933, National Aeronautics and Space Administration, Washington, DC, 1965, p. 6.
4. See orbit parameter tables in SIPRI, *Outer Space—Battlefield of the Future?* (Taylor & Francis, London, 1978), pp. 49-81; and Jasani, B. (ed.), *Outer*

Space—A New Dimension of the Arms Race (Taylor & Francis, London, 1982), pp. 331-40 [a SIPRI book].

5. Perry, G.E., 'Identification of military components within the Soviet space programme', in Jasani (note 4), p. 142.
6. Katz, A.H., *Verification and SALT: The State of the Art and the Art of the State* (Heritage Foundation, Washington, DC, 1979), p. 16.
7. SIPRI 1978 (note 4), p. 17.
8. Jasani (note 4), p. 332; see SIPRI, *World Armaments and Disarmament, SIPRI Yearbook 1983* (Taylor & Francis, London, 1983), p. 448.
9. Richelson, J.T., *The Keyhole Satellite Program,* School of Government and Public Administration, The American University, Washington, DC, March 1984, pp. 27-33.
10. Most discussions of satellite photography show the light passing through a focusing lens, but large, high-resolution satellite cameras almost certainly use mirrors, since these can be made much lighter than lenses.
11. Bahcall, J.N. and Spitzer, L., Jr, 'The Space Telescope', *Scientific American,* Vol. 247, No. 1, July 1982, p. 39.
12. Mordoff, K.F., 'Company ends electrical tests on telescope', *Aviation Week & Space Technology,* Vol. 121, No. 13, 24 September 1984, p. 56.
13. Ondrjeka, R., 'Photoreconnaissance', in Tsipis, K., Hafemeister, D. and Janeway, P. (eds), *Arms Control Verification: The Technologies that Make it Possible* (Pergamon, Elmsford, NY, 1985).
14. Gelb, L., 'Keeping an eye on Russia', *New York Times Magazine,* 29 November 1981, p. 148.
15. Bahcall & Spitzer (note 11), p. 42.
16. Whitney, W.M., Mackin, R.J., Jr and Spear, A.J., *A Forecast of Space Technology; 1980–2000, Part Three: Management of Information,* NASA SP-387, National Aeronautics and Space Administration, Washington, DC, January 1976, p. 3-13.
17. Fante, R.L., 'Electromagnetic beam propagation in turbulent media', *Proceedings of the IEEE,* Vol. 63, No. 12, December 1975, p. 1669.
18. Richelson, J.T., *United States Strategic Reconnaissance: Photographic/Imaging Satellites,* ACIS Working Paper No. 38, Center for International and Strategic Affairs, UCLA, Los Angeles, May 1983, p. 13.
19. Bahcall & Spitzer (note 11), p. 42.
20. Hafemeister, D., 'Advances in verification technology', *Bulletin of the Atomic Scientists,* Vol. 41, No. 1, January 1985, p. 36.
21. Colby, W., in *Military Implications of the Treaty on the Limitation of Strategic Offensive Arms and Protocol Thereto (Salt II Treaty),* Hearings before the Committee on Armed Services (SASC Hearings), US Senate, 96th Congress, First Session (US Government Printing Office, Washington, DC, 1979), Part 3, 9, 10, 11 and 16 October, p. 1015.
22. Previously published in Jasani (note 4), p. 47.
23. Scoville (note 2).
24. Scoville (note 2), p. 172.
25. 'Satellite pictures show Soviet CVN towering above Nikolaiev shipyard', *Jane's Defence Weekly,* Vol. 2, No. 5, 11 August 1984, pp. 171-73.
26. Hudson, R.D. and Hudson, J.W., 'The military applications of remote sensing by infrared', *Proceedings of the IEEE,* Vol. 63, No. 1, January 1975, p. 123.
27. Sabins, F.F., Jr, *Remote Sensing: Principles and Interpretation* (W.H. Freeman, San Francisco, 1978), p. 121.
28. Kellogg, W.W., Buettner, K.J.K. and May, E.C., *Meteorological Satellite Obser-*

vation of Thermal Emission, RM-4392-NASA, Rand Corp., Santa Monica, CA, December 1964, p. 47.

29. Hudson & Hudson (note 26), p. 121.
30. Cannon, T.M. and Hunt, B.R., 'Image processing by computer', *Scientific American,* Vol. 245, No. 4, October 1981, p. 215; see also Sabins (note 27), pp. 49-50.
31. Greenwood, T., 'Reconnaissance and arms control', *Scientific American,* Vol. 228, No. 2, February 1973, p. 19.
32. Hudson & Hudson (note 26), p. 120.
33. Sabins (note 27), p. 120.
34. Constant, J.N., *Fundamentals of Strategic Weapons: Offense and Defence Systems,* Part 2 (Martinus Nijhoff, The Hague, 1981), p. 350.
35. 'USAF admits weather satellite mission', *Aviation Week & Space Technology,* Vol. 98, No. 11, 12 March 1973, p. 18.
36. 'Defense infrared payload loaded in Shuttle Orbiter', *Aviation Week & Space Technology,* Vol. 116, No. 24, 14 June 1982, p. 21.
37. Von Hippel, F. and Levi, B., *Controlling the Source: Verification of a Cutoff in the Production of Plutonium and High-Enriched Uranium for Nuclear Weapons,* Report PU/CEES-167, Princeton University Center for Energy and Environmental Studies, Princeton, NJ, July 1984, p. 25.
38. Hudson & Hudson (note 26), p. 124.
39. Kellogg, Buettner & May (note 28), p. 33.
40. Hudson & Hudson (note 26), p. 112.
41. Hudson & Hudson (note 26), p. 110.
42. Schultz, J. and Russell, D., 'New staring sensors', *Defence Electronics,* Vol. 16, No. 7, July 1984, p. 45.
43. Schultz & Russell (note 42), pp. 46-47.
44. Amelio, G.F., 'Charge-coupled devices', *Scientific American,* Vol. 230, No. 2, February 1974, pp. 22-31
45. Klass, P.J., 'Interest rises in infrared search, track', *Aviation Week & Space Technology,* Vol. 117, No. 9, 30 August 1982, p. 68.
46. Hudson & Hudson (note 26), p. 112.
47. Smith, B.A., 'Tests confirm Teal Ruby design', *Aviation Week & Space Technology,* Vol. 115, No. 1, 6 July 1981, pp. 23-24.
48. Smith, B.A., 'Problems double costs of Teal Ruby', *Aviation Week & Space Technology* (note 47), pp. 23-24.
49. Elachi, C., 'Spaceborne imaging radar: geologic and oceanographic applications', *Science,* Vol. 209, No. 4461, 5 September 1980, p. 1073.
50. Brookner, E., 'A review of array radars', *Microwave Journal,* Vol. 24, No. 10, October 1981, pp. 25-28; see also Brookner, E., *Radar Technology* (Artech House, Dedham, MA, 1977), chapter 1.
51. Brookner, *Microwave Journal* (note 50), p. 25.
52. Rihaczek, A.W., *Principles of High-Resolution Radar* (McGraw Hill, New York, 1969), pp. 51-56.
53. Figure from Brookner, E., 'Radar of the '80s and beyond', Raytheon Company Equipment Division, Wayland, MA, May 1984, p. 4.
54. *McGraw Hill Encyclopedia of Science and Technology,* Vol. 11 (McGraw Hill, New York, 1982), p. 230.
55. *Jane's Weapon Systems, 1982–83* (Macdonald & Co, London, 1982), p. 499.
56. Aspin, L. and Kaplan, F.M., 'Verification in perspective', in Potter, W.C. (ed.), *Verification and SALT: The Challenge of Strategic Deception* (Westview Press, Boulder, CO, 1980), pp. 180-81.

57. SIPRI, *World Armaments and Disarmaments, SIPRI Yearbook 1980* (Taylor & Francis, London, 1980), p. 298.
58. Stein, K.J., 'Backscatter radar unit enters production phase', *Aviation Week & Space Technology,* Vol. 117, No. 7, 16 August 1982, p. 68.
59. Stein (note 58), p. 69.
60. SIPRI (note 57), p. 295.
61. SIPRI (note 57), p. 295.
62. Brookner, *Microwave Journal* (note 50), p. 28.
63. Clear explanations of the principles of synthetic aperture radar are also given in Brown, W.M. and Porcello, L.J., 'An introduction to synthetic-aperture radar', *IEEE Spectrum,* Vol. 6, No. 9, September 1969, pp. 52-62; Jensen, H. *et al.,* 'Side-looking airborne radar', *Scientific American,* Vol. 237, No. 4, October 1977, pp. 84-95; and Brookner in *Radar Technology* (note 50), chapters 16-18.
64. Sherwin, C.W., Ruina, J.P. and Rawcliffe, R.D., 'Some early developments in synthetic aperture radar systems', *IRE Transactions on Military Electronics,* Vol. MIL-6, April 1962, p. 113; Brookner, *Radar Technology* (note 50), chapter 17.
65. Elachi (note 49), p. 1074.
66. Ulsamer, E., 'Military imperatives in space', *Air Force,* Vol. 68, No. 1, January 1985, pp. 92-93.
67. Whitney, Mackin & Spear (note 16), p. 3-12.
68. Chapman, J., 'New eyes for NATO', *Military Technology,* October 1983, p. 42.
69. Kinnucan, P., 'Machines that see', *High Technology,* Vol. 3, No. 4, April 1983, pp. 30-36; Rhea, J., 'DARPA pushes strategic computing technology', *Defense Electronics,* Vol. 16, No. 6, June 1984, pp. 112-30.
70. Constant (note 34), p. 356.
71. Waldrop, M.M., 'The infrared astronomy satellite (II)', *Science,* Vol. 221, 1 July 1983, pp. 43-44.
72. Constant (note 34), p. 343.
73. Hunt, B.R., 'Image enhancement by digital computer', in Hafemeister, D.W. and Schroeer, D. (eds), *Physics, Technology and the Nuclear Arms Race,* AIP Conference Proceedings No. 104 (American Institute of Physics, New York, 1983), p. 135.
74. Oppenheim, A.V., Schafer, R.W. and Stockham, T.G., 'Nonlinear filtering of multiplied and convolved signals', *Proceedings of the IEEE,* Vol. 56, No. 8, August 1968, pp. 1264-92.
75. Hunt (note 73).
76. Pratt, W.K., *Digital Image Processing* (Wiley, New York, 1978), chapter 12.
77. Hunt (note 73), pp. 147-48.
78. A binary number is related to the 'base' 2 in the same way that an ordinary decimal number is related to the base 10. Binary numbers are therefore strings of zeros and ones. For example, the decimal number 2 is written in binary form as 10, and the decimal 4 is written as 100.
    Each digit of a binary number is called a 'bit', so an 8-bit binary number would encompass all the decimal numbers from 0 (written 00000000) to 255 (written 11111111).
79. Kristian, I. and Blouke, M., 'Charge-coupled devices in astronomy', *Scientific American,* Vol. 247, No. 4, October 1982, p. 54.
80. Boehm, B.W., *Some Information Processing Implications of Air Force Space Missions: 1970–1980,* Rand Memorandum RM-6213-PR, January 1970, Rand Corp., Santa Monica, CA, p. 13.
81. Pratt (note 76), pp. 319-21.
82. Hunt (note 73), p. 145.

83. Pratt (note 76), pp. 311-18; Sabins (note 27), pp. 248-53.
84. Sabins (note 27), p. 250.
85. Peli, T. and Lim, J.S., 'Adaptive filtering for image enhancement', *Optical Engineering,* Vol. 21, No. 1, January/February 1982, pp. 108-12.
86. Ebersole, J.F., 'Optical image subtraction', *Optical Engineering,* Vol. 14, No. 5, September/October 1975, pp. 436-47.
87. Quatieri, T.F., *Object Detection by Two-Dimensional Linear Prediction,* Technical Report 632, Massachusetts Institute of Technology Lincoln Laboratory, Lexington, MA, 28 January 1983.
88. See Pratt (note 76) for a more complete survey.
89. Hunt (note 73), p. 143; Woods, R.E. and Gonzalez, R.C., 'Real-time digital image enhancement', *Proceedings of the IEEE,* Vol. 69, No. 5, May 1981, pp. 643-54.
90. Ebersole, J.F. and Wyant, J.C., 'Real-time optical subtraction of photographic imagery for difference detection', *Applied Optics,* Vol. 15, No. 4, April 1976, pp. 871-76.
91. Boehm (note 80), p. 12.
92. Whitney, Mackin & Spear (note 16), p. 3-83.
93. Robinson, A.L., 'Experimental memory chips reach 1 megabit', *Science,* Vol. 224, No. 4649, 11 May 1984, pp. 590-92.
94. 'New circuits expected to exceed projections', *Aviation Week & Space Technology,* Vol. 121, No. 5, 30 July 1984, p. 47.
95. Preston, G.W., 'The very large scale integrated circuit', *American Scientist,* Vol. 71, No. 5, September/October 1983, pp. 466-73.
96. Brookner, E. and Hunt, B.R., 'Synthetic aperture radar processing', *Trends and Perspectives in Signal Processing,* Vol. 2, No. 1, January 1982, p. 3; see also Elachi (note 49), pp. 1073-82.
97. Cutrona, L.J. *et al.,* 'On the application of coherent optical processing techniques to synthetic aperture radar', *Proceedings of the IEEE,* Vol. 54, No. 8, August 1966, pp. 1026-32.
98. Jensen, H. *et al.,* 'Side-looking airborne radar', *Scientific American,* Vol. 237, No. 4, October 1977, p. 94.
99. Brookner & Hunt (note 96), p. 3.
100. Bicknell, T., 'Real-time digital processing of SAR data', Spaceborne Imaging Radar Symposium, 17-20 January 1983, Jet Propulsion Laboratory, Pasadena, CA, 1 July 1983, pp. 96-97.
101. Brookner & Hunt (note 96), p. 4.
102. Carver, K.R., 'Spaceborne SAR sensor architecture', Spaceborne Imaging Radar Symposium (note 100), p. 19.
103. Sykes, L.R., Evernden, J.F. and Cifuentes, I., 'Seismic methods for verifying nuclear test bans', in Hafemeister & Schroeer (note 73), p. 86.
104. Dahlman, O. and Israelson, H., *Monitoring Underground Nuclear Explosions* (Elsevier, Amsterdam, 1977); Bolt, B.A., *Nuclear Explosions and Earthquakes: The Parted Veil* (W.H. Freeman, San Francisco, 1976); Douglas, A., 'Seismic source identification: a review of past and present research efforts', in Husebye, E.S. and Mykkeltveit, S. (eds), *Identification of Seismic Sources—Earthquake or Underground Explosion* (D. Reidel, Dordrecht, 1981), pp. 1-48; Sykes, L.R. and Evernden, J.F., 'The verification of a comprehensive nuclear test ban', *Scientific American,* Vol. 247, No. 4, October 1982, pp. 47-55; *Bulletin of the Seismological Society of America,* Vol. 72, No. 6, December 1982.
105. Ringdal, F. and Husebye, E.S., 'Application of arrays in the detection, location and identification of seismic events', in *Bulletin of the Seismological Society of America* (note 104), pp. S201-S224.

106. Herrin, E., 'The resolution of seismic instruments used in treaty verification research', in *Bulletin of the Seismological Society of America* (note 104), pp. S61-S67.
107. Wallerstedt, R.L., *Marine Seismic System (MSS) Deployment. Phase IV. Investigation of Techniques and Deployment Scenarios for Installation of Tri-Axial Seismometer in a Borehole in the Deep Ocean,* Report No. MSSA02-SYS-R003, Global Marine Development, Inc., Newport Beach, CA, 31 May 1983.
108. Taylor, S.R., 'The regional seismic test network', *Energy and Technology Review,* Lawrence Livermore National Laboratory, Livermore, CA, May 1983, pp. 20-29; Pomeroy, P.W., Best, W.J. and McEvilly, T.V., 'Test ban treaty verification with regional data—a review', in *Bulletin of the Seismological Society of America* (note 104), pp. S89-S129; Blandford, R.R., 'Seismic discrimination problems at regional distances', in Husebye & Mykkeltveit (note 104), pp. 695-740.
109. See for example Sykes & Evernden (note 104), p. 53 and Hannon, W.J., Jr, 'Seismic verification of a comprehensive test ban', *Energy and Technology Review* (note 108), pp. 50-65.
110. Dahlman & Israelson (note 104), pp. 56 and 67.
111. Dahlman & Israelson (note 104), p. 136.
112. Dahlman & Israelson (note 104), pp. 66 and 69.
113. Pomeroy, Best & McEvilly (note 108), p. S111 and Blandford (note 108).
114. Douglas, A. *et al.*, 'Earthquakes that look like explosions',*Geophys. J. R. Astr. Soc.*, Vol. 36, 1974, pp. 227-33.
115. See, for example, Dahlman & Israelson (note 104), chapter 9.
116. Sykes, Evernden & Cifuentes (note 103), p. 96.
117. Kerr, R.A., 'The deepest hole in the world', *Science,* Vol. 224, 29 June 1984, p. 1420.
118. Sykes, Evernden & Cifuentes (note 103), p. 106.
119. Sykes, Evernden & Cifuentes (note 103), p. 94.
120. Sykes & Evernden (note 104), p. 49.
121. Sykes, Evernden & Cifuentes (note 103), p. 108.
122. Bache, T.C., 'Estimating the yield of underground nuclear explosions', *Bulletin of the Seismological Society of America* (note 104), p. S133.
123. Bolt (note 104), p. 39.
124. Dahlman & Israelson (note 104), pp. 306-16.
125. Sykes, L.R. and Cifuentes, I.L., *Yields of Soviet Underground Nuclear Explosions from Seismic Surface Waves: Compliance with Threshold Test Ban Treaty,* Lamont-Doherty Geological Observatory and Department of Geological Sciences, Columbia University, NY, 7 December 1983, p. 3.
126. Sykes & Cifuentes (note 125), p. 15.
127. Dahlman & Israelson (note 104), chapter 13.
128. Glenn, L.A., 'Verification limits for test-ban treaty', *Nature*, Vol. 310, 2 August 1984, pp. 361-62.
129. Evernden, J.F. and Archambeau, C.B., 'Seismological aspects of monitoring a comprehensive test ban treaty', in Tsipis, Hafemeister & Janeway (note 13).
130. Evernden & Archambeau (note 129).
131. Husebye & Mykkeltveit (note 104), p. xii.
132. Ringdal & Husebye (note 105), p. S203.
133. Dahlman & Israelson (note 104), pp. 149-56.
134. Dahlman, O., private communication, 21 August 1984.
135. Ringdal, F., 'Automatic processing methods in the analysis of data from a global seismic network', in Husebye & Mikkeltveit (note 4), p. 807.

136. Singer, S., 'The Vela satellite program for detection of high-altitude nuclear detonations', *Proceedings of the IEEE,* Vol. 53, No. 12, December 1965, p. 1935.
137. Jungk, R., *Brighter than a Thousand Suns* (Harcourt Brace Jovanovich, New York, 1958).
138. Singer (note 136).
139. Argo, H.V., 'Monitoring atmospheric nuclear explosions', in Tsipis, Hafemeister & Janeway (note 13).
140. Argo (note 139). The origins of the term 'bhangmeter' are obscure, but according to one source it was coined in the early years of the US nuclear testing programme as a pun on the words 'bang' for an explosion and 'bhang', a narcotic drug made from hemp (private communication from H.V. Argo).
141. Argo (note 139).
142. Singer (note 136), p. 1942.
143. Argo (note 139).
144. Bell, J., 'Navigation for everyman, and his bomb', *New Scientist,* Vol. 104, No. 1425, 11 October 1984, pp. 36-40.
145. Powers, T., 'The ears of America', *New York Review of Books,* 3 February 1983, p. 12.
146. Bamford, J., *The Puzzle Palace: America's National Security Agency and its Special Relationship with Britain's GCHQ* (Sidgwick and Jackson, London, 1983), Chapter 6.
147. Powers (note 145).
148. Holloway, D., *The Soviet Union and the Arms Race* (Yale University Press, New Haven, CT, 1983), p. 18.
149. Pearson, D., 'KAL 007: what the US knew and when we knew it', *The Nation,* Vol. 239, No. 4, 18-25 August 1984, pp. 113-14.
150. Bamford (note 146), chapter 5.
151. Greenwood, T., *Reconnaissance, Surveillance and Arms Control,* Adelphi Paper No. 88 (IISS, London, 1972), p. 23.
152. SIPRI (note 4), pp. 39-42.
153. Moncrief, F.J., 'SALT verification: how we monitor the Soviet arsenal', *Microwaves,* September 1979, p. 42.
154. Bamford (note 146), p. 197.
155. *Two-line Orbital Elements,* NASA–Goddard Space Flight Center, Greenbelt, MD, daily until June 1983.
156. Treaty between the USA and the USSR on the limitation of Anti-Ballistic Missile Systems, reprinted in Goldblat, J., *Agreements for Arms Control: A Critical Survey* (Taylor & Francis, London 1982) [a SIPRI book]. See the Agreed Interpretation F (p. 199) and Article II (p. 197).
157. Compliance with SALT I Agreements, US Department of State, Bureau of Public Affairs, Special Report No. 55, Washington, DC, July 1979, pp. 2-3.
158. Moncrief (note 153), p. 46.
159. Perry, G.E. and Flagg, R.S., 'Telemetry from Russian Spacecraft', *Journal of the British Interplanetary Society,* Vol. 23, 1970, pp. 451-64; Perry, G.E., 'Identification of military components within the Soviet space programme', in Jasani (note 4), pp. 135-54.
160. Perry & Flagg (note 159), p. 458.
161. Moncrief (note 153), p. 46.
162. Hussain, F., *The Impact of Weapons Test Restrictions,* Adelphi Paper No. 165 (IISS, London, 1981), p. 45.
163. SASC Hearings (note 21), Part 1, p. 138.
164. Treaty between the USA and the USSR on the Limitation of Strategic Offensive

Arms (SALT II Treaty), Second Common Understanding to Paragraph 3 of Article XV, in Goldblat (note 156), p. 280.

165. Hussain (note 162), p. 39.
166. SIPRI, (note 57), pp. 293-300.
167. *The SALT II Treaty,* Hearings before the Committee on Foreign Relations (SFRC Hearings), US Senate, 96th Congress, First Session (US Government Printing Office, Washington, DC, 1979), Part 2, p. 275.
168. Talbot, S., *End Game: The Inside Story of SALT II* (Harper & Row, New York, 1979), p. 266.
169. Blair, B.G. and Brewer, G.D., 'Verifying SALT agreements', in Potter, W.C. (ed.), *Verification and SALT—The Challenge of Strategic Deception* (Westview Press, Boulder, CO, 1980), p. 33.
170. Moncrief (note 153), p. 47.
171. Ball, D., *The Rhyolite Programme,* Reference Paper No. 86, Research School of Pacific Studies, Canberra, November 1981, p. 4.
172. Moncrief (note 153), p. 47.
173. Blair, B.G., 'Reconnaissance satellites', in Jasani (note 4), p. 133.
174. Biddle, W., 'Initial orbit of new satellite different from usual', *New York Times,* 26 April 1985, p. A19; see also Richelson, J.T., *The US Intelligence Community* (Ballinger, Cambridge, MA, 1985), p. 122.
175. Marriott, J., 'Tactical crypt: the art of secure communications', *Military Technology,* Vol. 5, No. 26, August 1981, pp. 12-14.
176. Sullivan, J., 'Cryptography: securing computer transmissions', *High Technology,* Vol. 3, No. 11, November 1983, p. 31-36.
177. Kolata, G., 'Factoring gets easier', *Science,* Vol. 222, 2 December 1983, pp. 999-1001; 'Another promising code falls', *Science,* 16 December 1983, Vol. 222, p. 1224.
178. NPT Newsletter, *IAEA Bulletin,* Vol. 26, No. 1, March 1984, p. 36.
179. *The Structure and Content of Agreements between the Agency and States Required in Connection with the Treaty on the Non-Proliferation of Nuclear Weapons,* INFCIRC/153, IAEA, Vienna, May 1971, para. 28.
180. Barnard, C.I. *et al.* 'A report on the international control of atomic energy, 16 March 1946', *Peaceful Nuclear Exports and Weapons Proliferation: A Compendium,* Committee on Government Operations, US Senate (US Government Printing Office, Washington, DC, April 1975), p. 167 [emphasis in original].
181. Grümm, H., 'IAEA safeguards—where do we stand today?', *IAEA Bulletin,* Vol. 21, No. 4, August 1979, p. 35.
182. *IAEA Safeguards Glossary* (IAEA, Vienna, 1980), para. 89.
183. Jennekens, J., 'International safeguards—the quantification issue', *IAEA Bulletin,* Vol. 22, No. 3/4, August 1980, pp. 42-43.
184. IAEA (note 182), para. 90.
185. IAEA (note 182), para. 87.
186. 'The present status of IAEA safeguards on nuclear fuel cycle facilities', *IAEA Bulletin* (note 183), p. 24.
187. Krass, A.S., Boskma, P. , Elzen, B. and Smit, W.A., *Uranium Enrichment and Nuclear Weapon Proliferation* (Taylor & Francis, London, 1983) [a SIPRI book], p. 45.
188. IAEA (note 182), paras 109-49.
189. IAEA (note 179), paras 31-32.
190. 'The safeguards analytical laboratory: its functions and analytical facilities', *IAEA Bulletin,* Vol. 19, No. 5, October 1977, pp. 38-47.

191. IAEA, *IAEA Safeguards: Techniques and Equipment*, IAEA/SG/INF/5 (IAEA, Vienna, 1984), pp. 2-11.
192. Prial, F.J., 'Sweden releases Soviet sub; finds signs of nuclear arms', *New York Times,* November 1981, pp. 1, 12.
193. *The Annual Report for 1983* (IAEA, Vienna, 1984), p. 59.
194. IAEA (note 193), pp. 68-69.
195. IAEA (note 182), paras 119, 135-37.
196. IAEA (note 182), para. 12.
197. IAEA (note 193).
198. Imber, M.F., 'Arms control verification: the special case of IAEA-NPT "special inspections"', *Arms Control,* Vol. 3, No. 3, December 1982, pp. 66-67.
199. IAEA (note 182), para. 216.
200. Klik, F., 'Field experience of safeguards inspectors', *IAEA Bulletin,* Vol. 23, No. 4, December 1981, p. 20.
201. 'Surveillance and containment measures to support IAEA safeguards', *IAEA Bulletin* (note 190), p. 22.
202. IAEA (note 193), p. 59.
203. IAEA (note 182), para. 217.
204. *IAEA Bulletin* (note 201), pp. 21, 24.
205. *IAEA Bulletin* (note 201), p. 22.
206. Pieragostini, K., 'RECOVERing verification', *Arms Control Today,* Vol. 12, No. 11, December, 1982, pp. 4-5.
207. United States of America, United Kingdom and Australia, 'Technical evaluation of "RECOVER" techniques for CW verification', Committee on Disarmament documents CD/271, CD/CW/WP.32, Committee on Disarmament, Geneva, 7 April 1982, p. 1.
208. Pieragostini (note 206), p. 5.
209. Sheaks, O.J., US Arms Control and Disarmament Agency, private communication, 15 October 1984.
210. Fischer, D.A.V., 'Safeguards—a model for general arms control?', *IAEA Bulletin,* Vol. 24, No. 2, June 1982, pp. 45-49.
211. United States of America, 'Illustrative on-site inspection procedures for verification of chemical weapons stockpile destruction', Committee on Disarmament document CD/387, Committee on Disarmament, Geneva, 6 July 1983.
212. United States of America, 'The declaration and interim monitoring of chemical weapons stockpiles', Conference on Disarmament document CD/516, Conference on Disarmament, 13 July 1984.
213. SIPRI, *World Armaments and Disarmament, SIPRI Yearbook 1978* (Taylor & Francis, London, 1978), pp. 73-79.
214. Scoville (note 2), pp. 178-79.
215. 'Debate on a comprehensive nuclear weapons test ban: pro and con', *Physics Today,* Vol. 36, No. 8, August 1983, pp. 24-25.
216. Kessler, R. and Knapik, M., 'Argentine enrichment pronouncement characterized as startling', *Nucleonics Week,* Vol. 24, No. 47, 24 November 1983, pp. 1-2.
217. Katz (note 6), p. 32.
218. Kahan, J.H., *Security in the Nuclear Age* (Brookings Institution, Washington, DC, 1975), p. 333.
219. Biddle, W., 'Senate defeats a proposal to ban sea-based nuclear cruise missiles', *New York Times,* 20 June 1984, p. 1.
220. 'Minuteman studied for airfield attack', *Aviation Week & Space Technology,* Vol. 121, No. 2, 9 July 1984, p. 21.
221. Rowny, E. in SASC Hearings (note 21), Part 2, p. 687.

222. FAS Public Interest Report, Vol. 36, No. 9, November 1983, pp. 13-16.
223. Sykes & Evernden (note 104), p. 55.
224. Kincade, W.H., 'Over the technological horizon', *Daedalus,* Vol. 110, No. 1, Winter 1981, p. 116.
225. Toth, R.C., 'Some experts doubt value of arms pacts', *Los Angeles Times,* 23 May 1984, p. 1.
226. Chayes, A., 'An inquiry into the workings of arms control agreements', *Harvard Law Review,* Vol. 85, No. 5, March 1972, p. 968.
227. Toth (note 225).

Chapter 3. The politics of verification

I. Introduction

While the development of the remarkable technological monitoring capabilities described in the previous chapter has solved many problems in arms control verification, the most serious problems remain the political ones. In this area progress has been slow, erratic and ambiguous. The gap between technical capabilities and political will has consequently grown very wide, and while progress in technique is essentially unidirectional (a technical problem once solved is never unsolved), political 'progress' can change direction rapidly; *détente* can become confrontation almost overnight.

The politics of verification is intimately connected to the politics of arms control, which in turn cannot be separated from the politics of national security. These intimate connections make any attempt to single out verification risky and somewhat misleading. Nevertheless there do exist a few well-defined political issues which focus on problems of compliance and verifiability in arms control agreements, and it is worthwhile to identify these, as long as it is kept in mind that verification is not an end in itself, but only a small part of the total political relationship between states. This means that it is far more likely that political attitudes towards verification will be affected by political shifts in other areas than that progress in the verification area will be the cause of more sweeping changes in the political atmosphere.

This chapter first considers the two main protagonists in the arms race, the USA and the USSR, and examines their political actions and positions with respect to verification. Then an attempt is made to identify the roots of these actions in the domestic political situations of the two states. Next, the very considerable contributions of other states to the question of verification are examined and the political positions of such 'third parties' analysed. Finally, an attempt is made to analyse the subtle concepts of 'adequacy' in verification and 'trust' between parties to a treaty. Both of these concepts are fundamental to the problem of verification and both are of an essentially political or subjective nature, ensuring that they will be interpreted in widely divergent ways by groups with different interests and perceptions. The existence of such subjective concepts at the core of the verification problem, a core virtually

114

impenetrable by technology, is the basic cause of most of the frustration and misunderstanding this problem has created.

II. The USA and the USSR as international actors

The United States and the Soviet Union have been discussing arms control with each other in bilateral, multilateral and international contexts for over 40 years. If one focuses only on the official records of these negotiations it is easy to conclude that the problem of ensuring compliance with agreements has been by far the most important obstacle to progress in meaningful arms control or towards disarmament.

However, such a conclusion would be highly misleading. While concerns about verification have certainly been a constant factor in arms control negotiations, it has never been clear to what degree these concerns represent a genuine desire for enforceable and lasting agreements, or to what degree they represent a convenient device for prolonging negotiations and preventing agreement in areas where limitations are not really desired. For example, the Reagan Administration has maintained that a ban on anti-satellite weapons would be unverifiable.[1] But one analysis of the Administration's position has concluded that: "While verification figures to be the public argument employed by Administration opponents of an agreement, in fact many of these officials oppose the very concept of an anti-satellite weapons pact".[2]

Meanwhile other analysts have established a strong case that such a ban would in fact be highly verifiable, adding further to the suspicion that claims of non-verifiability are really a cover for opposition to an agreement.[3]

Despite such examples of political posturing, there remain genuine concerns about verifiability in the great majority of arms control proposals. It is the difficult task of the analyst and the citizen to find the shifting and indistinct line that separates the real from the spurious concerns about verification.

The debate on "agreement in principle"

Arguments over verification generally focus on the amount and type of monitoring or inspection as well as the relationship between these activities and the arms control or disarmament goals being negotiated. In fact the first important argument between the USA and the USSR over a disarmament issue was not about how much inspection would be needed but how the control measures adopted would relate to the goal, which was the elimination of nuclear weapons.

The first US plan to eliminate nuclear weapons was presented by Bernard Baruch on 14 June 1946. The USA advocated the creation of an International Atomic Development Authority "to which should be entrusted all phases of the development and use of atomic energy...".[4] According to the plan:

> Once a charter for the Authority has been adopted, the Authority and the system of control for which it will be responsible will require time to become fully organized and effective. The plan of control will, therefore, have to come into effect in successive stages... As the successive stages of international control are reached the United States will be prepared to yield, to the extent required by each stage, national control of activities in this field to the Authority.[5]

The plan leaves no doubt that the creation of a workable control mechanism must precede any US commitment to relinquish its sovereign right to produce and retain nuclear weapons.

Five days later the Soviet representative, Andrei Gromyko, presented an alternative proposal:

> ...the Soviet delegation proposes ... an international convention prohibiting the production and employment of weapons based on the use of atomic energy for the purpose of mass destruction ... This act should be followed by other measures aiming at the establishment of methods to ensure the strict observance of the terms and obligations contained in the above-mentioned convention.[6]

The Soviet proposal makes clear that the commitment to and the act of nuclear disarmament must precede discussions of methods to ensure compliance.

The dichotomy between the US and Soviet perspectives can be simplified as follows: to the USA promises to disarm without assurance of adequate control are empty gestures, while to the USSR attempts to verify military activities in the absence of disarmament are tantamount to espionage. There is little reason to doubt that both of these positions are held with deep conviction and sincerity, their wide difference being a result of the very different historical, cultural and social experiences of the two nations.

The Soviet philosophy had not changed much by the late 1950s when discussions were under way on a nuclear test ban treaty. It was summed up graphically by Soviet ambassador Tsarapkin:

> It is as though we started to argue here on how to preserve a bearskin when the bear itself was still in the woods. We would be arguing about whether to put the bearskin in the refrigerator or to pack it in moth-balls in a trunk at home. In the end, we would disagree with you on which brand of moth-balls to buy and from which firm. The bear would be in the woods, alive and well, and we would have fallen out among ourselves over moth-balls.[7]

This imagery is highly illuminating but does not do justice to the US position. Tsarapkin sees the US delegates as wanting to argue about which method is best for preserving a bearskin, while a US delegate might argue that the problem is more fundamental, that is, whether any satisfactory method exists to preserve the bearskin. If the two sides agree to go out and shoot the bear before assuring themselves that the skin is indeed preservable, they might have wasted their time. So it is prudent first to make certain that adequate bearskin preservatives exist and are obtainable.

However, if the US approach is taken, the question immediately arises of how effectively the bearskin should be preserved. What constitutes 'adequate preservation'? Here there is indeed a possibility, even a probability, for all kinds of disagreement and endless wrangling over details and subtle value judgements. Here the Soviet point of view seems to have real advantages. If both sides can agree in principle to shoot the bear and take the skin, then this agreement in itself ought to be sufficient to overcome smaller disagreements over details and justify a search for the best feasible preservation method. Once the skin is taken it becomes imperative to preserve it in the best possible way, and it is in the interests of both parties to collaborate on the preservation. It is better to have the bearskin—which is presumably valuable to both parties—and to do the best one can with preservation, rather than let the bear get away while the parties conduct an endless search for the perfect preservation method.

It is a constantly recurring theme in US–Soviet arms control negotiations that to the Soviet side agreements in principle are vital prerequisites to discussions of control mechanisms. A recent Soviet analysis has reiterated the same philosophy:

> The Soviet proposals closely connect control with the process of limiting and eliminating armaments. Control cannot and must not play a separate and superior role, and its scope, means and forms should be geared to the character and volume of disarmament measures.[8]

In other words, *agreement in principle* on what is to be controlled should precede discussions of how the control is to be implemented, thereby preventing "the kind of 'control' that is designed not for effective disarmament, but for very different purposes".[9]

These "very different purposes" are, of course, espionage, that is, an illegitimate desire to gain valuable military intelligence under the cover of arms control agreements. There is no denying that such fears are to some extent justified. As the previous chapter has shown, the technologies and methods of arms control monitoring are indistinguishable from those of military intelligence gathering, and the same data which are used in one government agency to provide evidence of compliance can be used by another to target nuclear missiles more accurately or effectively.

A good example of this dual nature of monitoring is provided by the so-called "Open Skies" proposal made by President Eisenhower in 1955.[10]

This proposal was made ostensibly to reduce "the fears and dangers of surprise attack" and would have involved complete freedom for reconnaissance aircraft of both countries to survey the territory of the other as well as an exchange of "complete blueprints of our military establishments".[11]

There is now solid documentary evidence that fears of a possible surprise attack by the Soviet Union against the United States were seriously held at the highest levels of the US government.[12] Therefore, the proposal for an Open Skies inspection scheme represented a genuine desire to reduce the suspicion and tension resulting from this concern. In this sense the Open Skies plan was a potential arms control verification measure.

The same collection of documentary evidence shows, however, that in 1955 the United States possessed all the necessary weapons for a counterforce nuclear attack against the Soviet Union. The major obstacle to confidence that such an attack could be carried out without a massive Soviet counter-attack was the lack of accurate and complete targeting data. The US Strategic Air Command was faced with a rapidly expanding target list, the expansion being "largely attributable to identification of additional 'counterforce' targets . . . and to the poor quality of target intelligence through the 1950s, which encouraged creative guesswork".[13] In this context the Open Skies plan can be seen as a military intelligence measure of the highest importance, one which would strengthen the weakest link in US nuclear war-fighting plans.

The Open Skies plan was, of course, unacceptable to the Soviet Union, mainly for this latter reason. It was not simply obstructionism or a penchant for secrecy which caused this rejection, any more than it was a pure desire by the USA to carry out espionage which motivated its proposal in the first place. Given good intentions on both sides, an Open Skies agreement would have indeed reduced tension and fear of surprise attack and could have contributed to real disarmament. But given a continued commitment to military competition, a hostile political atmosphere and a clear imbalance of military forces, such an arrangement could in fact be dangerous to the weaker party and is obviously unacceptable. Indeed, many believe that the Open Skies proposal was made with the knowledge that it would be rejected by the Soviet Union.[14] However, now that the Soviet Union has accepted the legitimacy of satellite reconnaissance (see below) and perceives itself to be in a state of military parity with the United States, at least one suggestion has been made that the time may be ripe to resurrect the Open Skies idea.[15]

That such an idea still has little hope of success can be deduced from the continued high level of suspicion by the USSR of any Western efforts to increase 'transparency'. A recent article in a Soviet military journal has attributed to "evil intentions" NATO proposals for new confidence-building measures at the Stockholm Conference on Confidence- and Security-Building Measures and Disarmament in Europe. Such transparency it is argued "only introduces suspicion into interstate relations" and "boils down to legitimized espionage" designed to "facilitate the targeting of Pershing II and cruise missiles". The alternative, according to the Soviet author, is "the adoption by all nuclear states of a pledge not to be the first to use nuclear weapons and the conclusion of a treaty on the mutual non-use of military force and the maintenance of relations of peace". If such treaties were agreed to, "the need to ... monitor the opposite side's military activities would disappear".[16]

The intimate connection between monitoring for arms control and for military intelligence provides a substantial basis for the Soviet claim that discussions of verification techniques in the absence of an "agreement in principle" are premature and unproductive. Such attempts to obtain agreement in principle have been a consistent feature of Soviet negotiating behaviour.[17] But to the US side such efforts are baffling and frustrating and generally seem just as clearly to have been made with the knowledge that they would be unacceptable. To most Americans this notion of agreement in principle seems empty without solid confidence that the agreement can in fact be implemented. It is just as easy to conceal indecision, insincerity and cynicism behind demands for agreement on vague and grandiose 'principles' as behind nit-picking demands for foolproof monitoring schemes.

For example, the two sides might agree in principle to repeal the second law of thermodynamics or invent an anti-gravity machine. Such goals would clearly be of great mutual benefit to both sides, but there is every reason to expect that despite the best efforts of their most brilliant scientists the "details" of the implementation would prove insurmountable. It is probably fair to say that to most US negotiators the "principle" of general and complete disarmament (a favourite principle of Soviet negotiators in the 1950s) appeared about as realizable as an anti-gravity machine. Ironically, the USA did commit itself to this principle in 1961 by signing a "Joint Statement by the USA and the USSR of Agreed Principles for Disarmament Negotiations".[18] But no sooner had the statement been signed than Presidential Advisor John McCloy informed his Soviet counterpart Deputy Foreign Minister V. Zorin that US adherence to the principles was contingent on a US interpretation of the verification provision which stated that "not only [should] agreed limitations or reductions take place but also that *retained armed forces and armaments* do not exceed agreed levels at any stage."[19]

Mr Zorin's reply was that while "The Soviet Union favours the most thorough and strict international control over the measures of general and complete *disarmament...* [it] is at the same time resolutely opposed to the establishment of control over armaments".[20] Here again the contrast is starkly drawn between the Soviet preference for deciding first where one wants to go and then looking up the best route to get there, and the US preference for looking for passable roads before deciding where it might be both desirable and possible to go.

The debate on on-site inspection

A second major area of disagreement, already implicit in some of the examples cited above, is the degree of intrusiveness necessary or desirable in a monitoring system. It is clear from the entire history of US–Soviet negotiations that even when agreements can be reached on desirable goals for arms control measures, significant differences remain on the need for intrusive inspection, in particular on-site inspection. A thorough analysis of the technical feasibility and political sensitivity of on-site inspection proposals is made in chapter 4. Here it is intended only to examine the difference in attitude and behaviour of the two states on this issue.

A recent compilation of the historical record of arms control negotiations shows that 91 per cent of all US verification proposals involve some form of 'intrusive' monitoring procedure, while only 50 per cent of these proposals included non-intrusive methods. [21] Soviet proposals tended to contain both types in roughly equal proportions, but it is important to note that there are far fewer Soviet proposals in the total sample, only 9 compared to the US total of 22. This means that while the United States has made 20 proposals including intrusive elements, the Soviet Union has made only 6. The two states have jointly proposed 4 measures including intrusive measures. A chronological ordering of the proposals including on-site inspection provisions reveals no significant changes in this frequency for either side in the period from 1960 to 1980. [22]

While this evidence supports the widely held belief that the USA is far more interested in on-site inspection than the USSR, it should also lay to rest the disturbingly common assertion by US officials that "the Soviets have never been willing to discuss onsite inspection". [23]

Unfortunately, the effort to infer actual US and Soviet attitudes from these data is greatly complicated by the need to ascertain how seriously or cynically each proposal was made. The history of arms control negotiations is replete with examples of proposals put forward in the full knowledge that they would be rejected by the other side. This game has even been given the name "onus-shifting" by one historian. [24]

For example, a few of the Soviet proposals were made in the context of calls for general and complete disarmament, always a guaranteed non-starter. Similarly, many US proposals were made in much the same spirit as the Open Skies proposal, under the assumption that they would be unacceptable to the Soviet side. An example is the US attitude towards a ban on multiple independently targetable re-entry vehicles (MIRVs) in the SALT I negotiations. Gerard Smith, the Chief US negotiator, writes that President Nixon "had directed us to raise the flag of on-site inspection if the Soviets proposed a MIRV ban. But he must have known that such a condition had little or no chance of being accepted". [25] Indeed, there has always been a serious question as to just how enthusiastically the United States would embrace on-site inspection should the

Soviet attitude suddenly change. In response to the suggestion of a US Senator that "the US is probably . . . unwilling to have communists running around our defense plants", William Colby, former head of the US CIA, responded: "Well, I am not sure that Lockheed would particularly like to see Soviet colonels walking through their secret skunk works".[26] So, while it is clear from the public record that the United States has placed far more emphasis on on-site and other physically intrusive forms of monitoring than has the Soviet Union, it is *not* clear what this record really means in terms of attitudes towards realistic verification possibilities. It is certainly true that both the excessive demands for on-site inspection by the USA and the excessive resistance to it by the Soviet Union have been in some measure simply negotiating postures intended to put pressure on the other side and play to public opinion while delaying or preventing progress. Just how large this proportion is cannot be assessed with any precision, but it is not the entire story. There remains some level at which there is an honest and fundamental divergence of views between the two sides on the need for and the propriety of physically intrusive inspection to ensure compliance. This means that even if both sides can stop their posturing on this issue and work sincerely towards an agreement, such an agreement will not necessarily be easy to achieve.

Evidence of convergence

Having established two major differences in the two sides' approach to verification it is now important to show that these differences are in no sense static or immutable. Each side has found itself playing roles more associated with the other side from time to time and, in the passage of nearly 40 years since the Baruch and Gromyko exchanges of 1946, there has been some tendency towards convergence, although the past few years have shown this to be a fragile and uncertain trend.

Just one year after the presentation of the Gromyko proposal (see above) the Soviet Union elaborated its concept of monitoring and controlling a ban on nuclear weapon production.[27] This involved the creation of an International Control Commission with extensive powers of inspection and analysis. However, the plan was carefully stated to be "in addition and in development of" the Gromyko proposal, implying that there had been no change in the Soviet demand that all nuclear weapons be destroyed before any control mechanism was activated.

The Soviet position began to become noticeably more flexible after the change in leadership in 1953, and in the following two years there was considerable movement towards the Western position. This movement is best illustrated by a series of events in the spring of 1955, in the meetings of the United Nations Disarmament Subcommittee. On 8 March, the participating Western states (Canada, France, the UK and the USA) introduced a draft resolution which included the prohibition of nuclear weapons and major reductions in all armed forces and conventional armaments.[28]

As usual this resolution placed a heavy emphasis on effective verification and included provisions for an international "control organ". The Western philosophy towards verification was expressed in the explicit statement that no stage of the disarmament process was to begin until "the control organ reports that it is able effectively to enforce" it.[29]

This resolution was followed by a Soviet Draft Resolution on 19 March which expressed commitment to all the same goals but which followed the traditional Soviet line of calling for substantive acts of disarmament and various pledges, undertakings and conferences before the creation of a control organ with extensive powers of inspection.[30] Only after significant disarmament had taken place and a "complete prohibition of atomic, hydrogen and other weapons of mass destruction" had been put into effect would a "standing international organ" be created with "powers to exercise supervision, including inspection on a continuing basis".

The Soviet proposal was followed by an amended Western proposal in the form of an Anglo-French memorandum, which made some relatively minor concessions to Soviet demands for more "coordination" between the reductions of conventional and nuclear weapons.[31] Then on 10 May 1955 the Soviet delegation submitted an extensive new proposal (not a 'draft' proposal) which made significant concessions to Western demands for effective verification. This proposal was made up of many parts, but the most important for verification was the suggestion that "during the first stage" of the disarmament process "the international organ shall establish on the territory of the States concerned, on a basis of reciprocity, control posts at large ports, at railway junctions, on main motor highways and at aerodromes".[32] According to the Soviet proposal this would provide assurance against any attempt to mobilize forces for a surprise attack and would "create the necessary atmosphere of trust between States, thereby ensuring the appropriate conditions for the extension of the functions of the international control organ".[33]

This wording reveals an interesting divergence between Soviet and US attitudes towards "trust", a divergence which is analysed further below. More relevant for this discussion is the expressed Soviet willingness to institute major control mechanisms at the earliest stages of the disarmament process. The seriousness of the Soviet proposal was underlined in a speech by Soviet Premier Bulganin to a Warsaw Treaty Organization conference the following day.[34]

The Soviet concessions were seen as highly significant by Western delegates. The US delegate, James Wadsworth, stated on 11 May that "the Soviet Union has reversed its line and this time seems to be using ideas and language which are similar in many respects to the views put forward for many years by [the Western states]. We welcome this development".[35] Wadsworth's enthusiam was tempered by the reservation that Soviet inspection proposals "still appear to fall short of the minimum safety requirements", but the overall tone of the assessment was positive. One week later this positive mood was reaffirmed in the statement that "what is important is the fact that, to a measurable degree, the gaps between us seem to have been lessened".[36] Unfortunately this positive assessment was offered in the context of a US decision to break off the negotiations temporarily, even though the Soviet delegation was anxious to continue them.[37] The negotiations were never resumed, and the United States subsequently withdrew "all of its pre-Geneva substantive positions taken in this Subcommittee or in the Disarmament Commission or in the UN on these questions in relationship to levels of disarmament".[38] Instead the USA shifted its ground completely when President Eisenhower made the Open Skies proposal in July 1955 (see above). Rather than capitalizing on the movement shown by the Soviet Union in the Disarmament Subcommittee, this proposal sent the whole issue of the relationship between disarmament and inspection back to square one.

This incident is the first but certainly not the last in which the Soviet Union has indicated its willingness to relax its insistence that agreements in principle must precede detailed provisions for control. The SALT negotiations have also demonstrated a slow but measurable progress in Soviet flexibility on this issue. For example, at an early stage of the SALT I negotiations the USA was insisting on specific numerical limits on various missile types, while "The Soviets never budged from the principle that numbers would be disclosed and discussed only after agreement on principles".[39] But a few years later, in the latter stages of the SALT II negotiations, the Soviet Union provided the US delegation with official data on Soviet heavy bomber and launcher numbers, a marked break with traditional Soviet behaviour. In fact, when these data were handed over the head of the Soviet delegation, V. Semyonov, informed his US counterpart that this action had "just repealed four hundred years of Russian history. But on reflection, maybe that's not a bad thing".[40] The great significance of this change also impressed US negotiators who had persistently pointed out both the technical and political advantages of an agreed data base as a benchmark for future negotiations.[41] Unfortunately, by its failure to ratify the SALT II Treaty the USA has also missed the opportunity to capitalize on this concession.

As a final comment on "agreement in principle" it is interesting to note that there has been at least one instance of the USA itself seeing the virtues of the Soviet position. At one point during the long and frustrating wrangling in the SALT I negotiations, US National Security Advisor Henry Kissinger said: "the only way to make progress was to *agree in principle* on a freeze and then negotiate the ABM agreement and details of the freeze".[42]

While history has shown the Soviet Union moving from unrealistic and extreme positions on matters of principle to more pragmatic ones, a similar story holds true for the United States on the issue of on-site or intrusive inspection. Early US positions in this area were highly intrusive and tended to exacerbate, either wittingly or unwittingly, Soviet feelings of military vulnerability and fears of espionage.

The original Baruch Plan would have created an international authority with virtually total powers to intervene in national atomic energy programmes, and all through the 1950s US insistence on on-site inspection in many areas of arms control was a constant obstacle to agreement. But in the late 1950s and early 1960s, especially in connection with negotiations for a comprehensive nuclear test ban, the USA began to show some flexibility on this issue, moving from an initial position that *any* unidentified seismic event should be subject to on-site inspection, to a proposal that the number of on-site inspections be some small fraction of the annual number of unidentified seismic events, and then to a demand for a fixed quota of 20 on-site inspections per year. Meanwhile the Soviet position moved from accepting no on-site inspections at all to accepting a quota of three per year. Throughout this evolution the USA insisted that the required number of on-site inspections was a technical question while the Soviet Union insisted that it was a political question.[43]

With the advent of the Kennedy Administration in 1960 the USA showed further flexibility in the number of on-site inspections, dropping the number to a minimum of 10 and a maximum of 20.[44] Then the demand dropped to eight,[45] and then to seven, with a "fall-back" number of six which was not revealed.[46] There was even a growing body of expert opinion in the USA that the quota of three proposed by the Soviet Union would in fact be adequate to deter violations.[47] Meanwhile the Soviet Union, while refusing to raise its own offer of three on-site inspections, was the first to suggest the use of so-called 'black boxes', unmanned seismic stations placed on the territories of states agreeing to a test ban. The stations were to be placed in seismically active areas, and the host country would agree to allow international scientific personnel to visit them for data collection and maintenance.[48] There were good reasons at the time to believe that such a network of black boxes would greatly reduce or eliminate the need for on-site inspections, and there is even more reason to believe this now (see chapter 4, pp. 218–23).

However, the United States did not accept the black box proposal, and given the political and technical problems associated with any system of 'challenge' or 'demand' on-site inspections (see chapter 4) the significance of the US progression to lower numbers is easily exaggerated. The two sides remained much further from agreement than the numbers suggest. Nevertheless the US concessions did represent a substantial movement from the principle of unlimited on-site inspections which the USA had held to for many years. Meanwhile in the years since 1960 the steady improvement in the capabilities of national technical means of verification along with the development of a number of co-operative measures for the exchange of geological data and observers have pushed on-site inspection further into the background. The 1974 Threshold Test Ban Treaty[49] and the 1976 Peaceful Nuclear Explosions

Treaty[50] both contain innovative and significant co-operative measures to improve the efficacy of national technical means. Unfortunately these Treaties remain unratified by the United States, so these measures have not been put into operation.

It is fair to conclude that the United States has shown growing flexibility on the issue of on-site inspection, largely as a result of the improvements in national technical means, but also as the result of a willingness to explore and adopt other types of measure involving a greater degree of voluntary co-operation and mutual respect. The extent of the US change of heart can be grasped from a 1976 statement by the US Arms Control and Disarmament Agency (ACDA):

> In estimating the role of inspection measures in future arms control agreements, it is important to distinguish between the symbolic or political value of such measures and their actual value for verification. Future progress in some areas of arms control may well depend on a greater readiness on the part of other nations to consider arrangements of this kind. At the same time, their role will remain limited, and they should be regarded primarily as a supplement to national technical means.[51]

At the same time the Soviet Union has come to recognize that some on-site inspection is unavoidable and has shown a willingness to accept it within certain narrow limits. An example is the acceptance of permanent on-site monitoring of the destruction of chemical weapon stocks under a treaty banning the possession of chemical weapons.[52]

Another encouraging sign of convergence is the similarity in assessments of the two sides of the 1972 Biological Weapons Convention.[53] This treaty embodies a very weak verification mechanism involving only an agreement "to consult one another and to cooperate in solving any problems which may arise" either bilaterally or "through appropriate international procedures within the framework of the United Nations".[54]

Such a provision might be expected to satisfy the Soviet Union, and this seems to be the case. A recent Soviet commentary asserts:

> Comparatively limited verification measures have been envisaged with regard to agreements banning weapons which of their very nature can be controlled without particular difficulty and do not require far-reaching inspection measures. Examples in point are the ban on bacteriological weapons and the modification of the environment for military purposes.[55]

What is more remarkable is the similarity between this statement and a US assessment made in 1976. The US Arms Control and Disarmament Agency suggests that the extent of verification required is related to the degree of risk posed by possible violations. Referring to the Biological Weapons Convention as a case in point the ACDA analysis states:

> Its prohibitions on the development, production or stockpiling of biological weapons are difficult to verify, particularly in countries with relatively closed societies. On the other hand, the utility of such weapons is at best questionable ... and possession of them would not significantly affect the military balance between nuclear powers or provide a political advantage. Accordingly, the agreement was judged to be in the interests of the United States in spite of the difficulties of verification...[56]

A final example of the progress that had been made up to 1980 in reconciling US and Soviet approaches is the Tripartite Report to the Committee on Disarmament concerning a comprehensive nuclear test ban.[57] Significant compromises by both sides are apparent in the agreement that "additional measures under negotiation to facilitate verification of compliance... must first be agreed in principle and then drafted in detail"[58] and the agreement that: "If a party has questions regarding an event on the territory of any other party it may request an on-site inspection... If the party which receives the request is not prepared to agree to an inspection... it shall provide the reasons for its decision".[59] Provisions such as these represent a serious attempt by each side to recognize and adapt to the concerns of the other.

These signs of convergence are encouraging, but more recent events suggest that they cannot serve as grounds for excessive optimism, at least in the short run. For example, the current US attitude towards the Biological Weapons Convention is far less sanguine than the one embodied in the ACDA quote. Vice-President George Bush, in presenting a new US draft treaty on chemical weapons, called attention to reports of alleged violations of the 1925 Geneva Protocol and 1972 BW Convention and asserted that one important reason for the persistence of such allegations is that neither treaty "includes any form of effective verification and enforcement".[60]

In fact, the traditional patterns of US and Soviet negotiating behaviour are still easily perceptible in current negotiations. For example, in the same address quoted above Vice-President Bush described a US plan for "open invitation" on-site inspection of suspicious activities related to chemical weapon production or stockpiling. Under such a plan a state would be required to "open for international inspection on short notice all of its military or government-owned or government-controlled facilities".[61]

Vice-President Bush asserted that such a broad verification proposal "goes way beyond what we would have done a few years ago",[62] and in this he is correct. In fact, it has all the aspects of a return to the much older US position of demanding virtually total access and freedom of movement by international inspectors on the territory of sovereign states. Even the name of the proposal, "open invitation", recalls the name "Open Skies", and Mr Bush's enthusiastic predictions that such a measure can "engender the kind of openness among nations that dissipates ungrounded suspicions"[63] suggests early US efforts to use verification as a means of "opening" Soviet society.

That such hopes are still premature can be seen from the rapid condemnation of the plan by the Soviet Union.[64] The Soviet position on such "open" inspection schemes remains firm: "The USSR is categorically opposed to 'inspections', like the notorious 'Baruch Plan', the 'Open Skies' concept, and others that were put forward by the USA in the past and had the nature of intelligence-gathering operations. The Soviet Union will not agree to such 'verification' ".[65]

And Soviet negotiators continue to stress that satisfactory compliance mechanisms can be arranged only *after* agreements in principle or goals and objectives have been achieved. The Soviet representative to the CD chemical weapons negotiations has made this clear: "The problems which we have to solve in order to reach agreement on the prohibition of chemical weapons are many. They concern the scope of the prohibition, the arrangements and deadlines for compliance with the various obligations under the future convention and, *lastly,* control".[66] While it does seem that agreement in principle *has* been achieved on a chemical weapons treaty and that the remaining arguments are over control, this statement serves as a reminder that the Soviet approach to arms control verification is still different in important ways from the US approach. These differences can be expected to persist for the foreseeable future, but history has shown that they need not prevent the achievement of agreements when the will to reach agreement is present.

III. Domestic politics

Public opinion and Congress

It is a commonplace observation among arms control experts that "for all practical purposes verification is strictly an American concern".[67] A similar thought was expressed by an analyst of Soviet attitudes towards SALT, who devotes less than one out of 110 pages of his study to Soviet views on verification and concludes that "verification is primarily an American problem and thus not likely to be of much concern to members of the Soviet ruling elite".[68]

In what sense are these statements true? They certainly do not imply that Soviet leaders require no reassurance in the form of hard evidence that the USA is living up to its obligations. Soviet leaders harbour at least as much mistrust of US intentions as do US leaders of Soviet intentions. And there is also evidence from the historical record of arms control negotiations of Soviet concern for the verifiability of certain proposals. For example, during the SALT II negotiations the Soviet negotiators expressed great concern over the deployment of cruise missiles, because they can carry either conventional or nuclear warheads, an obviously important difference which cannot be detected by national technical means. At one point the Soviet side reportedly offered a major concession in the form of a limited ban on telemetry encryption if the USA would accept a total ban on cruise missiles. [69]

The Soviet offer can be seen in two ways: either as an expression of genuine concern about verifiability or as a way of using US concerns about verifiability to extract concessions on actual weapon deployments. [70] These motivations are not mutually contradictory, so both can be present to some degree. However, given the difficulty of distinguishing nuclear-armed from conventionally armed cruise missiles and the unquestionable military importance of the distinction, it seems likely that verifiability was a major Soviet concern.

Nevertheless, despite the evident Soviet distrust of US motives and occasional examples of Soviet concern for the verifiability of certain treaty provisions, and even at least one instance of an attempt to reassure the Soviet people on the issue of verifiability, [71] it remains true that verification is far more a US than a Soviet concern.

The difference is the result of two important asymmetries between the two sides. First, information relevant to military and arms control issues is almost totally absent from open Soviet sources, while the United States produces a veritable glut of such information. A list of open US sources from which important (sometimes ostensibly secret) information can be obtained would include the annual report of the Secretary of Defense and posture statement of the Joint Chiefs of Staff, the budget documents released by the President, Congressional hearings and debates, and dozens of military and trade journals which carry articles, editorials and advertising which discuss in detail US military strategy, tactics, hardware and R&D programmes. Even the daily newspapers and weekly or monthly magazines frequently run articles based on investigations by journalists, opinion pieces by knowledgeable insiders and outsiders, and the ever-present 'leaks', often from sources close to sensitive information. This plethora of information is in reality far more than any thoughtful citizen or diligent researcher can handle, and much of it is inaccurate, speculative or politically inspired. Yet in its totality it provides Soviet intelligence agencies with a picture of the US military posture and plans which is far more complete and useful than that which US analysts can gather from Soviet sources, which are tightly controlled and of far less diversity and breadth of coverage.

The second major asymmetry derives from the contrast between the sharply pyramidal structure of decision-making power in the Soviet Union and the pluralistic and diluted system in the United States. The Soviet form of government ensures that only a few people near the top need to be reassured by being given access to intelligence information. This group, which, despite its frequent disagreements on arms control philosophy and policy, [72] is politically quite homogeneous, can relatively easily reach a consensus, either on the evaluation of intelligence data or on a willingness to take risks on less than absolutely verifiable agreements.

By contrast US national security policy is an overtly political matter marked by deep differences among a number of powerful interest groups, all of whom have ample access to the mass media and other means of influencing public opinion. Achieving any consensus in this climate is extremely difficult, and if risks are to be taken (and inevitably they must if real progress is to be made in arms control) then even the most cautious and resistant must either be convinced that the risks are acceptable, or be overridden by a substantial majority. In the latter case the dissatisfied group then has the option of pressing its case in the mass media and working through sympathetic members of Congress to undermine the decision.

Herbert York has emphasized two serious problems in the US system with respect to arms control, neither of which is faced by the Soviet Union. One is the requirement for a two-thirds vote in the US Senate to ratify treaties, and the other is the long presidential campaign that takes place every four years.[73] With regard to verification it is the former problem that has proven to be most serious. In order to get the necessary two-thirds majority for Senate ratification, treaties must often be tailored to fit the concerns of certain influential senators, and very often these concerns focus on the verifiabilty of the treaties. Throughout the SALT I and II negotiations the concerns of Senator Henry Jackson were constantly on the minds of the negotiators,[74] and Senators Jackson, John Glenn and Howard Baker all played important roles in the later stages of the SALT II negotiations and in the ratification hearings by emphasizing their concern that the loss of the US "listening posts" in Iran combined with Soviet encryption of missile-test telemetry would render crucial provisions in the treaty unverifiable.[75]

Of the two asymmetries the second is considerably more important than the first. While the absence of open Soviet sources undoubtedly makes intelligence gathering (and therefore verification) more difficult and expensive, US intelligence agencies do not seem to suffer from a serious lack of information about Soviet military activities. The intelligence problems created by the closed nature of Soviet society seem to be exaggerated. Former CIA director William Colby has stated: "While this is obviously a simpler process for the Soviet Union than for the United States, the fact is that we have been able over the past thirty years' development of our modern intelligence system to penetrate the screen of secrecy the Soviets raise around these weapons and forces".[76]

It must also be kept in mind that this extensive gathering of intelligence has gone on and will certainly continue to go on whether or not arms control agreements exist to be verified. According to former US Secretary of Defense Harold Brown, "Our need for such information did not begin with SALT.... With or without SALT we have a vital interest in keeping track of Soviet strategic forces. Doing so is our highest intelligence priority".[77]

The problem created by the first asymmetry, that of gathering intelligence in a tightly controlled society, is primarily technical and therefore more likely to be manageable. In contrast, the second asymmetry, the very different roles played by intelligence information in the domestic politics of the two states, is far more subtle and difficult to reconcile. Difficulties arise most often in the USA in the interaction between the President's Administration and the Senate, where problems of verification and allegations of Soviet violations of existing agreements have become the major focus of a vocal group of US senators,[78] who are kept well supplied with arguments and information by current and former members of the intelligence community.[79]

The Senate has no formal role in the negotiation of treaties, and in particular in questions of verification, other than to ratify or refuse to ratify the final version of the treaty. It also has no alternative authoritative sources of information on which to base a critique of the Administration's assertion that a treaty is adequately verifiable.[80] The Senate is routinely given classified briefings, and attempts were made by the Carter Administration to involve certain senators in the negotiation process itself. In the case of SALT II this produced little or no ultimate benefit and had to be carried out over the objections of the Soviet negotiators.[81]

One other possibility is for the President to negotiate *agreements* rather than *treaties* on arms control. The former require only simple majorities in both houses of Congress rather than the difficult two-thirds majority in the Senate. For example, SALT I consisted of both a treaty (the ABM Treaty) and an "Interim Agreement" setting temporary limits to certain categories of strategic weapon.[82] The former was ratified by the Senate while the latter was approved by both houses. President Carter kept open the option of submitting SALT II as an 'agreement' up until the last stages of the process and then committed himself to submitting it as a treaty.[83] He was concerned that the use of the 'agreement' device would be seen as an attempt to evade effective Senate advice and consent, and this concern appears to be well founded. The US Arms Control and Disarmament Act of 1977 strongly limits presidential freedom of action in negotiating arms limitations or reductions, and the legislative history of this Act makes clear that the Congress intended to preclude unilateral presidential actions in arms control.[84] This law makes it highly unlikely that a future president will attempt to evade the Senatorial ratification process by negotiating agreements rather than treaties. It also makes clear the fact that future presidents who desire arms control treaties will have to involve the Senate more creatively and fully in the negotiating process than has been done in the past.

It has even been suggested that the Congress should play a much more active role in verification. An important argument for such involvement has been given by Representative Les Aspin: "When we involve Congress we also involve members of the out-party. And that minority participation is essential both to give public credibility to the verification process and to assure the out-party that the process is not being tampered with for political purposes".[85] The legislation introduced to implement this involvement was not passed in 1979 and since then there has been no formal change in the nature of Congressional activity relative to verification. There are also serious questions about the way the Congress would handle problems of secrecy and confidentiality. Nevertheless, such a proposal may help in reducing the impact of leaks (see below, pp. 157–58) and in preserving the political legitimacy of the compliance process.

Bureaucratic politics

Arms control agreements are not only the product of bilateral negotiations between governments; they are also the product of internal negotiations within blocs and alliances, as well as within the individual governments themselves. One study of Soviet bargaining behaviour analyses Soviet actions and positions in the nuclear test-ban negotiations within three separate frameworks: East versus West, Sino-Soviet relations, and internal Soviet bureaucratic and political controversies.[86] Another study highlights the shifting balance of power between 'arms-controllers' and 'militarists' within the Soviet government.[87] Meanwhile, analyses of US negotiating behaviour emphasize the sensitivity of West European allies to certain US negotiating positions[88] as well as the intense bureaucratic conflict within the US government which has accompanied all arms control negotiations.[89]

When one focuses on the narrow issue of verification, one finds very few instances of intra-alliance controversy. A possible exception is that of West European attitudes towards the Reagan Administration's 1984 charges of Soviet violations of previous agreements. According to testimony of Richard Perle, US Assistant Secretary of Defense for International Security Policy, the USA was delayed in making its charges public for "political reasons". According to Perle, "There are other members of the Alliance who don't take these violations as seriously as we do".[90] Aside from this politically sensitive area the most common West European view is that verification is much more a US problem than a European problem, "imposed by the political culture of the United States as much as by technical necessity".[91]

This West European attitude raises interesting questions in the context of concern over the threat of surprise attack in Europe and the efforts to improve and expand confidence-building measures at the Stockholm Conference on Security and Co-operation in Europe.[92] These questions are dealt with in more detail in chapter 4.

Bureaucratic and interest-group competition over verification can affect the arms control process in two major ways. First, the need to reach a compromise or consensus among competing agencies has a major impact on the kinds of proposal which are brought to the negotiations by each side. Bureaucratic rivalries can limit the effective uses of either monitoring or information-processing technologies, and bureaucratic perspectives and interests can use (or even create) verification problems to eliminate or water down proposals they find threatening to their interests. Second, internal conflicts can express themselves in the day-to-day operation of the monitoring and compliance mechanisms once a treaty has been signed. Control of monitoring information and the analytical capabilities necessary to interpret it can be powerful bureaucratic weapons in an area as complex, ambiguous and sensitive as arms control compliance.

The role of verification in US bureaucratic politics is pronounced, although it must be kept in mind that concerns about verification are often expressed as surrogates for more substantive objections to agreements. Historically, it was generally true that the US State Department and the Arms Control and Disarmament Agency were more active proponents of making agreements and more willing to accept less-than-perfect verifiability than the Pentagon. [93] This changed, however, with the advent of the Reagan Administration when negotiators and bureau chiefs such as Paul Nitze, Eugene Rostow, Edward Rowny, Richard Perle and Kenneth Adelman were appointed. These were all people who had previously taken a much tougher stand on verification issues than such predecessors as Gerard Smith, Ralph Earle, Paul Warnke and Cyrus Vance. The Reagan Administration now presents a more united, albeit less flexible, front on this issue than did previous administrations.

The CIA presents an interesting example of bureaucratic conflict. During the SALT I negotiations in the early 1970s the CIA could be described as having "a strong bias in favor of the venturesome approach to SALT" and as taking a "cheerier view [on verification] than any competitor". [94] However, in the mid-1970s, as attitudes towards arms control began to harden in US domestic politics, the CIA's estimates of Soviet capabilities came under intense pressure from other bureaucratic interests. This culminated in the so-called 'Team-B' review of the CIA's intelligence activities in 1976, a review which called into serious question many CIA estimates of, for example, Soviet military spending and missile accuracy. [95] The Team-B review produced a major shift in CIA estimates creating a "new intelligence consensus... reflecting a growing general dissatisfaction with détente and accompanying doubt regarding the intentions of the Soviet Union". [96] This shift in consensus was accompanied by a series of rapid shifts in leadership of the CIA connected with the Watergate scandals and revelations of covert and illegal activities in various parts of the world. [97]

The chastisement of the CIA must be seen in the larger context of an old bureaucratic rivalry between the CIA and the military intelligence agencies, especially that of the US Air Force. In fact, much of the authority of the CIA in verification was given to it in the late 1950s when the Agency was given its own aerial reconnaissance mission "to be certain that the utilization of the photographic 'take' not be left solely in the hands of the Air Force". [98] An early manifestation of this bureaucratic rivalry was the struggle between the CIA and the Air Force over control of U-2 flights over Cuba, a struggle that delayed significantly the discovery of the construction of Soviet missiles sites there in 1962.[99] In a later battle the Air Force gained control over the SR-71 high-altitude reconnaissance aircraft despite CIA objections.[100]

Such intense bureaucratic struggles have serious implications for current and future monitoring of arms control agreements. It can be argued that because a civilian intelligence agency such as the CIA has no weapon programmes or strategic doctrines to protect or promote, it is therefore more able to evaluate intelligence data without bias than an intelligence unit with explicitly military connections.

But the CIA has its own bureaucratic imperatives. One analysis points out that:

> ...the role of the intelligence community is somewhat ambiguous. Its dual role in building and operating intelligence collection systems on the one hand, and assessing verification matters ... on the other appears to represent a potential conflict of interest ... there is always the temptation for the intelligence community to promote treaty provisions that make intelligence collection easier, regardless of their direct relevance to arms control issues.[101]

It is quite clear that as long as monitoring for verification remains an offshoot of the much larger and more comprehensive military intelligence-gathering process, military interests will influence the processing and interpreting of data. Such biases can be expected to show up both in the kinds of verification arrangement embodied in treaties and in the day-to-day operation of the compliance mechanisms as well. It is an old maxim that "where you stand [on verification] depends on where you sit [in the bureaucracy]",[102] and this maxim seems particularly appropriate to US approaches to verification.

Another very clear illustration of this general principle is the position of the US national nuclear weapon laboratories on the issue of a comprehensive nuclear test ban (CTB). Throughout the efforts of the 1950s and 1960s to negotiate such a ban, influential scientists and administrators such as Edward Teller, Ernest Lawrence and Harold Agnew argued forcefully against a nuclear test ban, and encouraged their laboratories to produce data and evasion scenarios which would cast doubt on the ability of the USA to verify a ban on underground nuclear tests.[103] The idea of concealing an underground explosion by conducting it in a large cavity (called 'decoupling') was first proposed in 1959–60 as part of an effort to demonstrate the unverifiability of an underground test ban.[104] This evasion technique, which is discussed further in chapter 4, has remained one of the most popular in the arguments of those who oppose a comprehensive test ban. Years later, when the Carter Administration showed a serious interest in negotiating a comprehensive test ban, arguments by the administrators of the national laboratories were again influential in causing him to change his mind.[105]

The vested interest of the US national laboratories in continued testing of nuclear weapons remains strong. The director of the US Department of Energy's Office of Military Applications has stated:

> Like any good corporation, we have an investment strategy which we have been pursuing for the last couple of years and we intend to pursue it in the decade of the eighties ... We think we need to increase our manpower in research, development, and technology by about 15% above what it was a couple of years ago. We think we need to increase the level of underground testing. [106]

And among the recent spate of assessments by seismologists of the verifiability of an underground test ban the one published by the Lawrence Livermore Laboratory is certainly the most conservative and cautionary. [107] But verification is not the central concern of the Livermore scientists. For example, one anti-CTB argument directed to a scientific audience by a Livermore scientist never even mentions verification as a drawback. Instead, it presents a number of reasons having to do with military security and technological progress why such a treaty would not be in the best interest of the USA, verifiable or not. [108]

None of these activities necessarily implies a lack of professional integrity or lack of desire for meaningful arms control measures. Indeed, they can derive from a high sense of professional integrity, as they have, for example, in the Peaceful Nuclear Explosions Treaty. [109] The verification provisions of this Treaty represent, according to a Livermore physicist who helped to negotiate them, a higher level than any other treaty of "substantive scientific and technical provisions". These provisions go on for many pages of extremely fine detail, a "prolixity" which "followed from a basic premise of the U.S. that verification provisions should be spelled out in full detail as precisely as possible in the treaty text". [110] Unfortunately, even this high level of technical comprehensiveness and precision has not been sufficient to permit the Treaty to be ratified by the US Senate or even for the Administration to press for such ratification.

Such an experience should cast some doubt on the necessity and desirability of expending so much effort to obtain so much precision. However, as long as the negotiation of such treaties remains the special province of lawyers and scientists, as it has traditionally been in the United States, such heroic efforts at comprehensiveness and precision seem inevitable. There is no question that the political content and impact of a treaty can be literally buried in the "prolixity" of technicalities, and this argues for a greater degree of political sensitivity than is ordinarily found in contract lawyers and physicists.

The other side of the coin of excessive professional zeal is the defence of bureaucratic interests, and even here it is not necessary to be disingenuous or unethical to interpret data to one's own advantage. Whether considering an estimate of another state's missile accuracy or the ability to identify relatively small seismic events, there are always margins of error, sometimes rather large ones. The choice of a conservative or hopeful interpretation of such uncertain information will almost certainly be influenced by other factors, and bureaucratic or institutional bias is one such factor.

Do such bureaucratic conflicts exist in the Soviet Union? Any answer to this question must be strongly qualified, given the very fragmented and incomplete information available on the functioning of Soviet bureaucracy, especially in the military and intelligence areas.[111] The essence of verification is information, and while information is a precious and guarded commodity in any bureaucratic setting, the nature of Soviet society suggests that the handling of monitoring data and the production of intelligence estimates must be a source of awkwardness, at least, and probably considerable tension among various agencies. Analyses of the role of secrecy in other aspects of Soviet military activities have turned up signs of such tensions,[112] and in the peculiarly sensitive area of intelligence data: "Students have noted a high degree of compartmentalization in the Soviet bureaucratic structure, which may make it easier for the right hand to be kept in ignorance of what the left is doing".[113]

Western analysts do not present a consistent picture of Soviet intelligence activities. On the one hand, one learns that within the Committee on State Security (KGB) the First Main Administration (the Foreign Directorate) "is responsible for the collection of foreign *strategic intelligence* and the supervision of other Soviet intelligence organizations".[114] On the other hand, one learns that "the Soviet system does not contain the major non-military sources of military information found in U.S. politics—there is no equivalent to the CIA or to private consulting firms such as the RAND Corporation".[115]

From Soviet sources one can learn very little. One reliable source notes that Soviet military intelligence is divided into a number of branches with different functions, such as radio and radar, aircraft and satellites, naval intelligence and the monitoring of foreign publications, radio and television broadcasts, and so on.[116] When one adds to this the reasonable assumption that all of the information gathered by these agencies must be co-ordinated with economic and political intelligence gathered by civilian agencies, the implication is that there must be some interaction between military and civilian agencies and this must involve some flow of information from the military to the civilian sector.

Still, the historical evidence does suggest a stronger control by the military over strategic intelligence in the Soviet Union than in the United States. This was quite evident, for example, in the early stages of the SALT negotiations when Soviet negotiators from the diplomatic side were found to be quite poorly informed on the details of the weapon systems and deployment and testing procedures under discussion, and negotiators from the military side were reluctant to give them the necessary information.[117] Although this situation seems to have improved considerably since the early 1970s,[118] it can still be seen as an aspect of what many Western analysts have interpreted as a serious mutual distrust between the military and political hierarchies.[119]

Just how this combination of secrecy and specialization affects Soviet negotiating positions is extremely unclear. Only some vague hints of bureaucratic conflicts over verification provisions have been detected by US negotiators. For example, Ralph Earle II, the chief US negotiator in the later stages of SALT II, suggests that Soviet willingness to accept unmanned seismic stations and even on-site inspection on their territory in the context of a comprehensive test ban does not imply a willingness to do so in other circumstances, for example, in a chemical weapons ban. This may reflect a difference of bureaucratic attitudes between different agencies.[120]

If it were true that arms control monitoring data are almost totally controlled by the military, this would have serious implications for Soviet conduct of the compliance process. High-level policy makers are inevitably dependent on analyses by experts, especially on such complex technical questions as those which arise in arms control verification. It has already been noted in the US context that the temptation for such experts to bias their analyses is great, especially when major bureaucratic or economic interests are involved. However, the historical record of Soviet handling of compliance issues does not show evidence of such a pro-military bias, so it seems reasonable to conclude that the Soviet political leadership has found ways to keep this problem under control. Just what those ways are, however, is not possible to determine.

IV. The role of other states

So far this discussion of the politics of verification has focused almost entirely on the internal and mutual interactions of the Soviet Union and the United States. Such a focus misses the substantial international interest which verification has generated, even before there was a US–Soviet confrontation. In fact, disarmament has traditionally been far more an international concern, discussed at international conventions and embodied in international treaties, than it has been a purely bilateral concern of two great powers.[121]

Since the end of World War II and the creation of the United Nations, international interest in disarmament has remained high, but the realities of the world distribution of military power, and especially nuclear weapons, have made bilateral agreement between the United States and the Soviet Union an essential condition for the achievement of successful international agreements.

Discouragement and even anger over this unequal situation are common among neutral, non-aligned and developing nations: "First and foremost it should not be tolerated that the two superpowers exercise a world hegemony based largely on their incessant arms race and at the same time play an insincere game of disarmament at the negotiating tables."[122] Similarly, from a different part of the world: "Common security has to be based on a sense of common destiny binding all nations together. The concept will be robbed of all its meaning if it were to stop at endorsing the fashionable cult of arms control which would perpetuate the dominance of nuclear weapon powers..."[123]

This inequality or "hegemony" is not confined to the weapons themselves but extends to the technological capabilities "to exercise the legal rights of states parties to arms control/disarmament agreements to verify compliance to these agreements".[124] Without these technological capabilities states remain either insecure or militarily dependent on one of the great powers (or quite often both). Their insecurity is increased by the ability of more technologically, militarily and economically powerful states to monitor their resources, military capabilities and economic development. Noting that "it seems unfair that legal rights have been established allowing the space powers to practice certain space reconnaissance activities without somehow protecting the rights of other states", two Egyptian authors list three important consequences of this asymmetry in technical capabilities: (a) the threat to the interests and security of developing states from their lack of control over military reconnaissance of their territories; (b) the possibility that strategic data gathered by satellites might be supplied to other states without the approval of the monitored state; and (c) the general trend in international law tending to legitimate the unilateral exploitation of space for reconnaissance purposes.[125]

Similar concerns could apply to the many other intelligence-gathering technologies controlled only by the rich and powerful states. It is also clear that the USA and the Soviet Union are not unconscious of this asymmetry in power, and on at least one occasion concern has been expressed that "other nations could create great difficulties if they were compelled to admit that many of their tightly protected secrets were in fact not secret at all".[126]

There is one important way that third countries do participate in verification, but it is a passive participation based on the same inequalities in power just mentioned. Many countries serve as 'platforms' for the intelligence operations of one of the superpowers. NATO and Warsaw Treaty Organization (WTO) states, Australia, Japan, China, Cuba and others permit their territory to be used for air bases, electronic listening posts and communications links. These serve important intelligence and verification functions for the USA and the USSR.[127] This use of the territories of third parties as part of 'national' technical means is one of the least discussed but potentially most controversial of all arms control issues.[128] In return for the use of their territory these states may receive economic concessions or military aid or protection, but what they do *not* receive is the right of access to the information collected on their territories. While some of the data may on occasion be shared with the host country, this sharing remains at the discretion of the state that owns the equipment.

As long as a handful of states retain control over the technology which can monitor arms control agreements, such agreements cannot be truly international, no matter how many states subscribe to them. An interesting case in point is the Sea-Bed Treaty,[129] which forbids the emplacement of weapons of mass destruction on the ocean floor and which provides for open and equal rights to observe suspicious activities by all states party to the Treaty.[130] But this equality of access is not achievable in practice, since only the two major powers possess the technology to gain access to the ocean floor for the purpose of monitoring activities there. So while the Treaty gives any state party the right to "consult and cooperate" with other parties to investigate possible violations, such consultations will in effect be "reduced to consultation between a less-developed party and one superpower in opposition to the other superpower".[131] Such problems would seem to be inevitable as long as the most sophisticated and effective monitoring technologies remain under the exclusive control of states.

It is ironic that the nuclear weapon,which has to a great extent produced the situation of hegemony criticized above, has also produced the one genuinely international verification mechanism: the safeguards system administered by the International Atomic Energy Agency. But even here the problem of nuclear hegemony cannot be avoided, since the IAEA safeguards are administered largely under the Non-Proliferation Treaty (NPT), which itself enshrines the fundamental asymmetry between nuclear weapon and non-nuclear weapon states.[132] The two classes of state are subjected to different restrictions; in particular, only the non-nuclear weapon states are required to submit to safeguards.[133] Such agreements on the part of nuclear weapon states are entirely voluntary. A number of states have refused to sign the Treaty and accept the safeguards ostensibly because of this asymmetry.

The persistence of these problems has led a number of states to become more active in promoting international verification mechanisms to accompany such international treaties as a comprehensive nuclear test ban, a chemical weapons ban, the Biological Weapons Convention and others. The forum for these proposals has generally been the Committee on Disarmament (CD) in Geneva, which now consists of 40 states and which has on its permanent agenda a wide range of disarmament and arms control problems.[134]

The most active states in making verification proposals, more active in fact than the USA and USSR, have been Sweden and Japan (see table 7). Both have been consistent advocates of international verification agencies with control over such technical means as reconnaissance satellites and seismic networks, as well as authorization for carrying out inspections on a routine or challenge basis.

For example, Sweden has been a leader in developing the concept and the detailed elaboration of an international seismic monitoring network. The current proposal for such a network suggests the use of more than 50 well-equipped seismological stations around the globe, an international exchange of data from these stations over the existing telecommunication system of the World Meteorological Organization (WMO), and the processing of these data at several special International Data Centres to which all participating states would have access.[135] Work on this system has progressed to the point of a

Table 7. State verification proposals according to arms control objective[a]

State	Nuclear weapons	Chemical/biological weapons	Other weapons of mass destruction	Other arms control objectives (cumulated)	Total
Sweden	24	15	2	2	43
Japan	24	14	1	0	39
USA	17	13	3	5	38
UK	22	11	0	0	33
USSR	7	7	5	4	23
Netherlands	9	8	1	0	18
Canada	11	3	0	3	17
Finland	1	11	0	0	12
Italy	4	2	1	4	11
Australia	6	1	1	0	8
France	0	4	0	2	6
FRG	1	3	1	0	5
Socialist states (joint)	0	4	1	0	5
USA/USSR (joint)	0	2	0	2	4

[a] The numbers in this table represent a sum of actual verification proposals made by each state up to 1981 in four categories plus comments it has submitted in response to the proposals of others. It therefore "reflects state participation in a sense which is broader than the making of verification proposals alone" (Crawford, A. and Gilman, E., *Quantitative Overview of the Second Edition of the Compendium of Arms Control Verification Proposals*, ORAE Report No. R89 (Dept of National Defence, Ottawa, April 1983), p. 79).

Sources: Adapted from Crawford & Gilman (see note above), p. 80; and personal communication with A. Crawford.

detailed design for an experimental test of the system and acceptance by the WMO of the use of its communication system for the experiment.[136]

While there remain technical and administrative problems to be resolved in this system, there is little doubt that given sufficient motivation and support they could be resolved in a relatively short time to create a highly satisfactory international seismic-monitoring network. This, coupled with the national networks and analytical capabilities of the major states and the supplemental monitoring capabilities of satellites, would provide ample assurance against any significant clandestine nuclear weapon testing programme anywhere in the world.

Unfortunately, the fundamental problems are not technical and administrative; they are political. It is a fact of international political life that no real progress in nuclear arms control can be made until the two major nuclear powers are willing to commit themselves to such progress. Therefore until the United States and the Soviet Union can come to terms on a nuclear test ban, there is little that states like Sweden or Japan can do except to continue to prepare the foundations for administering and verifying a treaty if and when it does become a reality.

An effective political mechanism which smaller states can use to exert pressure on the major nuclear powers simply does not exist. The Non-Proliferation Treaty stands as evidence of the inherent asymmetry of political power in the field of nuclear energy and nuclear weapons. This asymmetry makes any approach to international forms of verification extremely difficult as is shown in chapter 4.

V. Adequacy

How much verification is enough? This question has been the focus of an intense and virtually continuous debate in the United States since the beginning of the SALT process, that is, since the time when actual arms control agreements began to be negotiated between the United States and the Soviet Union. Before that time the only agreements reached were those which were either easy to verify with very high confidence by national technical means (the Partial Test Ban Treaty) or for which verification was thought to be unimportant (the Outer Space Treaty of 1967). However, when negotiations began to deal with systems having real or potential military and/or symbolic value, the question of verification came to the fore and has remained there ever since.

Soviet versus US views of adequacy

While the United States has had to grapple constantly with the question of a minimum acceptable level of verification, the Soviet Union has never faced this problem, at least in public. Indeed, the Soviet Union has faced the opposite problem, that is, what is the maximum amount of monitoring and 'inspecting' it would tolerate.

Soviet attitudes towards verification have been summarized in the following seven 'basic principles':

> 1. The conduct of verification should in no way prejudice the sovereign rights of states or permit interference in their internal affairs.
> 2. Verification cannot exist without disarmament but must stem from a precise and clear agreement on measures for the limitation of armaments and for disarmament.
> 3. The scope and forms of verification should be commensurate with the character and scope of the specific obligations established...
> 4. The detailed elaboration of the verification provisions is possible only after an agreement on the scope of the prohibition has been mapped out.
> 5. We proceed from the assumption that a State becomes a party to a convention not in order to violate it but in order to abide strictly by the

obligations it has assumed under it, and therefore that verification should not be built upon the principle of total distrust by States of one another...

6. International forms of verification should be limited.

7. ...in the conditions of the present-day development of science and technology, any fairly less serious violation of an agreement in the field of disarmament ... has no chance of remaining undetected for very long. [137]

To discern a definition of 'adequacy', that is, what would be a minimum acceptable level, in these principles is not easy, since most of them deal with upper limits instead of lower ones. However, principles 3, 4 and 7 seem to suggest a vague concept of adequacy. The means of verification must be commensurate with the specific obligations, should derive directly from these obligations and should take into account the deterrent effect of the risk of detection.

As abstract 'basic principles' these form a coherent and logical approach to verification, but problems begin to arise immediately when they are applied to practical situations. Unfortunately it is not possible to find in Soviet writings on verification any attempt to derive specific guidelines for decision making on arms control agreements. Instead, the chief function of the above principles has been to act as constraints on US demands for more extensive verification.

It is therefore not surprising that the phrase 'adequately verifiable' was invented in the United States. President Nixon, in his charge to the US SALT delegation used the phrase, [138] and it is used as well in the law establishing the US Arms Control and Disarmament Agency which was amended in 1977 to require that "adequate verification" accompany any arms control agreement. [139] The term "adequate" was preferred by the Senate to the word "effective" suggested by the House of Representatives on the grounds that it was less ambiguous. Interestingly, the word "effective" has now been resurrected by the Reagan Administration as the new standard of acceptability for verification measures. [140] The significance of this change is analysed below.

An official formulation of the US view of the abstract principle of adequacy is given by the following list of basic principles analogous to those offered by Issraelyan from the Soviet side. A US Arms Control and Disarmament Agency publication addresses the question "when is verification adequate?" and produces the following list of factors which must be taken into account in answering the question:

(*a*) the existing degree of friendship or hostility between the states in question; (*b*) the degree of risk posed by possible violations; (*c*) the ease or difficulty of responding to possible violations; and (*d*) the political benefits to be gained from the treaty. [141]

It is clear from these principles that a very high level of verifiability would be required in a treaty dealing with militarily significant weapons negotiated with a hostile or untrustworthy state. On the other hand, a treaty of high symbolic value dealing with a marginal military system and negotiated among friendly states would require very little verification.

Such self-evident generalities are not very helpful as policy guidelines and, just as in the Soviet case, it is necessary to bring these basic principles down to the real world of arms control negotiations, a world in which it must unfortunately be assumed that at least two of the negotiating states maintain a hostile relationship with each other. Under the Nixon, Ford and Carter Administrations a treaty would have been considered adequately verifiable if "any Soviet cheating which would pose a significant military risk or affect the strategic balance would be detected by our intelligence in time for the United States to respond effectively".[142]

This definition, or very slight variations from it, formed the core of the argument that the SALT agreements were adequately verifiable. But this definition has come under increasing attack and has now been abandoned by the US government. The balance of this section is devoted to an attempt to understand the significance of this change.

The first problem with the definition is that it begs more questions than it answers. It depends for its usefulness on a consensus as to the meanings of phrases such as "significant military risk", "strategic balance" and "respond effectively". But the debates of the past decade over SALT and other arms control proposals have revealed that these are in fact highly controversial phrases in the USA. Their meaning seems to depend heavily on individual attitudes towards more fundamental questions such as the political utility of marginal advantages in military power and the proper goals of arms control.

One analysis of US attitudes towards verification had divided the spectrum of attitudes into three 'schools': the "substantive", the "legalistic" and the "metaphysical".[143] The definition quoted above is characteristic of the concept of adequacy held by the substantive school, and its demands on verifiability are actually comparatively low. They depend on the assumption that the levels of armaments on both sides are already very high and that a *de facto* state of strategic equivalence exists. Therefore, any attempt to affect this balance in a significant way would require a substantial effort, and the very scale of this effort would make any attempt to do it clandestinely almost certain of failure. This connection was made clear by Secretary of Defense Harold Brown in testimony on the SALT II Treaty:

> In short, there is a double bind which serves to deter Soviet cheating. To go undetected, any Soviet cheating would have to be on so small a scale that it would not be militarily significant. Cheating on such a level would hardly be worth the political risks involved. On the other hand, any cheating serious enough to affect the military balance would be detectable in sufficient time to take whatever action the situation required.[144]

This "double bind" concept has been called the "basic canon of the arms control community"[145] and it formed the basis of arguments made by the Nixon, Ford and Carter Administrations for the ratification of the SALT treaties.

Members of the substantive school are not greatly concerned with "minor" violations, as witnessed by the response of Gerard Smith, the chief US negotiator in SALT I, to recent charges of Soviet violations by the Reagan Administration: "Smith added that the alleged violations had no 'substantial' military significance and did not alter the balance of power between the two countries."[146]

In contrast to this view the "legalistic" school considers *all* violations important, even if from a purely military or strategic point of view they are minor. According to this school the degree to which the parties adhere rigorously to all the provisions of a treaty is an important measure of the good-will and trustworthiness of those parties. For example, "The principle effect of the violations is not the immediate military consequences, but the issue of how we conduct negotiations in the future and the expectations we set for these negotiations. We just have to be more careful".[147]

Another argument of the legalistic school is that small violations of an agreement can be used to test the resolve of another party. In this view: "We should not tolerate non-adherence in small things lest we lose our credibility in insisting on adherence in large".[148]

This perceived need to enforce adherence in small or militarily insignificant matters places a far greater burden on verification efforts and raises the standard of adequacy well above that of the substantive school. It forces the monitoring systems to observe much more closely and comprehensively and therefore inevitably raises the false alarm rate. It places a heavy demand on the analytical capabilities of the intelligence agencies and it strains the resilience of the political commitment to maintaining the viability of treaties.

It is in the matter of proof that the legalistic approach encounters its greatest problems. In this view an arms control treaty is a 'contract' whose individual provisions are to be scrupulously adhered to, in analogy with contracts made within the US legal system. But it is almost never mentioned that this system also has as one of its fundamental principles that parties are assumed to be innocent until proven guilty. In this legal tradition violations of a contract must be proved before they in fact become violations. If this same standard were applied rigorously to arms control treaties, the legalistic approach would at least be logically consistent. But such a consistency has not always been manifested in US approaches to verification, where an insistence on rigid adherence to the letter of a treaty has often been accompanied by the presumption that the Soviet Union will probably attempt to cheat. It is far too easy for suspicion to become its own 'proof' under such conditions.

Suspicion is raised to the status of a fundamental principle in the metaphysical school where "even strict compliance with some provisions could be interpreted as 'sinister' ".[149] The basic approach to verification of this school is best summarized by the so-called 'theorem': "We have never found anything that the Soviets have successfully hidden".[150]

Analysis of such a statement must begin with the recognition that it is not in any sense a theorem. A theorem is defined as "a proposition that is not self-evident but that can be proved from accepted premises".[151] But the statement in question *is* self-evident; it is a tautology, that is, a "needless repetition of an idea in a different ... phrase". Something which has never been found has obviously been successfully hidden; no proof of such a statement is either necessary or possible, nor does it require any evidence of either a positive or negative nature to sustain it.

The constant repetition of such a tautology (and it is found repeatedly in the more conservative assessments of verification) can serve only one purpose: to create and sustain an attitude of constant suspicion and fear. That this is its inventor's purpose can be inferred from his paraphrase of Hamlet in the same article: "There are more ways to hide ICBMs in heaven and earth than are dreamt of in your philosophy".[152] The "game" is one of "hiders and finders", and the hiders always seem to have the advantage.[153] It is undoubtedly this attitude that the Soviet Union is reacting to when it refers to the "principle of total distrust of one another", a principle which it sees as fundamentally incompatible with a successful verification mechanism (see principle 5 on p. 140).

The essential demand of the metaphysical school is not that the Soviet Union demonstrate *compliance* with arms control treaties, but that it prove the *absence of non-compliance*. The essence of this demand can be illustrated in the following challenge by a senator of the metaphysical school to Harold Brown who was explaining the concept of adequate verifiability: "... the repeated use of the word 'adequately' bothers me. And I guess Mrs Brown would be a little suspicious of you if you were to come home tonight and tell her that you were adequately faithful to her, wouldn't she?"[154] Dr Brown's interesting answer to this question is given below, but for now the focus should be on the implications of the question itself. First, the question attempts to compare a standard of behaviour with a standard for monitoring behaviour. Second, it suggests a standard of international behaviour in which treaty obligations are in some sense equivalent to marriage vows. What the question ignores is the fundamental assumption of trust on which a marriage is based and which often is sufficient to establish a shared understanding of what "adequately faithful" means.

One can call upon Shakespeare again to see what happens when this understanding is undermined. Othello, with the help of Iago, finds certain evidence of Desdemona's non-compliance with their agreement and, in effect, demands proof of the absence of non-compliance. Such proof cannot be given, and Shakespeare makes very clear what lies at the end of this particular road.

What separates the metaphysical school from the substantive and legalistic schools is the question of "whether monitoring is expected to prove compliance against the presumption of violation or prove violation against the presumption of compliance".[155] It must be made very clear that while the latter task may be made more or less difficult, it is at least in principle possible.

The former task, as Desdemona learned so tragically, is in principle impossible. In the face of such a demand the concept of verification itself becomes meaningless.[156] Verification means the ascertaining of truth or correctness of a statement by the use of evidence. It therefore deals only with "the *fulfilment* and confirmation of an *anticipated* result", that is, compliance.[157] To require a verification system to demonstrate the complete absence of non-compliance is to ensure that it will fail.

The approach to verification of the Nixon, Ford and Carter Administrations can be characterized as a mixture of the substantive and legalistic schools, although the arguments for ratification in Senate hearings tilted strongly towards the substantive end of the spectrum. During the 1970s the metaphysical school acted as an outside critic, which grew progressively in influence, but which had little or no effect on the actual negotiations. With the advent of the Reagan Administration the centre of gravity of US verification policy now lies somewhere between the legalistic and the metaphysical. The demise of the substantive school has been symbolized by the change in standard from "adequately" to "effectively" verifiable.

The meaning of this change in terminology can be seen first by another reference to a dictionary, where "effective" is equated with words like "operative", "active" or "impressive". On the other hand "adequate" is defined with terms like "sufficient", "suitable" or "barely satisfactory".[158] The change seems to imply a more active role for verification than had been contemplated under the previous administrations. To be "effective" rather than merely "adequate" the verification process must have goals beyond those of simply verifying compliance with treaty provisions; it seeks to "effect" something. One way to put this is: "We need a positive assessment that the agreement is being carried out, not just a negative one that no violations of any importance have been detected."[159]

Just how the goals of the new standard are seen by the Reagan Administration has still not been made entirely clear. However, some idea can be obtained from the following principles laid down by Eugene Rostow, the Reagan Administration's first director of ACDA:

> First we shall not confine ourselves to negotiating only about aspects of the problem which can be detected by national technical means. We shall begin by devising substantive limitations that are strategically significant, and then construct the set of measures necessary to ensure verifiability.
>
> Secondly we shall seek verification provisions which not only ensure that actual threats to our security resulting from possible violations can be detected in a timely manner, but also limit the likelihood of ambiguous situations developing.[160]

The first of these principles can be interpreted as essentially equivalent (with only a change in rhetorical emphasis) to principles 3 and 4 stated by Soviet Ambassador Issraelyan (see p. 140). The second principle uses the previous concept of adequate verifiability (i.e., that actual military threats can be detected in a timely manner) as a base and then extends this to a limitation of the possibility of "ambiguous situations".

The problem of ambiguity

"Ambiguity is the problem." [161] "Ambiguous provisions result in compliance questions and compliance questions, *even if ultimately resolved*, strain the atmosphere for arms control negotiations." [162] So one operative 'effect' to be achieved in 'effective verification' is the reduction or removal of ambiguity. This can be done in two ways, both of which have been suggested by officials of the Reagan Administration. One way would be "to go for simpler arms control agreements that are not involving such arcane requirements of verification". [163] The other would be to demand of the Soviet Union a greater willingness to consider "cooperative measures" [164] to improve the verifiability of agreements. Such a willingness would serve as "a litmus test of their commitment to serious limitations". [165]

Both of these alternatives pose their own problems. While 'simpler' arms control agreements may reduce the ambiguity of the verification process, they may not achieve meaningful objectives. For example, a restriction to unambiguously verifiable agreements would rule out such vital measures as a chemical weapons ban or a comprehensive nuclear test ban. On the other hand, demanding more "cooperative measures" from the Soviet Union as a "litmus test of their commitment to serious limitations" sounds suspiciously like earlier US efforts to force the Soviet Union to conform to US standards of openness, a favourite goal of the metaphysical school. The Bush proposals for a chemical weapons ban (see p. 126) appear to be consistent with this interpretation. But such proposals can be predicted in advance to be unacceptable, especially when they are presented as "litmus tests".

The goal of reducing ambiguity in arms control agreements is certainly a desirable one, especially in view of the volatility of the US political process. And it is undeniable that the previous standard of adequate verifiability left ample room for ambiguity. But not even the most ardent advocate of effective verification would argue that ambiguity can be removed entirely, and a case can even be made that some ambiguity may be desirable in certain cases to permit some flexibility in interpretation and implementation. But even if absolute precision is the goal, it can never be possible to eliminate the possibility of differences in interpretation, technical limitations and other sources of ambiguity.

If some ambiguity is inevitable, then the problem has come full circle and the question boils down to how much ambiguity can be tolerated. In other words when does verification become "adequately effective"? Such playing with words is only partially facetious. It illustrates the ultimate frustration encountered in any attempt to make the inherently subjective objective. It cannot be done.

Quantitative approaches to adequacy

Ambiguity is frustrating to many people, especially scientists, and from time to time efforts are made to find objective measures of adequacy or effectiveness. The most common approach to this problem is to compare the risks inherent in a given arms control proposal to the benefits expected from it. In order to make such a comparison both risks and benefits must be quantified in some way and must be commensurable, that is, measurable in the same units.

It is enough to define the problem in this way to see how difficult (many would say impossible) it is to solve. While risks can be quantified to some degree under certain assumptions in certain special cases, there is virtually no way to measure quantitatively the benefits of most arms control or disarmament measures. While there may sometimes be measurable economic benefits, and while some quantitative estimates might be made for the reduction of risks of accidents, the greatest proportion of the benefits are in their contribution to the reduction of international tensions and the risk of war. Such benefits cannot be measured quantitatively, and few analysts attempt to do so.

The risk inherent in a particular provision is proportional to both the probability of successful violation and the magnitude of the consequence of such a violation.[166] This assures that relatively inconsequential violations pose little risk even if they are easy to accomplish, while serious violations (often called 'break-outs') pose significant risks even if their probability of execution is relatively low. This methodology may be familiar to many from the debate over the safety of nuclear power plants in the USA during the 1970s. It is now widely used in many areas of risk assessment.

In order to quantify risk both probability and consequences must be quantified. The former can in fact be quantified for a number of possible agreements. One example is in the detection of underground nuclear explosions. A seismograph in a certain location is subjected to a known level of seismic noise (see chapter 2) and, therefore, can detect signals from actual events with a probability that depends on the ratio of the signal strength to the noise level (S/N).[167] Knowing how seismic signals decrease in amplitude with distance from the source then allows the computation of a relationship between the probability of detection of an event and its distance from the seismograph. These individual probabilities can then be combined mathematically to give the detection probability of a network of seismographs spread over many locations. It is then possible to design a network adequate to detect and identify seismic events of a given strength anywhere in the world with a known probability.[168] This procedure leads to a well-defined and credible value for the probability that an underground nuclear test of a given yield could be carried out without detection.

The next question, however, is how large this probability should be to serve as an 'adequate' deterrent to potential violators. Already at this stage subjective values begin to enter the calculation. Does one take the point of view of the detector and demand a high probability of assurance of detection, say 90 per cent?[169] Or does one work on the assumption that a potential violator would be effectively deterred by even a relatively low probability (say 30 per cent) that a clandestine test would be identified?[170]

There is no objective answer to this question; the answer clearly depends on the level of hostility and suspicion between the parties at the time the agreement is negotiated. It also depends on the other half of the risk calculation, that is the consequences of a successful or unsuccessful violation. But how does one estimate quantitatively the gain or loss of military and/or political advantage from the successful execution of a clandestine test or series of tests of warheads small enough to evade detection? And how does one estimate the political costs of being caught in an attempt to cheat?

There are several other approaches to the problem of defining a quantitative standard of adequacy. One set uses the mathematical theory of games in an attempt to see how two 'players' will behave in a situation in which cheating successfully and unsuccessfully has certain risks and benefits (called payoffs).[171] While this technique can provide an interesting qualitative description of certain kinds of decision making, the simplifying asumptions which must be made to make it analytically soluble render it hopelessly inadequate for the treatment of real verification problems. Another approach formulates 'breakout scenarios' of various magnitudes in order to test the 'sensitivity' of the strategic balance to clandestine weapon deployments.[172] But such scenarios also suffer from highly simplified analytical assumptions and tend to be devoid of political content, making their usefulness questionable even as heuristic aids.

A possibly more promising quantitative approach begins from the assumption that small marginal changes in some measure of military power become less and less significant as the absolute magnitude of the measure becomes larger. For example, one proposal for a cut-off on the production of fissionable materials assumes that a "fissile production cutoff agreement would be adequately verifiable if it were possible to detect with a reasonable probability the clandestine production or diversion of an amount of fissile material greater than ten percent of the current US stockpile over a period of ten years".[173]

This implies that an adequate monitoring system would be incapable of reliably detecting any production capability less than one per cent per year of the current US stockpile, equal to either 6.5 tonnes per year of highly enriched uranium or 1 tonne per year of weapon-grade plutonium.

From one point of view this definition seems quite reasonable and conservative; one can hardly imagine the 'strategic balance' being upset by the secret expansion of nuclear explosive stockpiles by one per cent per year. But from another point of view there are serious political problems with such a definition, since one per cent of the US stockpile of fissionable materials could be used to produce at least 1 000 nuclear weapons.[174] How does a government reassure a suspicious public and Senate that a monitoring system which can permit as many as 1 000 secret new nuclear weapons per year on the other side is 'adequate'?

The actual problem of clandestine weapon production is, of course, more complicated than this question implies. It is one thing to produce the necessary explosives clandestinely, but it is quite another thing to turn them into weapons, provide them with delivery systems and integrate them into military plans clandestinely. Still, the numbers themselves are so large that such careful qualifications are likely to be overwhelmed in the inevitable simplifications of public debate. Former US Defense Secretary Harold Brown has made clear the political difficulties: "For an American president, the political problem is the real one. For President Carter (or even President Reagan) to be accused of . . . taking a position . . . that allowing the USSR that many bombs a year in violation of an agreed ban is adequate verification . . . would quite likely make the front page of the *New York Times*".[175] This example raises as clearly as any other the complex and controversial distinction between politically significant violations and militarily significant ones, a distinction which is examined in detail in chapter 4.

The role of doctrine

The debate on adequacy of verification must ultimately be considered in the context of the debate on military-strategic doctrine. This boils down to the question of whether marginal advantages in military forces, in particular in nuclear weapons, carry with them corresponding marginal political advantages. There seems to be an intimate connection between the position people hold on this doctrinal issue and the standards of adequacy they apply to verification of arms control agreements.[176]

The two poles of the debate are delineated by the following statements. The first is by Gerard Smith, the chief US negotiator in SALT I: "If there was to be success at SALT, I felt that the two sides would to some extent have to pursue a similar strategic doctrine, that the prime (but not necessarily sole) purpose of strategic nuclear weapons is to deter the use of such weapons by the other side. . . This in simple terms is the doctrine of 'assured destruction' ".[177] It is implicit in the doctrine of assured destruction that nuclear threats, even when made from a position of considerable superiority, are incredible and therefore have no political utility. A state with a secure retaliatory capability need not fear such threats and can tolerate even rather substantial shifts in the strategic balance.

On the other side can be found the following views: "Weapons imbalances can be as useful for deterrence and coercion as for war fighting, a circumstance both the USSR and the US obviously appreciate".[178] And "If one assumes that no capabilities beyond those required for a 'minimum deterrent' are significant, then none of the SALT II limitations are 'strategically significant': they may assure the Soviet Union strategic nuclear superiority, without denying us a 'minimum deterrent' ".[179] In this view marginal weapon imbalances or strategic superiority are (or at least can be) politically significant and, by implication, must be preventable if an arms control agreement is to be meaningful.

When this abstract doctrinal argument is brought down to the level of verification one tends to find assured destruction advocates belonging to the substantive school and agreeing with the 'double bind' analysis offered by Harold Brown.[180] The other side, who believe that nuclear superiority remains a useful political tool even in the face of an opponent with an assured destruction capability, tend to be found in the legalistic and to some extent in the metaphysical schools and to deny that there is any logical or practical connection between the verifiability of a particular issue and its military-political significance.[181]

This is not the place for a careful discussion of the doctrinal issues involved in this debate. It must suffice to emphasize that this debate, which has raged almost unabated in the United States ever since the nuclear age began, is at the root of much of the internal dissension that marks US approaches to arms control in general and verification in particular.

On this level a very similar comment can be made about the Soviet Union, which has been conducting its own debate on strategic nuclear doctrine ever since the death of Josef Stalin in 1953.[182] It is interesting to speculate that the two sides of this debate may be distinguished by different approaches to the problem of 'co-operative measures' in arms control verification. Those in the Soviet Union who consider nuclear parity or assured destruction sufficient may argue for a greater willingness to share information and make concessions on on-site inspection in order to reach agreements which will preserve this parity. That such concessions are from time to time made indicates that they are being advocated by reasonably strong political forces. On the other hand, those who believe in the usefulness or danger of superiority, when held by the Soviet or the US side, will tend to see the ability to withhold military information as an important Soviet advantage, one which it would be reckless to negotiate away without equally significant concessions from the other side.

There is no hard evidence with which to test this hypothesis, but one former US negotiator has noted that:

> ...the Russians rightly understand every verification provision that gets into a treaty to be a concession that they are making to us ... every stage is an extraordinarily difficult effort—which the Soviets expect to be a two-way process, with Soviet concessions on verification (both monitoring and

precision) compensated by U.S. agreement on points of concern to the USSR. [183]

One would need to add to this observation only the additional suggestion that some part of the "extraordinary difficulty" may occur in the political debates within the Soviet Union itself.

One loose end remains to be tied in this discussion of adequacy in verification: Harold Brown's response to the senator's question about the adequacy of his fidelity to Mrs Brown (see above, p. 144). Dr Brown's answer was, "In that case as in this, I suppose it would depend upon the alternative offered". [184] The alternative in arms control to a working consensus on the definition of adequate verifiability is no arms control at all, so it is essential to draw some conclusions from the above analysis as to what sort of consensus might be possible.

In choosing among the substantive, legalistic and metaphysical approaches one must consider the technical and political demands each places on the verification process. From this point of view the metaphysical approach is clearly unacceptable, and the legalistic approach seriously problematic. The former, in fact, if not in explicit words, denies the possibility of meaningful arms control or disarmament, while the latter places so much emphasis on sensitive and comprehensive monitoring that it promises constantly to create at least as many problems as it solves. The substantive approach would set a much higher threshold on violations and in some cases may appear to involve some risks, but it has the virtue of focusing on the military significance of possible violations, a criterion which seems less vulnerable to ambiguities, false alarms and shifts in political attitudes than more legalistic, technically arcane and sensitive criteria.

It cannot be emphasized too strongly that no matter what criterion of adequacy is chosen it will always be subject to strong influence by the prevailing political climate. As is stated at the beginning of this chapter, it is far easier for shifts in political relations to affect attitudes towards verification than it is for verification, no matter how adequate or effective, to improve the political climate. This leads to the conclusion that the best approach is one which does not place unreasonable demands on a system which is inherently fragile. The substantive approach based on military criteria of adequacy shows the best promise of staying within this limitation. It also has the virtue of focusing the public debate on arms control onto issues of military-strategic doctrine and the role of military force in international politics. This is where the debate belongs.

As to the distinction between 'adequate' and 'effective' verification, this seems little more than a semantic and symbolic device with which the Reagan Administration has attempted to establish its break with previous US approaches to arms control. As the above analysis has shown, changing the word does not change the problem. The problem remains to find the appropriate level of verification necessary to reassure governments and citizens that arms control agreements are being complied with. If this problem can be solved the word used to describe the solution will not matter very much. The achievement of a public and leadership consensus on a substantive criterion of adequacy will not be easy. It will require much education and reassurance from a government strongly committed to arms control. And it will also require a high level of commitment by all parties to bilateral or international treaties to a scrupulous adherence to their obligations. Finally, there is no escaping the need for trust, a much maligned and misunderstood concept, which is the next subject for analysis.

VI. Trust

No word is more fundamental to the problem of verification than 'trust', and no word has suffered more from both hypocrisy and scepticism in the history of arms control efforts. It is a concept on which US and Soviet positions seem furthest apart, yet the processes by which trust might be enhanced through verification measures are never examined in detail by either side. That which is not taken for granted is dismissed out of hand. But no discussion of verification would be complete without an attempt to analyse two of the most basic assumptions of Western approaches to verification: first, that verification can operate as a substitute for trust and, second, that verification can lead to the building of trust.

A particularly clear statement of these assumptions is the following: "Verification systems which are now essential because of lack of trust, can, by the assurance of compliance they can provide, become one of the most powerful tools for building the sought-for mutual trust... In sum we have the following equation: the more absolute the verification—born in mistrust—the greater the progress toward absolute trust". [185]

Another suggests that "The successful verification of a cut-off [of fissionable materials production] would have great psychological and political importance. It might profoundly affect conventional beliefs that nothing can be done to halt the arms race". [186]

While these statements may exaggerate the intimacy of the cause–effect relationship between verification and trust, they nevertheless make clear the basic assumption underlying the role of verification as a 'confidence-building measure' (see chapter 1). It is therefore essential to examine this assumption critically, to ask in short: can confidence-building measures really build confidence?

Any approach to this question must recognize that trust operates on two quite distinct levels. First, there is the notion of trust between states who sign a treaty or agreement. On this level states are independent unitary actors whose degree of trust in each other's intentions is reflected in the compliance provisions embodied in the treaty. Second, there must be the recognition that states are not in fact unitary actors but carry out policies which are the result of internal political debate and compromise. Trust plays a crucial role in this internal process as well, especially in an area characterized by high degrees of both technical complexity and secrecy, not to mention occasional illegality. Those who do not have access to monitoring and intelligence data, and could not interpret them even if they did, must trust those who do see the information to interpret it with skill and integrity and to act appropriately on the basis of these interpretations. A strong argument can be made that this problem of internal trust is considerably more important to the success of arms control than the problem of trust between states.

Internal trust

As suggested above, the problem of maintaining internal trust derives from two major sources: technical complexity and secrecy. The technical sophistication of virtually all national technical means of monitoring implies that only highly trained specialists will be able to transform the raw data from photographs, seismographs, radar and radio antennas, infra-red sensors, radiation meters, and so on, into an understandable and useful form for policy makers. Meanwhile the dense cloud of secrecy under which the intelligence-gathering and interpreting process is carried out implies that very few people will have access to crucial information and be aware of the nature and reliability of its sources.

The need for political leaders to depend on expert technicians in order to make critical decisions is more and more a characteristic of modern life. In such highly technical areas as nuclear energy, environmental protection, military preparedness, economic policy and arms control those who must take responsibility for making decisions cannot begin to absorb and master all of the factual and analytical work that must precede such decisions. In the vast majority of cases policy makers have only the vaguest understanding of the technical details of the systems they are controlling.

It is not only the technical complexity of the data that is inaccessible to decision makers, but also their sheer volume. Just the interpretation of satellite photographs, which provide only a small fraction of all intelligence data collected, requires the sustained work of hundreds, possibly thousands, of highly trained professional photo-interpreters whose job is to extract important information from photographs on which the layperson would see only fuzzy blotches of varying shape and size. The classic example is the photographs of Soviet missile emplacements under construction in Cuba shown to President Kennedy in October 1962. To anyone who had not been trained to interpret such photographs and who was not already familiar with the configurations of Soviet missile emplacements such photographs would be useless. Indeed, acccording to McGeorge Bundy, an advisor to President Kennedy at the time: "it was the persuasive conviction of the experts and not the naked appearance of the first photographs which was immediately conclusive to President Kennedy on October 16. If he had not learned to know and trust those experts, he might well have doubted their story".[187]

A more recent example involved the showing to a selected group of journalists of infra-red and low-light motion pictures taken by US reconnaissance aircraft over the south-east coast of El Salvador.[188] The films were alleged to provide hard evidence of the shipment of weapons by Nicaragua to rebel forces in El Salvador. But the journalist writing the account could say only that he saw "fuzzy white objects", "a cluster of small white outlines", "white blots" or "small white forms" on the film (see figure 7, p. 33). The interpretation of these images was done for him by voice-over commentary on the films. To this journalist the evidence remained "inconclusive", and US embassy officials could only say that "in conjunction with other evidence we have, some of which is sensitive, they make an interesting case that arms are being infiltrated into the country, and from Nicaragua."

This example makes clear that the simple release of monitoring data will in most cases be useless in informing the public. Interpretation by experts will inevitably have to accompany any attempt to use intelligence data in the domestic political process, and it is not difficult to list the qualifications such experts must have if they are to do their job properly. They must have the best possible data-gathering and processing equipment, they must maintain a high standard of professional competence and, above all, they must confine themselves to purely objective, non-political assessments of the data they analyse. All political judgement must be left to those who carry political responsibilities.

These requirements clearly define the problems of expertise. However sophisticated the hardware becomes there will always be interesting, possibly critical, data which are just beyond its reach, and however well trained the experts, there will inevitably be mistakes, misinterpretations and lack of initiative to contend with. For example, it has been suggested that the US allegations of the use of 'yellow rain' by the Soviet Union or states friendly to it resulted from faulty interpretation of evidence by intelligence analysts who were scientifically incompetent. The question then arises as to "how far back . . . into the intelligence-evaluating channels . . . such deficiencies extend. And can we assume that the people in government who have to act on the intelligence appraisals have a proper capacity for distinguishing what may loosely be called a scientific fact from a scientific opinion?"[189]

These are serious problems, but they can be dealt with by careful hiring and training practices. Such problems are not crippling to the verification process as long as the condition of professional detachment is fulfilled. As long as confidence remains in the essential objectivity and integrity of the experts, their technical and human limitations can be accepted as a fact of life without compromising the value of what they do produce.

Unfortunately, however, this primary requirement is the most difficult to preserve precisely at the times when it is most necessary: when an issue has become politically controversial. Analysts are asked not only to describe what the data *say*, but also what they *mean*. They are pressured to resolve ambiguities which, as professionals, they would prefer to see remain as ambiguities. And their cautious and tentative interpretations are often introduced into the public debate and distorted beyond recognition by misunderstanding, oversimplification and misrepresentation.

The essence of the problem is that equally competent experts can be more or less in agreement on what the data say but be in bitter disagreement about what they mean. As these disagreements emerge into the public debate, people become confused and begin to lose confidence in the experts themselves. People are accustomed to disagreements between politicians, but disagreements among experts on arcane and dangerous technical issues are extremely discomforting. The public has no independent means of analysing the data and, as happened in the case of nuclear power plant safety in the USA, the issue can reduce to one of pitting 'our' experts against 'their' experts.

These pressures to take political positions in the debate external to the policy-making process are compounded by the pressures to produce politically and bureaucratically 'acceptable' analyses within the process. There are many bureaucratic levels between raw intelligence data and the final decision makers, and at these levels are career officials who "have a strong interest in cooking raw intelligence to make their masters' favorite dishes".[190] It is a rarely achieved ideal in which intelligence provides the objective facts that then determine policy choices. More often, "Policy is made and *then* supported by intelligence ... [T]his is partly ... to avoid giving the intelligence service any more power than can be helped. There is also a concern that intelligence operators interested in policy may become the advocates of some pet scheme at the expense of reporting facts".[191]

Fears of just these kinds of pressure made many in the CIA reluctant to take on the responsibility for verification in the 1960s.[192] And these fears seem to have been justified, especially during the Nixon Administration when the demands of the SALT negotiations caused National Security Advisor Henry Kissinger to put intense pressure on intelligence analysts to produce numbers and assessments which would be useful to him in negotiations with the Soviet Union. According to one account of this process:

> By early 1970 [CIA Director Richard] Helms had been convinced that it was far safer to misrepresent the intelligence than to do battle with the White House. The CIA no longer automatically analyzed intelligence data on critical issues, but immediately turned over the raw information to

Kissinger and the National Security Council (NSC) for them to analyze as they saw fit and draw whatever conclusions they chose.[193]

An example of the results of this process is the story of a former NSC staff member who was given the task of projecting Soviet nuclear submarine and submarine-lanched missile production capabilities. According to the analyst, "My clear task was to make sure that the Soviet proposals came up in the middle range. The NSC had no illusions about what they were being asked to do: falsify national intelligence estimates ... the numbers allegedly supplied by the Soviets ... had originated with Kissinger, not Brezhnev".[194]

A number of other such attempts to manipulate the intelligence process for political purposes could be mentioned. For example, there have been two recent resignations from the CIA over alleged pressures to make intelligence estimates conform to US policy in Central America.[195] And charges of political manipulation of intelligence data were at the heart of the legal action taken by General William Westmoreland against the Columbia Broadcasting System.[196]

Kissinger's manipulation of information during the SALT I negotiations caused problems for the US and Soviet negotiating teams[197] and might be interpreted by some as unethical manipulations of the professional intelligence process. At the same time others might defend such actions as legitimate on the grounds that the numbers themselves were not strategically significant and that the manipulation was necessary to achieve political goals which were far more important than some abstract notion of pure objectivity. But whatever value judgement one places on these activities there can be no illusions about the role such political manipulation plays in undermining trust in intelligence expertise. Once this trust is undermined there is little that can be done to restore it except to make available the controversial data and allow independent assessments to be made.

This immediately raises the difficult problem of secrecy. Some secrecy is both necessary and desirable in any system of verification. Not only must important sources of intelligence be protected, but some uncertainty on the part of all parties to a treaty as to the monitoring capabilities of other parties has a useful deterrent effect on violations. However, secrecy also creates serious obstacles to public confidence in the verification system as well as to the effective operation of the system itself.[198] And in an interesting reversal of the 'deterrent' argument Paul Warnke, the chief US negotiator on SALT II, has suggested that the deterrent effect of verification might even be *enhanced* by the release of more information: "I suspect that we are even better than [the USSR] think we are and, therefore, if they knew a little more, they would be even more worried about cheating".[199]

Unfortunately, increased openness faces major bureaucratic obstacles. In a sensitive area like intelligence, information becomes both a precious currency and a potent weapon, and access to secret information is both a tool and symbol of political power and bureaucratic status.[200] During the SALT I negotiations Henry Kissinger succeeded in gaining almost complete control over the flow of information within the national security bureaucracy, often withholding from both the Secretary of State and Secretary of Defense information essential to the performance of their official responsibilities.[201] During the negotiations Dr Kissinger relied almost entirely on Soviet-supplied interpreters because he did not trust intepreters supplied by the US State Department.[202] This can be compared with the Soviet willingness to use US-supplied data on force levels in order to avoid the need for Soviet military officials to reveal actual Soviet numbers in the presence of Soviet civilian diplomats (see above, p. 135). While much of what has been said so far about public trust has had a distinctly US context, this problem of information-as-weapon is common to bureaucracies everywhere and, were they free to do so, Soviet and US national security managers would certainly find many common problems in this area to discuss.

When the seemingly irresistible force of the need for public confidence meets the seemingly immovable object of the desire for absolute secrecy, something must give way. In the Soviet system, of course, the 'irresistible force' half of this equation is absent. Soviet citizens are simply assured that "in our century of developed electronics and space flights, those who are entrusted with such verification possess all the necessary facilities for immediately finding out any violation of the treaty if it occurs".[203] Still, even in the absence of serious concerns about public opinion, many Soviet officials are surely aware of the price that is paid for excessive secrecy and compartmentalization in the form of decreased efficiency and creativity in solving problems.

In the US system the usual method for reducing accumulated tensions between secrecy and public demand for information is for the system to spring leaks. Such leaks of supposedly secret information have become a standard part of the US political process and are used at all levels of the political and bureaucratic hierarchy to achieve various political goals. Certain journalists and journals have become well known as conduits for leaks, and outside critics and supporters of various policies learn to recognize these valuable bits of information as they appear. According to one US Congressman, disputes within the intelligence community can create "a field day for rumormongers": "A piece of evidence suggesting a violation is leaked and presented as positive proof of a violation. Then a piece of contrary evidence is counter-leaked as positive proof that nothing whatsoever happened. The end result is to discredit the whole verification process".[204] This is one of the problems that has led the Congressman to propose a much closer involvement of the US Congress in the entire verification process (see above, p. 130).

While leaks play, to some extent, the role of a safety valve in the US political system, they do not resolve the contradiction between the demands for secrecy and the need for public confidence in official decisions. Leaks are inevitably and properly seen as politically motivated, and they are almost never accompanied by enough supporting data to make them credible to someone who is not already convinced of their truth. In fact, politically or ideologically motivated leaks from the intelligence community ultimately serve only to undermine even further public confidence in the competence and objectivity of intelligence professionals even if, as is often the case, they are not responsible for the leaks.

Information, in order to inspire confidence, must be freely given and clearly credible or must come from a source which is seen to have no political interest at stake. The Carter Administration took several steps to release information which had previously been treated as secret. In 1978 President Carter acknowledged publicly the official 'secret' that the United States used reconnaissance satellites to photograph the territory of the Soviet Union.[205] This 'secret' had been common knowledge for almost 20 years but for political reasons, which are discussed in chapter 4, had never been admitted officially. The Carter Administration also released a summary of the issues which had been discussed in the Standing Consultative Commission regarding ambiguities and irregularities in Soviet and US behaviour under the SALT I Treaty.[206] The proceedings of this Commission are supposed to be absolutely secret, and President Carter risked serious criticism from the Soviet Union for breaking this secrecy. However, this criticism has turned out to be relatively mild,[207] indicating a willingness of the Soviet leadership to take into account the demands of the US political process.

As useful as these relaxations of secrecy were they were not sufficient to overcome the suspicions of opponents of the SALT agreements that other, possibly more damaging evidence was being withheld. Every government must face the prospect that in maintaining secrecy it can invite charges that it is covering up failures in the intelligence process or weakness and irresolution in the face of apparent violations.[208] Even the release of some information will often not solve the problem but only bring charges of selective manipulation and whet appetites for even more information.

As one might expect, opinions are deeply divided over the solution to this problem. On one side are those who would strengthen secrecy and plug the leaks. According to General David C. Jones, former Chairman of the US Joint Chiefs of Staff: "this whole subject of verification has been discussed too much in public, and continued discussion of the subject is likely to end up in jeopardizing some of our intelligence gathering systems".[209] But William Colby, former Director of the CIA, has advocated a significant relaxation of secrecy with respect to intelligence information: "Intelligence can contribute to the public debate... The functions of intelligence have to be shared with the people. This is very much a change in the operation of intelligence. It's an old myth ... that everything should be secret".[210]

In attempting to evaluate these two positions it must be kept in mind that information is a two-edged sword, and that its release will not necessarily reduce tensions or promote arms control objectives. For example, General Bernard Rogers, Commander of NATO forces in Europe, recently argued that aerial or satellite photographs of Soviet military deployments in Eastern Europe should be revealed. He told a group of newspaper reporters: "I wish we could have spent the afternoon here just showing you photographs from overhead platforms... How we can see the offensive orientation of the Warsaw Pact. They've got acres and acres, in various locations, of river crossing equipment. It isn't to cross rivers going east... It's to head west, you see".[211]

If General Rogers is correct in his interpretation of these photographs, their release would clearly not be helpful in reassuring the people of Western Europe of peaceful Soviet intentions. But if the pictures *were* released, others would also have the opportunity to examine them and might arrive at different interpretations. In particular it would be interesting and instructive to learn how one determines from pictures of bridging equipment in which direction it is intended to be used. But in the present situation in which such photographs are kept secret the concerned public has only its preconceived ideas and attitudes on which to decide whether to accept, reject or ignore General Rogers' interpretation.

Without minimizing the genuine problems involved it does seem that Mr Colby's approach offers the greater promise for real progress in arms control. US officials who seem quite eager to point out the negative effects on mutual trust of Soviet concerns for secrecy seem much less willing to understand the damaging effects of their own obsession with secrecy in dealing with the US electorate and Congress. Given a genuine interest in arms control, any present or future US Administration is going to have to rebuild the confidence which has been lost in US verification capabilities through the acrimonious debates over SALT. It is difficult to see how this confidence can be regained without the release of considerably more information than has been freely available in the past. If one picture is worth a thousand words, then one high-quality satellite photograph may prove more effective than a thousand exhortations to trust the experts.

However, even more fundamental than reassuring public concerns about verification is the re-establishment of a leadership consensus on the US approach to arms control. The loss of public confidence has resulted far more from the breaking up of this consensus than it has from concerns about technical inability to monitor Soviet behaviour.[212]

Rebuilding this consensus will not be easy. In a poll taken immediately after the 1980 election which brought the Reagan Administration to power, 90 per cent of respondents favoured continued US–Soviet negotiations on arms control, but about half of those in favour of negotiations also agreed with the statement that while the USA would keep its end of the bargain the Soviets probably would not.[213] The ensuing four years of Reagan Administration, characterized by extremely bellicose rhetoric in its early stages and numerous accusations of Soviet treaty violations (see chapter 4), can hardly have improved this situation.

Trust between states

It is assumed in the discussion that follows that the internal problems of confidence described in the previous section have been brought under control and that two (or more) states face each other as unitary actors in arms control negotiations. The question to be addressed is: can verification substitute for a lack of trust and actually lead ultimately to the growth of trust?

That one must begin from a baseline of very little mutual trust will not be difficult to demonstrate. On the US side the almost total absence of trust in the Soviet Union is generally asserted as the foundation of US compliance policy. For example, the final report on SALT II verification by the Foreign Relations Committee of the US Senate begins with the assertion by its Chairman: "It is agreed that the United States cannot rely upon or trust the Russians to comply with [the treaty's] terms".[214]

William Colby was once head of the CIA and is now a strong public advocate of arms control agreements. He can be categorized as a member of the substantive school of verification, and his views typify those of the more liberal US advocates of a nuclear freeze and a reduction of tensions between the USA and Soviet Union.[215] Yet even Mr Colby makes clear that "the first and most obvious fundamental is, of course, that we should not 'trust' the Russians".[216] More recently, Walter Mondale, the 1984 Democratic candidate for the US presidency, stated with considerable emphasis in a televised debate with President Reagan: "I don't trust the Russians".[217]

In the United States it has become *de rigueur* to begin discussions of verification with this almost ritualistic incantation. It serves the purpose of demonstrating that the speaker is not a sentimental disarmer or unwitting dupe of Soviet trickery. To some extent it is a 'credibility ritual' which Americans have come to expect of anyone with pretensions to expertise in arms control verification. This can partially explain the extraordinary frequency with which this assertion recurs in US politics, but it is also certainly true, as the previously cited public opinion survey indicates, that lack of trust of Soviet motives in signing arms control treaties is a pervasive attitude in the United States. It is probably useless to speculate on whether it is the prevailing public climate of distrust which forces politicians to emphasize their own distrust, or whether the politicians in fact create the public attitudes. Both views are certainly true to some extent and they tend to reinforce each other.

Expressions of lack of trust in the United States are far less common on the Soviet side. Gerard Smith, the chief US negotiator for SALT I, was impressed by the fact that during the entire two years of negotiations leading up to the agreements "the closest the Soviets ever came to suggesting that the United States might violate an agreement was a statement that a party to an agreement might evade its terms by helping to build up allied strategic forces".[218] Yet there are limits to such restraint, and occasionally a Soviet spokesman will remind the world that "we have no reason for trusting others any more than others trust us".[219] At the same time it remains one of the basic Soviet principles of arms control verification that it "should not be built upon the principle of total distrust by states of one another and should not take the form of global suspiciousness".[220]

On no other issue is the distinction between Soviet and US positions so clear. To the USA, verification must be based on the premise of distrust, that is, the assumption that states (or at least the Soviet Union) sign treaties while maintaining the option, if not the conscious intent, of secretly violating the agreements if an opportunity presents itself in the form of either complacency or irresolution on the other side. To the Soviet Union, verification must be based on the premise that states sign treaties with every intention of living up to their obligations. To the USA confidence is *a priori* non-existent and must be built by the accumulated evidence of compliance, while to the USSR initial confidence is assumed and can only be eroded by evidence of non-compliance.

It needs to be emphasized that these differences in attitude are not explained simply by the observation that Soviet society is 'closed' while US society is 'open'. There is in fact no logical connection between the tightness of control over information and political activity within a state and its trustworthiness in adhering to international agreements. Indeed, it can be argued that a state which exerts a strong control over its internal politics is far less likely to have its chief of state sign an arms limitation agreement only to have it fail in the ratification process because of political forces beyond his control. Similarly, if the intention does exist at the highest levels to adhere to an agreement there is less likelihood in a highly centralized state that independent bureaucratic and/or political actors will take initiatives which undermine the confidence of the other side in the stability of the agreement.

This argument is certainly not intended as an endorsement of highly centralized control over information and political expression. Its purpose is simply to emphasize that the presence of such control in no way constitutes a *prima facie* case for the inherent deceitfulness of the state which possesses it. It is quite possible for such a state to see its best interests served by meaningful and reliable arms control agreeements with potential adversaries and therefore to be committed to scrupulous adherence to the provisions of existing agreements. Nor is there anything inherently trustworthy about the behaviour of pluralistic states in foreign affairs. The interactions between domestic and international politics are far too subtle to allow for such generalizations.

Chronic distrust can exist, and often has existed, between states with very similar political systems, whether pluralistic or centralized. Therefore, the problem of building trust through verification of compliance with arms control agreements goes well beyond the question of the relative 'openness' or 'closedness' of US and Soviet societies.

The hypothesis that arms control verification can build trust must be examined against the background of the following constraints:

1. Arms control agreements are limited instruments which regulate only relatively narrow aspects of the military and political competition. It is assumed that the competition continues unabated in all areas not covered by the agreement. Anything not forbidden is permitted.

2. Verification, however adequate or effective, can never be absolute, and the comprehensiveness and sensitivity of any monitoring process are inherently limited by the need to keep information rates and false alarms to an acceptable level.

3. While it is possible to use evidence to prove non-compliance with an agreement, it is impossible to use evidence to prove total compliance. However much evidence of compliance is gathered, the possibility that some non-compliance remains undetected will always exist. The Katz tautology (see above, p. 143) is simply another way of stating the logical impossibility of proving the absence of non-compliance.

Within the context of these constraints, and assuming that the verification process starts from a lack of trust in the intentions of the other side, one can identify a number of very serious obstacles to the building of trust through verification. The first is ambiguity, something the Reagan Administration has already stated must be reduced substantially if verification is to be effective. Eugene Rostow (see p. 146) is correct when he points out that ambiguities increase suspicion, even if they are successfully resolved, but the unstated assumption underlying his argument is that the ambiguity arises in an atmosphere already characterized by distrust. In this atmosphere the presumption of guilt which is temporarily reinforced by the ambiguity is never fully removed by the clarification. In the USA in the 1950s, people who were accused by Senator McCarthy and others of being communists or communist sympathizers suffered heavily even if they were later shown to have been falsely accused. Similarly, even if it were demonstrated conclusively tomorrow that 'yellow rain' is a natural phenomenon unrelated to chemical warfare, this would not undo all of the damage that has been done to the political atmosphere by accusations that the Soviet Union is responsible for using or encouraging the use of such a weapon. Where there is a presumption of guilt, accusation based on ambiguous evidence leaves an added taint of guilt. Conversely, where there is a presumption of innocence, ambiguity can almost always be resolved to sustain and even enhance the presumption of innocence.

It is possible to construct quantitative models that illustrate the way in which the same evidence can be used to support both a positive and a negative prejudice.[221] The example assumes a mobile ICBM system in which some agreed number of launchers are moved around among some much larger number of shelters, similar to the Carter Administration's 'shell game' plan for the MX missile. However, to facilitate verification that the allowed number of launchers is not exceeded, some specified number of randomly chosen shelters is opened to allow satellites of the other side to see how many of them contain launchers. Then, on the basis of a statistical calculation, the monitoring side can decide whether the number of launchers actually observed is consistent with the number expected.

This is all straightforward except for the very last word: 'expected' on the assumption of compliance or 'expected' on the assumption of non-compliance? It can be demonstrated straightforwardly that *both* hypotheses can be 'confirmed' (in the statistical sense) with the *same* observed data. Even in this most objective of monitoring situations one can still see what one expects to see.[222]

This phenomenon has been demonstrated in many psychological experiments with individuals and groups. In one such experiment certain students were chosen from a group to act as supervisors of the work by other students on a set of assigned tasks.[223] Each of the supervisors was responsible for ensuring that the output of two student workers met specified standards. The situation was arranged so that the supervisor could closely watch the work of one student but could not easily monitor the actions of the other. The experiment was planned to ensure that, to the supervisor's knowledge, both of his workers produced the same amount of work. After several periods of work, the supervisor was instructed to choose which worker he needed to watch more closely. In almost all cases, the supervisor's choice indicated that he perceived the student who had been working without close monitoring to be more trustworthy. The reason should be clear—while the outputs were the same (and, hence, the supervisor was confronted with the same stimuli), the supervisor had reason to suspect that the observed student might have been working only because he was being watched. However unjustly, the supervisor's perception of trustworthiness was influenced by this extraneous knowledge.

This example makes clear the very real possibility that the institution of more and more comprehensive and intrusive inspection measures in an atmosphere already poisoned by distrust can serve to reinforce distrust between the parties: "If we assume something approaching a 100 percent willingness to cheat, then verification by technical means becomes politically ineffective. In an atmosphere of intense distrust the verification system will be asked to verify things that resist verification and to provide unreasonable reassurances".[224]

Another possible consequence of attempting to accomplish too much with verification could be to institutionalize distrust. Institutionalized distrust is a familiar feature of modern societies. It is manifested in the auditing of income tax returns, the 'frisking' at airport boarding areas, the searching of baggage at customs counters and in breath tests for alcohol on highways. Encounters with such manifestations of official distrust can range in impact from the mildly annoying to the deeply humiliating, depending on the sensitivity with which they are carried out. They are never pleasing or flattering. Citizens submit to such experiences either because they recognize and accept the legitimate authority of those who conduct them or because they have no alternative.

It is an entirely different matter to institutionalize such distrust among equals. Unless inspections are conducted with sensitivity and skill by an authority with universally recognized legitimacy, they can become an irritant leading to even greater hostility and distrust than would have existed without them. And to maintain a consensus of legitimacy for an inspection programme, the programme must adapt to the widely varying cultural and political characteristics of the states to be inspected. While these two constraints do not rule out an effective inspection mechanism, they do make the design of one extremely difficult, even when the political atmosphere is relatively cordial. When the atmosphere is hostile the task becomes virtually hopeless, since there is no authority with the power to impose it on the states involved.

So far the problems identified have had to do with ambiguous behaviour. But even more insidious than the confidence-eroding nature of ambiguities is the probability that in an atmosphere of distrust even clear evidence of compliance can be seen as having sinister implications. If one knows one is dealing with a cheater, then when one observes evidence of compliance it is natural to assume that this evidence has been planted in order to distract attention from the real cheating which is going on elsewhere.

For example, Katz argues that what appears to be US success in gathering intelligence on Soviet missile forces is due to the fact that "the Soviets have been cooperating with the US intelligence systems". They have not made the task easy; "Rather, they don't make things impossible". He then argues that since success has been based on Soviet co-operation, it is impossible to say how effective US intelligence methods would be if the Soviet Union were actually hiding missiles.[225] In short, it is not what is seen which is worrisome; it is what is *not* seen.

A bizarre example of this phenomenon is related by Steinberg in his account of the 'missile gap' scare of the late 1950s, when a number of Democratic presidential candidates accused President Eisenhower of allowing the Soviet Union to gain an enormous lead over the USA in ICBMs. There was no hard evidence for this gap but: "Maxwell Taylor and John Kennedy saw the lack of evidence of large-scale Soviet missile deployment as *evidence that such deployment was imminent*".[226]

It is one thing to be pessimistic and always assume the worst, but it is quite another to use in support of one's pessimism evidence for precisely the opposite conclusion. This is very close to the thinking of the hypochondriac who sees the absence of illness as evidence that he will soon get sick, and the obverse of the chronic optimism of the compulsive gambler who sees every losing streak as evidence that his luck is about to take a turn for the better.

One final example will illustrate the self-fulfilling nature of distrust. It concerns what de Rivera has called the "construction of reality"[227] and is best typified by Goethe's observation that "in the end we are all dependent on monsters of our own creation".[228] John Foster Dulles, US Secretary of State from 1953 to 1957, believed that "a communistic government was essentially evil"[229] and "feared that if we were drawn into agreements with the Kremlin on particular issues the effect on public opinion might be to undermine our ability to keep up our guard".[230] These assumptions made Dulles incapable of interpreting the evidence of change in Soviet behaviour following Stalin's death in 1953 in a way that would cause a change in his basic assumptions. A study of Dulles' publicly expressed attitudes towards the Soviet Union showed that there was no correlation between Soviet behaviour and Dulles' attitude. This raises the important question:

> If there were factions in the Soviet Union who desired friendlier relations with the United States, what could they have done (in the realm of political practicality) to convince the Secretary of State of their sincerity? It would appear that no matter what the Soviet Union could have done, the Secretary would have interpreted the very acts that should have led him to *change* his beliefs in such a way as to *preserve* his beliefs.[231]

While these examples effectively illustrate the destructive effects of distrust, one cannot ignore the fact that the same self-magnifying mechanisms can operate to produce unwarranted complacency. US officials were so convinced in 1941 that Pearl Harbor could not be attacked that they attributed evidence of Japanese intelligence gathering to "Japanese diligence".[232] And Josef Stalin was so convinced that Adolf Hitler would not betray their non-aggression pact that he ignored obvious evidence of German preparations for an invasion of the Soviet Union.[233]

The lesson to be learned from these examples is not that pessimism is necessarily more or less dangerous than optimism, but that whatever prejudice one starts with will have a strong tendency to be reinforced by the evidence one obtains from monitoring. This calls into serious question the notion that a verification system intended as a "substitute for trust" can ever result in a building of trust. This may have been what Soviet Premier Brezhnev had in mind when he told a US Senator: "The danger today is not that the current methods of verification are inadequate, but that this issue might be used to fuel a propaganda campaign that would only trigger distrust between our countries and poison the political atmosphere".[234]

Recognition of this possibility is not confined to the Soviet Union. Many of these potential problems of arms control agreements were recognized by

Western analysts years ago,[235] and according to a more recent Western assessment:

> Transparency has revealed defense establishments of great technical complexity, in the process of constant change. Where the meaning of certain activities is inherently obscure, greater amounts of information are bound to lead to conflicts of interpretation and thus of policy choice. Transparency has a confidence-eroding as well as a confidence-building dimension.[236]

How then can confidence be built? There exists a vast amount of solid evidence of compliance with arms control agreements which could serve to reinforce trust. There also exists a vast amount of highly ambiguous evidence of possible non-compliance (see chapter 4) which can serve to reinforce the absence of trust. It seems clear that in order for the first process to prevail some modicum of trust must be created to begin it.

An analogy which suggests itself is a cloud of water vapour in which the temperature and density have the correct values to produce condensation and rain, but in which rain does not form. The drops will not form unless the cloud also contains small 'nuclei' (for example dust particles or ice crystals) onto which the water vapour can condense. In fact rain can often be produced artificially by seeding saturated clouds with ice or silver halide crystals. These nuclei are an indispensible initiating factor which are qualitatively different from the water which condenses on them to form rain.

The building of confidence can be seen as very similar to the building of raindrops. The political atmosphere can be full of evidence of compliance, but confidence will not grow unless a nucleus of some kind is present. This nucleus must be of an essentially different nature, that is, it cannot itself be constructed out of evidence of compliance. It is more a willingness to be convinced or a "disposition to be reassured".[237] It was precisely this willingness that was absent in Secretary of State Dulles and which others find so threatening today. It represents a certain leap of faith and must ultimately derive from a sense of shared danger and shared interest in the reduction of this danger.

This does not imply that all conflicts and tensions between the USA and USSR must be resolved before the process of building trust can begin: "Compliance issues can be handled satisfactorily even if superpower relations are far from ideal. But the essential precondition for success is that both sides believe it is in their interest to maintain the viability of previous agreements".[238]

Another US statesman, hardly less anti-communist than Dulles, recognized the need for this leap very early in the nuclear age. Henry Stimson, Secretary of War in the Roosevelt and Truman Administrations, at first held hopes that by maintaining its monopoly over nuclear weapons the United States could coerce the Soviet Union into accepting US plans for the post-war world. However, in 1945 Stimson became the first senior administration official to become disillusioned with this notion and advocated that a direct approach be made to the Soviet Union to negotiate a sharing of information on atomic energy.[239] In his letter of resignation to President Truman, Stimson wrote: "The chief lesson I have learned in a long life is that the only way you can make a man trustworthy is to trust him; and the surest way to make him untrustworthy is to distrust him and show your distrust".[240] However impressive the technological progress in verification capabilities may have been over the nearly 40 years since these words were written, their essential truth remains undiminished.

VII. Trust and adequacy

In the 1950s the frustration bred by unsuccessful efforts at disarmament led to the ascendency of the concept of arms control. If the arms race could not be ended it would have to be managed, and verification would become an essential tool in this management. This led to many attempts to formulate some general principles connecting the demands for verification with the overall state of the arms competition, some of which are examined briefly above.

Probably the most influential and lasting of these efforts was one put forward in 1961 by Jerome Wiesner, President Kennedy's Chief Science Advisor.[241] Wiesner assumed that disarmament would have to begin and proceed in an atmosphere of mutual distrust between the disarming parties, both of whom would begin the process from some relatively high level of armaments. Both sides would first agree to dismantle some relatively small fraction of their forces. At this stage, since both sides retain a powerful nuclear force, the importance of verifying that no cheating took place on the size of this reduction would not be great, so the inspection effort could be relatively minor.

As subsequent steps were taken and the sizes of the retaliatory forces on both sides became smaller and smaller, so the potential danger of one side cheating would increase, since a marginal superiority which is innocuous at high levels might become (or appear to become) decisive at low levels. Extending this argument to its logical conclusion leads to the prediction that complete nuclear disarmament is an unstable and potentially very dangerous situation, since a marginal advantage of only a few weapons could give its possessor enormous power.

The most important implication for verification of Wiesner's analysis is that the amount of inspection must increase as the level of armaments is reduced. That this conclusion is still widely accepted is illustrated by the following statement of the Palme Commission: "The more deeply a treaty bites into existing arsenals or the more tightly it binds possible future developments of military technology, the more comprehensive must be the means of verification

specified in the agreement".[242] The same connection between reduced arma-
ment levels and increased verification demands is suggested in the concluding
paragraph of the study which looks at the verification of a cut-off in fissile
material production (see pp. 148–49): "Of course, if and when nuclear
disarmament proceeds to the point where the stockpiles have been greatly
reduced, the task of adequate verification may become more difficult".[243]

The relationship between verification and disarmament implied by these
statements is illustrated in figure 40, usually called the 'Wiesner curve'.[244] The
graph shows the progress of nuclear arms reduction over time as well as the
degree of inspection required to prevent significant violations. The final objective, to be reached at time *A*, is some minimal level of nuclear weapons on
both sides—in other words, a permanent stable balance. Along with the curve
showing a decreasing number of 'legal' weapons, Wiesner draws another curve
to illustrate the acceptable uncertainties at each period of time. As the legal
number of weapons decreases, so must the uncertainty, so the two curves get

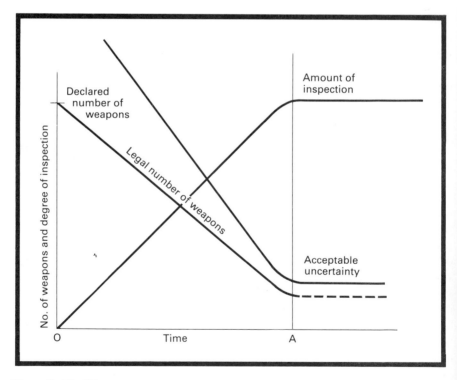

Figure 40. The Wiesner curve
The curve shows the relationship between the degree of disarmament achieved and the demand
for inspection. All of the variables are plotted without units, so the sizes of the final 'minimal
deterrents', the final magnitude of the inspection system, and the time required to complete the
process are all unspecified. In particular, time 'A' may be 5, 10 or even 50 years in the future.

closer together, and the curve for 'amount of inspection' goes steadily upward. Wiesner does not state it explicitly, but is is implicit in his analysis that if the disarmament curves were extended to zero, the uncertainty would also have to be zero (or at least extremely small), and the amount of inspection would therefore be intolerably high.

The evidence accumulated over the more than 20 years since this model was proposed suggests that while it may have some usefulness in dealing with certain special cases of quantitative arms limitation, it is almost certainly invalid, and even misleading as a general description of the relationship between the degree of disarmament and the demand for verification.[245] Since the model was proposed in 1961 the numbers of weapons on both sides have grown substantially, suggesting that demands for verification should have decreased. They most certainly have not; if anything they have become even more stringent and politically sensitive than they were in 1961. The historical experience is therefore more consistent with a model in which the level of suspicion and fear, instead of remaining constant, is proportional to the level of armaments.

To understand the failure of the Wiesner model it is necessary only to state clearly the assumptions on which it is based. First, it assumes that the task of inspection is to effect disarmament "in a context of acute distrust between powerful nations".[246] This high level of distrust is implicitly asumed to remain constant during the disarmament process. Second, the model assumes that only militarily significant violations need to be deterred, and that the military significance of violation depends on the marginal advantage it achieves relative to the existing levels of armaments. In other words, 10 clandestine nuclear weapons are assumed to be far more significant when measured against a base of 50 than against a base of 5 000. These assumptions will be recognized as those of the substantive school of verification described above.

There are a number of reasons for the failure of Wiesner's model to predict the course of events since its formulation. The first is the essentially quantitative approach to both armaments and inspection implied by the graphical presentation in figure 40. Both armaments and inspection are plotted in terms of amounts or numbers, ignoring the extremely important qualitative dimensions of both of these factors. The most important changes in armaments since 1961 have been qualitative rather than quantitative, and this trend is still accelerating. The actual number of nuclear weapons possessed by the United States in 1984 is not much greater than the number in 1960, but the accuracy, reliability, flexibility, survivability and mobility of these weapons have been increased enormously. Similar trends are well advanced on the Soviet side.

Increases in monitoring capabilities have been both quantitative and qualitative since Wiesner constructed his model, but in recent years the emphasis has shifted almost entirely to qualitative improvements—better sensitivity and resolution, improved reliability and survivability, more rapid data processing, and so forth. Future developments in sensor and information-processing technology promise to be almost entirely qualitative. Unfortunately, as has already been noted (see chapter 2), the improvements in monitoring technology are not keeping pace with the qualitative improvements and proliferation of weapon technology. Models based on purely quantitative approaches to arms limitation are not very useful even as conceptual guides to the evolving connection between verification and arms control.

Another problem with Wiesner's model is the implicit assumption that the political significance of possible violations is closely related to their military significance. As a member of the substantive school Wiesner may believe that this is the way things ought to be, but the history of arms control negotiations shows that the reality is quite different. Along with the commitment to qualitative improvements in weapons has come what appears to be an increasing belief in the political utility of even small marginal military advantages.[247] This belief is rarely expressed in the positive sense of a state openly exploiting its own perceived advantage. Instead it manifests itself in an exaggerated sensitivity to perceived marginal advantages of the other side and the concern that they have acquired this advantage because they see political utility in it. How much of this concern is genuine and how much is rationalization is very difficult to determine. Under these conditions the legalistic and metaphysical concepts of verification are more logically appropriate, and these have in fact come to dominate the US approach to the problem. The result of such an approach is that the "balance of terror" becomes "delicate",[248] and more monitoring rather than less is required to prevent the clandestine development of some supposedly potent advantage.

Even if the above-mentioned difficulties could be solved by constructing a more sophisticated model, there would remain an even more fundamental flaw in the Wiesner curve. This can be found in its assumption that a constant level of distrust will be maintained during the process of disarmament. One criticism which appeared soon after the publication of Wiesner's model argued:

> If the process of disarmament, once commenced, were to continue, it would almost necessarily transform both the attitudes of states toward one another and the general character of international society. It seems most implausible to postulate as constant the political atmosphere that exists today during the course of disarmament from beginning to end. Either trust and harmony would emerge to a much greater extent than they exist today or the disarmament process would not proceed very far.[249]

This argument is consistent with the results of other psychological experiments similar to those cited above in the analysis of trust (see pp. 163–66). These experiments showed that people who had previously engaged in some form of co-operative activity showed a significantly enhanced tendency to trust each other in subsequent competitive situations relative to people who had had no previous co-operation.[250]

All of this suggests that there would almost certainly be a strong correlation between the degree of disarmament and the level of trust, precisely the reverse of the apparent growth of distrust in lock-step with an escalating arms race. The question comes down to finding some way to reverse the arms race, and this must confront another 'double bind': hostile states will not begin to disarm until they trust each other but will not trust each other until they begin to disarm. This dynamic feedback relationship suggests that disarmament and trust must progress closely together or they will not progress at all. Such a feedback loop, however, gives very little guidance as to how much verification is necessary to help the process, and, as has already been argued, too much verification could even interfere with it.

In the end the political role of verification remains elusive. The problem cannot be reduced to a scientific formulation, and it remains in the very apt words of Amrom Katz "the art of the state".[251]

Notes and references

1. 'Antisatellite ban called unsound', *New York Times,* 16 March 1984, p. 8.
2. Strauss, R. and Wollack, K., 'Pursuit of arms talks divides Reagan advisers', *Los Angeles Times*, 15 July 1984, p. 3E.
3. Pike, J., *FAS Public Interest Report* (Washington, DC) Vol 36, No. 9, November 1983.
4. The Baruch Plan, Statement by the United States Representative (Baruch) to the United Nations Atomic Energy Commission, 14 June 1946, in *Documents on Disarmament 1945–1959,* Vol. I, US Department of State Publication 7008 (US Government Printing Office, Washington, DC, August 1960), p. 10.
5. *Documents on Disarmament 1945–1959* (note 4), p. 15.
6. Address by the Soviet Representative (Gromyko) to the United Nations Atomic Energy Commission, 19 June 1946, in *Documents on Disarmament 1945–1959* (note 4), p. 18.
7. Jönsson, C., *Soviet Bargaining Behavior: The Nuclear Test Ban Case* (Columbia University Press, New York, 1979), p. 72.
8. Zheleznov, R., 'Monitoring arms limitation measures', *International Affairs* (Moscow), July 1982, p. 75.
9. Issraelyan, V., 'Soviet initiatives on disarmament', *International Affairs* (Moscow), July 1977, p. 55.
10. Statement by President Eisenhower at the Geneva Conference of Heads of Government: Aerial inspection and exchange of military blueprints, 21 July 1955, in *Documents on Disarmament 1945–1959* (note 4), pp. 486-88.
11. Statement by President Eisenhower (note 10), p. 487.
12. Rosenberg, D.A., 'The origins of overkill: nuclear weapons and American strategy, 1945–1960', *International Security,* Vol. 7, No. 4, Spring 1983, p. 38.
13. Rosenberg (note 12), p. 50.
14. Steinberg, G.M., *Satellite Reconnaissance: The Role of Informal Bargaining* (Praeger, New York, 1983), p. 96.
15. Perry, R., *The Faces of Verification: Strategic Arms Control for the 1980s*, Rand Report P.5986 (Rand Corp., Santa Monica, CA, August 1977), p. 19.
16. Kuzar, B., *Krasnaya Zvezda*, 24 April 1984, 1st edition, p. 2, translated in *Cur-

rent News: Foreign Media Edition (US Department of the Air Force, Washington, DC, 21 May 1984), pp. 40-41.

17. Jönsson (note 7), pp. 71-74.
18. Goldblat, J., *Agreements for Arms Control: A Critical Survey* (Taylor & Francis, London, 1982), pp. 153-54 [a SIPRI book].
19. Goldblat (note 18), p. 154 [emphasis added].
20. Goldblat (note 18), p. 155 [emphasis added].
21. Crawford, A. and Gilman, E., *Quantitative Overview of the Second Edition of the Compendium of Arms Control Verification Proposals,* ORAE Report No. R89, Department of National Defence, Ottawa, April 1983, pp. 84-87.
22. Crawford, A. *et al., Compendium of Arms Control Verification Proposals,* 2nd edition, ORAE Report No. R81 (Department of National Defence, Ottawa, March 1982).
23. Moorer, Admiral T.H., *The Salt II Treaty, Hearings before the Committee on Foreign Relations* (SFRC Hearings), US Senate, 96th Congress, First Session (US Government Printing Office, Washington, DC, 1979), Part 2, p. 148.
24. Yergin, D., *Shattered Peace: The Origins of the Cold War and the National Security State* (Houghton-Mifflin, Boston, MA, 1978), p. 6.
25. Smith, G., *Doubletalk: The Story of SALT I* (Doubleday, New York, 1980), p. 170.
26. US Congressional Record, Senate, 28 June 1983, p. S9333. 'Skunk works' is the nickname of the Lockheed facility in California where the U-2 and SR-71 high-altitude reconnaissance aircraft were developed. The name is taken from another 'unapproachable' facility created by the US cartoonist Al Capp in his comic strip "L'il Abner".
27. Dupuy, T.N. and Hammerman, G.M., *A Documentary History of Arms Control and Disarmament* (R.R. Bowker, New York and T.N. Dupuy Associates, Dunn Loring, VA, 1973), pp. 345-48.
28. Western Draft Resolution introduced in the Disarmament Subcommittee, 8 March 1955, in *Documents on Disarmament 1945-1959* (note 4), pp. 448-50.
29. Western Draft Resolution (note 28), p. 449.
30. Soviet Draft Resolution introduced in the Disarmament Committee: Conclusion of an international convention (treaty) on the reduction of armaments and the prohibition of atomic, hydrogen, and other weapons of mass destruction, 19 March 1955, in *Documents on Disarmament 1945-1959* (note 4), pp. 450-52.
31. Anglo-French memorandum submitted to the Disarmament Subcommittee: Prohibition and elimination of nuclear weapons, 19 April 1955, in *Documents on Disarmament 1945-1959* (note 4), pp. 453-54.
32. Soviet Proposal introduced in the Disarmament Subcommittee: Reduction of armaments, the prohibition of atomic weapons, and the elimination of the threat of a new war, 10 May 1955, in *Documents on Disarmament 1945-1959* (note 4), pp. 456-67.
33. Soviet Proposal (note 32), p. 466.
34. Address by the Soviet Premier (Bulganin) at the Warsaw Conference of the Eastern European States (extracts), 11 May 1955, in *Documents on Disarmament 1945-1959* (note 4), pp. 467-71.
35. Statement by the Deputy United States Representative on the Disarmament Sub-committee (Wadsworth) regarding the new Soviet proposals, 11 May 1955, in *Documents on Disarmament 1945-1959* (note 4), p. 473.
36. Statement by the Deputy United States Representative on the Disarmament Sub-committee (Wadsworth), 18 May 1955, in *Documents on Disarmament 1945-1959* (note 4), p. 474.

37. Noel-Baker, P., *The Arms Race* (John Calder, London, 1958), pp. 12-30; Barnet, R.J., *Who Wants Disarmament?* (Beacon, Boston, MA, 1960), pp. 27-45.
38. Noel-Baker (note 37), p. 23.
39. Smith (note 25), p. 124.
40. Talbot, S., *End Game: The Inside Story of SALT II* (Harper & Row, New York, 1979), p. 98.
41. Earle, R.T., II, private communication, 16 October 1984.
42. Smith (note 25), p. 230 [emphasis added].
43. Seaborg, G.T., *Kennedy, Khrushchev, and the Test Ban* (University of California Press, Berkeley, 1981), p. 41.
44. Seaborg (note 43), p. 58.
45. Seaborg (note 43), p. 184.
46. Seaborg (note 43), pp. 188-89.
47. Seaborg (note 43), p. 191.
48. Seaborg (note 43), p. 177.
49. Treaty between the USA and the USSR on the limitation of underground nuclear weapon tests (Threshold Test Ban Treaty), in Goldblat (note 18), pp. 211-12.
50. Treaty between the USA and the USSR on underground nuclear explosions for peaceful purposes, in Goldblat (note 18), pp. 218-27.
51. ACDA, *Verification: the Critical Element of Arms Control,* US ACDA Publication No. 85 (US Government Printing Office, Washington, DC, March 1976), pp. 17-18.
52. 'Moscow yields on point of chemical war ban', *New York Times*, 22 February 1984, p. 4.
53. Convention on the prohibition of the development, production and stockpiling of bacteriological (biological) and toxin weapons and on their destruction (BW Convention), in Goldblat (note 18), pp. 193-95.
54. BW Convention, in Goldblat (note 18), p. 194.
55. Zheleznov (note 8), p. 79.
56. ACDA (note 51), p. 7.
57. SIPRI, *World Armaments and Disarmament, SIPRI Yearbook 1981* (Taylor & Francis, London, 1981), pp. 383-87.
58. SIPRI (note 57), para. 13, p. 385.
59. SIPRI (note 57), para. 18, p. 386.
60. Bush, G., Address before the Conference on Disarmament (CD), Geneva, 18 April 1984, *Current Policy*, No. 566 (US Department of State, Bureau of Public Affairs, Washington, DC), p. 1.
61. Bush (note 60), p. 2. This was later "clarified" to include "privately owned American factories that have government contracts"; see Pincus, W., 'U.S. clarifies stand on chemical pact', *Washington Post*, 1 May 1984, p. 12.
62. Bush (note 60), p. 5.
63. Bush (note 60), p. 3.
64. Schmemann, S., 'Moscow dismisses chemical arms plan', *New York Times*, 6 April 1984, p. 3.
65. Lebedev, Maj. Gen., 'Washington's speculations around verification issues', *Pravda,* 3 May 1984.
66. Statement by the Soviet Representative (Issraelyan) to the CD: Chemical Weapons, 6 March 1980; *Documents on Disarmament,* US ACDA Publication No. 116 (US Government Printing Office, Washington, DC, December 1983), p. 148 [emphasis added].
67. Slocombe, W., 'Verification and negotiation', in *The Nuclear Weapons Freeze and Arms Control*, Proceedings of a symposium held at the American Academy

of Arts and Sciences, 13–15 January 1983, Center for Science and International Affairs, Harvard University, 1983, p. 87.

68. Payne, S.B., Jr, *The Soviet Union and SALT* (MIT Press, Cambridge, MA, 1980), p. 81.
69. Talbot (note 40), p. 223.
70. Slocombe (note 67).
71. Cohen, S.A., 'The evolution of Soviet views on verification', in Potter, W.C. (ed.), *Verification and SALT: The Challenge of Strategic Deception* (Westview Press, Boulder, CO, 1980), p. 68.
72. Payne (note 68).
73. York, H.F., 'Bilateral negotiations and the arms race', *Scientific American*, Vol. 249, No. 4, October 1983, p. 110.
74. Talbot (note 40), pp. 52-54; Newhouse, J., *Cold Dawn: The Story of SALT I* (Holt, Rinehart and Winston, New York, 1973), p. 263; Smith (note 25), pp. 442-43.
75. Marshall, E., 'Senate skeptical on SALT verification', *Science,* Vol. 205, 27 July 1979, p. 373.
76. Colby, W.E., 'Verification of a nuclear freeze', in *The Nuclear Weapons Freeze and Arms Control* (note 67), p. 73.
77. Brown, H., in SFRC Hearings (note 23), p. 240.
78. Wallop, M., 'Soviet violations of arms control agreements: so what?', *Strategic Review*, Vol. 11, Summer 1983, pp. 11-20; Garn, J., 'The SALT II verification myth', *Strategic Review,* Vol. 7, Summer 1979, pp. 16-24.
79. Sullivan, D.S., 'The legacy of SALT I: Soviet deception and U.S. retreat', *Strategic Review*, Vol. 7, Winter 1979, pp. 26-41; Katz, A.H., *Verification and SALT: The State of the Art and the Art of the State* (Heritage Foundation, Washington, DC, 1979); Katz, A.H., 'The fabric of verification. The warp and the woof', in Potter (note 71), pp. 193-220.
80. Lowenthal, M.M., 'U.S. organization for verification', in Potter (note 71), pp. 91-93.
81. Talbot (note 40), p. 95.
82. Treaty between the USA and the USSR on the limitation of anti-ballistic missile systems (ABM Treaty), in Goldblat (note 18), pp. 197-201; Interim agreement between the USA and the USSR on certain measures with respect to the limitation of strategic offensive arms (SALT I Agreement), in Goldblat (note 18), pp. 202-205.
83. Talbot (note 40), p. 272.
84. Lowenthal, M.M., *Possible Means of Improving Congressional Oversight of SALT Verification and Other Arms Control Compliance Issues,* Congressional Research Service, Washington, DC, 22 August 1979, p. 2.
85. Aspin, L., 'Aspin proposes legislation giving Congress verification powers', Press release, US House of Representatives, Washington, DC, 22 August 1979, p. 2.
86. Jönsson (note 7).
87. Payne (note 68).
88. Talbot (note 40), pp. 141-42.
89. Talbot, S., *Deadly Gambits* (Knopf, New York, 1984).
90. *Washington Post,* 15 March 1984, p. 38.
91. Holst, J.J., 'A European perspective on the concept of a nuclear freeze', Norsk Utenrikspolitisk Institutet, NUPI Notat No. 260, Oslo, January 1983, p. 8.
92. Barton, D., Pöllinger, S. and Reinius, U., 'Negotiations for conventional force reductions and security in Europe', in SIPRI, *World Armaments and Disarmament, SIPRI Yearbook 1983* (Taylor & Francis, London), pp. 595-610.

93. Newhouse (note 74), pp. 43-45.
94. Newhouse (note 74), pp. 44-45.
95. Prados, J., *The Soviet Estimate* (Dial Press, New York, 1982), pp. 248-57.
96. Prados (note 95), p. 257.
97. Senate Select Committee to Study Governmental Operations with respect to Intelligence Activities, Final Report, 94th Congress, 2nd Session (US Government Printing Office, Washington, DC, 1976).
98. Richelson, J., 'The Keyhole satellite program', School of Government and Public Administration, The American University, Washington, DC, March 1984, p. 16.
99. Allison, G., *Essence of Decision* (Little, Brown & Co., Boston, MA, 1971), pp. 122-23.
100. Prados (note 95), p. 176.
101. Buchan, G.C., 'The verification spectrum', *Bulletin of the Atomic Scientists,* Vol. 39, No. 9, November 1983, p. 19.
102. Talbot (note 40), p. 201.
103. DeWitt, H.E., 'Debate on a comprehensive nuclear test ban: pro', *Physics Today,* Vol. 36, No. 8, August 1983, pp. 24, 29-34.
104. Latter, A.L., *Questions for the Vela Program on Decoupling of Underground Explosions*, Rand Corporation Report RM-2659-ARPA, 2 November 1960.
105. DeWitt (note 103), p. 29.
106. Hoover, Maj. Gen. W.W., quoted in DeWitt (note 103), p. 30.
107. Hannon, W.J., Jr, 'Seismic verification of a comprehensive test ban', *Energy and Technology Review*, Lawrence Livermore National Laboratory, Livermore, CA, May 1983, pp. 50-65.
108. Barker, R.B., 'Debate on a comprehensive nuclear weapons test ban: con', *Physics Today,* Vol. 36, No. 8, August 1983, pp. 25-29.
109. Treaty between the USA and the USSR on underground nuclear explosions for peaceful purposes, in Goldblat (note 18), pp. 218-27.
110. Heckrotte, W., 'Negotiating with the Soviets', *Energy and Technology Review* (note 107), p. 12.
111. Meyer, S.M., 'Soviet defense decisionmaking: what do we know and what do we understand?', ACIS Working Paper No. 33, Center for International and Strategic Affairs, UCLA, Los Angeles, January 1982.
112. Holloway, D., *The Soviet Union and the Arms Race* (Yale University Press, New Haven, CT, 1983), pp. 126-27.
113. Chayes, A., 'An inquiry into the workings of arms control agreements', *Harvard Law Review,* Vol. 85, No. 5, March 1972, p. 963.
114. Chayes (note 113), p. 926 [emphasis added].
115. Colton, T.J., 'The impact of the military on Soviet foreign policy', in Bialer, S. (ed.), *The Domestic Context of Soviet Foreign Policy* (Westview Press, Boulder, CO, 1981), p. 131.
116. Sokolovskiy, V.D., *Soviet Military Strategy,* 3rd edition, H.F. Scott (translator and editor), (Jane's, London, 1968), pp. 318-21.
117. Newhouse (note 74), pp. 55-56.
118. Colton (note 115), p. 131.
119. Meyer (note 111), p. 15.
120. Earle, R.T., II, 'Verification issues from the point of view of the negotiator', in Tsipis, K., Hafemeister, D. and Janeway, P. (eds), *Arms Control Verification: The Technologies that Make it Possible* (Pergamon, Elmsford, NY, 1985).
121. Goldblat (note 18), chapter 1.
122. Myrdal, A., 'The international control of disarmament', *Scientific American,* Vol. 231, No. 4, October 1974, p. 21.

123. Subrahmanyam, K., 'Common security: a new approach', in *Common Security and the Developing World* (Institute for Defence Studies and Analyses, New Delhi, 1983).
124. Jasani, B. and Karkoszka, A., 'International verification of arms control agreements', paper prepared for the Independent Commission on Disarmament and Security Issues (Palme Commission), December 1981, p. 2.
125. Abdel-Hady, M. and Sadek, A., 'Verification using satellites, feasibility of an international or multinational agency', in Jasani, B. (ed.), *Outer Space: A New Dimension of the Arms Race* (Taylor & Francis, London, 1982), pp. 275-76 [a SIPRI book].
126. Colby, W., quoted in Steinberg (note 14), p. 176.
127. Ball, D., *A Suitable Piece of Real Estate* (Hale & Iremenger, Sydney, 1980).
128. *Military Implications of the Treaty on the Limitation of Strategic Offensive Arms and Protocol Thereto (SALT II Treaty), Hearings before the Committee on Armed Services* (SASC Hearings), US Senate, 96th Congress, First Session (US Government Printing Office, Washington, DC, 1979) Part 1, pp. 39-40, 227-29.
129. Treaty on the prohibition of the emplacement of nuclear weapons and other weapons of mass destruction on the seabed and the ocean floor and in the subsoil thereof (Sea-Bed Treaty), in Goldblat (note 18), pp. 175-76.
130. Sea-Bed Treaty, Article III.1, in Goldblat (note 18), pp. 175-76.
131. Dore, I.I., 'International law and the preservation of the ocean space and outer space as zones of peace: problems and progress', *Cornell International Law Journal*, Vol. 15, No. 1, Winter 1982, p. 25.
132. Treaty on the non-proliferation of nuclear weapons (NPT), in Goldblat (note 18), pp. 172-74.
133. NPT, Article III in Goldblat (note 18), pp. 172-73.
134. Goldblat (note 18), pp. 350-53. Note: The CD is now called the Conference on Disarmament.
135. Dahlman, O., 'Letter dated 9 March 1984 from the Chairman of the *ad hoc* Group of Scientific Experts to Consider International Co-operation Measures to Detect and Identify Seismic Events to the President of the Conference on Disarmament Transmitting the Third Report of the *ad hoc* Group', Conference on Disarmament document CD/448, 9 March 1984, p. iv.
136. Dahlman (note 135), p. v.
137. Issraelyan, V., Final Record of the 119th Meeting, Committee on Disarmament document CD/PV.119, Geneva, 31 March 1981, pp. 16-17.
138. SFRC Hearings (note 23), Part 2, p. 261.
139. Colby, W., SASC Hearings (note 128), Part 3, p. 1025.
140. Krepon, M., *Arms Control: Verification and Compliance,* Headline Series No. 270, Foreign Policy Association, New York, 1984, pp. 16-20.
141. ACDA (note 51), pp. 6-8.
142. SFRC Hearings (note 23), Part 2, pp. 239-40.
143. Buchan (note 101), pp. 16-19.
144. *The SALT II Treaty, Report of the Committee on Foreign Relations* (SFRC Report), US Senate (US Government Printing Office, Washington, DC, 1979), p. 221.
145. Freedman, L., 'Assumed detection: needs and dysfunctions of verification', in Nerlich (ed.), *Soviet Power and Western Negotiating Policies,* Vol. 2 (Ballinger, Cambridge, MA, 1983), p. 245.
146. Mohr, C., 'U.S. charges on arms pact are criticized', *International Herald Tribune,* 20 January 1984, p. 2.

147. Getler, M. and Hiatt, F., 'Simpler pacts on arms eyed to bar deceit', *Washington Post,* 19 January 1984, p. 29.
148. Slocombe (note 67), p. 81.
149. Buchan (note 101), p. 17.
150. Katz, *Verification and SALT* (note 79), p. 11.
151. *Webster's New Universal Unabridged Dictionary,* 2nd Edition (Dorset & Baber, New York, 1983).
152. Katz, *Verification and SALT* (note 79), pp. 43-44
153. Katz, *Verification and SALT* (note 79), pp. 32-35.
154. SFRC Hearings (note 23), Part 2, p. 261.
155. Meyer, S.M., 'Verification and risk in arms control', *International Security*, Vol. 8, No. 4, Spring 1984, p. 122.
156. Buchan (note 101), p. 17
157. Imber, M.F., 'Arms control verification: the special case of IAEA-NPT "special inspections" ', *Arms Control*, Vol. 3, No. 3, December 1982, p. 57.
158. Websters (note 151).
159. Farley, P.J., 'Verification: on the plus side of the SALT II balance sheet', in Potter (note 71), p. 223.
160. Quoted in Schear, J.A., 'Verifying arms agreements: premises, practices and future problems', *Arms Control* (note 157), p. 77.
161. Perry, R. (note 15), p. 9.
162. Schear (note 160) [emphasis added].
163. Getler & Hiatt (note 147).
164. For a definition of "cooperative measures" see chapter 1.
165. Schear (note 160).
166. Katz, *Verification and SALT* (note 79), pp. 24-26.
167. Long, F.A., On Developments in Technical Capabilities for Detecting and Identifying Nuclear Weapons Tests, *Hearings before the Joint Committee on Atomic Energy,* Congress of the United States, 88th Congress, First Session (US Government Printing Office, Washington, DC, 1963), pp. 410-11.
168. Sykes, L.R. and Evernden, J.F., 'The verification of a comprehensive nuclear test ban', *Scientific American*, Vol. 247, No. 4, October 1982, pp. 53-54.
169. Douglas, A., 'Seismic source identification: a review of past and present research efforts', in Husebye, E.S. and Mykkeltveit, S. (eds), *Identification of Seismic Sources: Earthquakes or Underground Explosions* (D. Reidel, Dordrecht, 1981), p. 39.
170. Sykes, L.R., Evernden, J.F. and Cifuentes, I., 'Seismic methods for verifying nuclear test bans', in Hafemeister, D.W. and Schroeer, D. (eds), *Physics, Technology and the Nuclear Arms Race*, AIP Conference Proceedings, No. 104 (American Institute of Physics, New York, 1983), p. 109.
171. Bellany, I., 'An introduction to verification', *Arms Control* (note 157), pp. 1-13; Dresher, M., 'A sampling inspection problem in arms control agreements: a game-theoretic analysis', Rand Memorandum RM-2972-ARPA (Rand Corp., Santa Monica, CA), February 1962.
172. SIPRI, *Strategic Disarmament, Verification and National Security* (Taylor & Francis, London, 1977), pp. 105-171; Hafemeister, D., 'Sensitivity analysis of the threat to national security from the possibility of a breakout from arms control treaties', in Tsipis, Hafemeister & Janeway (note 120).
173. von Hippel, F. and Levi, B.G., *Controlling the Source: Verification of a Cutoff in the Production of Plutonium and High-Enriched Uranium for Nuclear Weapons*, Report PU/CEES-167, Center for Energy and Environmental Studies, Princeton, NJ, July 1984, p. 9.

174. von Hippel & Levi (note 173).
175. von Hippel & Levi (note 173), p. 10.
176. *Verification and Response in Disarmament Agreements*, Woods Hole Summer Study Summary Report, Institute for Defense Analysis, Washington, DC, November 1962, p. 6.
177. Smith (note 25), p. 24.
178. Perry (note 15), p. 11.
179. Nitze, P.H., SFRC Hearings (note 23), Part 1, p. 446. Although the terms are not seen by everyone as strictly equivalent, 'minimum deterrent' in this context can be read as 'assured destruction'.
180. SFRC Report (note 144).
181. Katz, *Verification and SALT* (note 79), p. 3.
182. Holloway (note 112), chapter 3; Payne (note 68).
183. Slocombe (note 67), p. 87.
184. *SRFC Hearings* (note 23), Part 2, p. 261.
185. Roberts, R.E., 'Verification problems—monitoring of conversion and destruction of chemical-warfare agent plant' in SIPRI, *Chemical Weapons: Destruction and Conversion* (Taylor & Francis, London, 1980), pp. 129-30.
186. Epstein, W., 'A ban on the production of fissionable material for weapons', *Scientific American*, Vol. 243, No. 1, July 1980, p. 48.
187. Katz, *Verification and SALT* (note 79), p. 15.
188. Rivard, R., 'New proof of infiltration?', *Newsweek*, 6 August 1984, p. 41.
189. Perry Robinson, J.P., 'The Soviet Union and the Biological Weapons Convention', *Arms Control* (note 157), p. 46.
190. Katz, *Verification and SALT* (note 79), p. 14.
191. de Rivera, J.H., *The Psychological Dimension of Foreign Policy* (Merrill, Columbus, OH, 1968), p. 58 [emphasis in original].
192. Freedman (note 145), p. 245.
193. Hersh, S.M., *The Price of Power: Kissinger in the Nixon White House* (Summit, New York, 1983), p. 207.
194. Hersh (note 193), p. 540.
195. Taubman, P., 'Analyst reported to leave C.I.A. in a clash with Casey on Mexico', *New York Times*, 28 September 1984, p. 1.
196. Farber, M.A., 'U.S. intelligence chief says he wasn't asked to falsify reports in Vietnam', *New York Times*, 25 October 1984, p. B6.
197. Smith (note 25), pp. 397-99.
198. *Challenges for US National Security, Final Report, Vol. 4: Verification*, Carnegie Endowment for International Peace, Washington, DC, 1983, p. 58.
199. Federation of American Scientists, *Seeds of Promise: The First Real Hearings on the Nuclear Arms Freeze* (Brick House Publications, Andover, MA, 1983), p. 108.
200. Nash, H.T., 'The bureaucratization of homicide', *Bulletin of the Atomic Scientists*, Vol. 36, No. 4, April 1980, pp. 22-27.
201. Hersh (note 193), chapters 12-13.
202. Smith (note 25), p. 245. Smith mentions this preference of Kissinger's only in the context of a single crucial meeting between Kissinger and Gromyko, but another US SALT negotiator asserts that this was standard practice for Kissinger (private comment to author).
203. Cohen (note 71), p. 68.
204. Aspin (note 85), p. 1.
205. Cohen (note 71), p. 54.

206. *Compliance with SALT I Agreements*, Special Report No. 55 (US Department of State, Bureau of Public Affairs, Washington, DC, July 1979).
207. 'The United States violates its international commitments', *News and Views from the USSR*, Soviet Embassy, Information Department, Washington, DC, 30 January 1984, p. 4.
208. Schear (note 160), p. 88.
209. SASC Hearings (note 128), part 1, p. 339.
210. 'End secrecy, says ex-CIA director', *Chicago Tribune*, 17 February 1984, p. 4.
211. Philpott, T., 'Gen. Rogers: show spy photos in Europe debate', *Air Force Times*, 23 July 1984, p. 6.
212. Einhorn, R.J., 'Treaty compliance', *Foreign Policy*, No. 45, Winter 1981–82, p. 44.
213. Einhorn (note 212), p. 29.
214. SFRC Report (note 144), p. 189.
215. Colby (note 76), pp.73-75.
216. SASC Hearings (note 128), Part 3, p. 1025.
217. Transcript of the Reagan–Mondale Debate on Foreign Policy, *New York Times*, 22 October 1984, p. B6.
218. Smith (note 25), p. 323.
219. Issraelyan (note 137), p. 16.
220. Issraelyan (note 137), p. 16.
221. Meyer (note 155), pp. 120-21.
222. Meyer (note 155).
223. de Rivera (note 191), p. 32.
224. Barnet, R.J., "Why trust the Soviets?", *World Policy Journal*, Vol. 1, No. 3, Spring 1984, p. 467.
225. Katz, *Verification and SALT* (note 79), p. 30.
226. Steinberg (note 14), p. 25 [emphasis added].
227. de Rivera (note 191), chapter 2.
228. Kennan, G.F., 'Soviet–American relations', *New Yorker*, Vol. 59, No. 33, 3 October 1983, p. 44.
229. de Rivera (note 191), p. 25.
230. de Rivera (note 191), p. 24.
231. de Rivera (note 191), p. 26 [emphasis in original].
232. de Rivera (note 191), p. 21.
233. Deutscher, I., *Stalin: A Political Biography*, 2nd edition (Oxford University Press, New York, 1966), pp. 455-60.
234. SFRC Hearings (note 23), Part 5, p. 261.
235. Hammond, P.Y., 'Some difficulties of self-enforcing arms agreements', *Journal of Conflict Resolution*, Vol. 6, No. 2, June 1962, pp. 103-115.
236. Schear (note 160), p. 91.
237. Freedman (note 145), p. 254.
238. Krepon, M., 'Both sides are hedging', *Foreign Policy*, No. 56, Fall 1984, pp. 167-68.
239. Herken, G., *The Winning Weapon: The Atomic Bomb in the Cold War, 1945–1950* (Random House, New York, 1982), pp. 23-42.
240. Stimson, H.L. and Bundy, McG., *On Active Service in Peace and War* (Harper Brothers, New York, 1948), p. 644.
241. Wiesner, J.B., 'Inspection for disarmament', in Henken, L. B. (ed.), *Arms Control Issues for the Public* (Prentice Hall, New York, 1961), pp. 112-40; Wiesner, J.B., 'Comprehensive arms-limitation systems', in Brennan, D.G. (ed.),

Arms Control, Disarmament and National Security (George Braziller, New York, 1961), pp. 198-233.
242. *Common Security: A Programme for Disarmament. The Report of the Independent Commission on Disarmament and Security Issues under the Chairmanship of Olof Palme* (Pan Books, London, 1982), p. 136.
243. von Hippel and Levi (note 173), p. 28.
244. Wiesner in Henken (note 241), p. 137.
245. Krepon, M., 'Political dynamics of verification and compliance isssues', in Tsipis, Hafemeister & Janeway (note 120).
246. *Common Security: A Programme for Disarmament* (note 242), p. 140.
247. Krass, A., 'The evolution of military technology and deterrence strategy', in SIPRI (note 57), chapter 2.
248. Wohlstetter, A., 'The delicate balance of terror', *Foreign Affairs*, January 1959, pp. 211-34.
249. Falk, R.A., 'Inspection, trust and security during disarmament', in Barnet, R.J. and Falk, R.A. (eds), *Security in Disarmament* (Centre for International Studies, Princeton, NJ, 1965), p. 47. See also Woods Hole Summer Study (note 176), p. 6.
250. de Rivera (note 191), pp. 379-80.
251. Katz, *Verification and SALT* (note 79).

Chapter 4. Technology and politics

I. Introduction

With the previous two chapters as background it is now possible to analyse a number of specific aspects of verification which illustrate the intense interaction between the technical and political dimensions. It is essential to understand this interaction in order to obtain a realistic picture of the capabilities and limitations of monitoring techniques and compliance mechanisms in arms control.

The first aspect examined is the legitimacy and/or legality of various monitoring techniques. Just as in so many other areas of modern life the development of intelligence-gathering technology has substantially outrun the international legal and institutional mechanisms for regulating it. This has led to much political friction in the past and promises much more in the future. It is therefore worthwhile to look at some examples of this friction including both past problems that seem to have been reasonably well resolved and current problems that are the subject of serious controversy.

The second aspect is the concept of violation or non-compliance. Violations come in many forms, as does the evidence used to establish them. An assessment of non-compliance usually involves far more than displaying a satellite photograph of a prohibited object or identifying a suspicious pattern in a seismograph. As shown in chapter 1 these are at best useful for identifying suspicious activities. The process of assessment of the evidence is far more subjective and cannot be abstracted from the political and psychological atmosphere in which it is conducted.

A third aspect is the use of so-called 'co-operative measures', in particular on-site inspection, as supplements to national technical means. The attitudes and negotiating postures of the two major powers towards on-site inspection are examined in chapter 3. This chapter first analyses a number of co-operative measures which do not involve on-site inspection, but which nevertheless add significantly to the effectiveness of the compliance process. In contrast, the analysis of on-site inspection (the fourth aspect examined) shows that it has serious political and technical limitations which make its utility considerably more dubious than many in the West appreciate.

A fifth aspect of verification which exhibits an intimate connection between technology and politics is the degree of internationalization of the process. It has already been noted in chapter 3 that the unilateral application of sophisticated national technical means by states able to afford them is highly unsatisfactory to many other states who would prefer an international approach. The final section of this chapter analyses the advantages and disadvantages of such an approach as well as its technical and political feasibility.

II. Legitimacy

National technical means

The phrase 'national technical means of verification' (NTM) has become a fixture in arms control agreements between the USA and USSR since its first use in the ABM Treaty of 1972.[1] It also appears in the Interim SALT I agreement limiting strategic weapons,[2] the Threshold Test Ban Treaty,[3] the Peaceful Nuclear Explosion Treaty[4] and the SALT II Treaty.[5]

Given this evidence of the usefulness and ubiquity of the concept of national technical means of verification it is surprising to learn that nowhere in any of the above-mentioned treaties, nor anywhere in the understandings and protocols that accompany them, is the concept defined in any way. Such relatively trivial or arcane items as ABM radars, 'new types' of ICBM, and the meaning of the phrase 'independently targetable warhead' are defined in meticulous detail in agreed statements and common understandings, especially in the SALT II Treaty, and one would expect at least as much attention would be devoted to defining national technical means, especially in view of the central importance of verification in all of the above treaties. Such is not the case, however, and this crucial concept remains open for interpretation by both sides, a situation which virtually guarantees misunderstanding and political friction.

Neither side has pressed for a clear definition of NTM. From the US point of view, "while some NTM are well known, such as photographic satellites, others are quite sensitive and we don't want to discuss them with the Soviets. An incomplete list would call into question [and could well place outside the protection of the agreement] those systems not on the list".[6] There is no clear public statement of the Soviet reasons for not pressing for a clear definition of NTM. The usual explanation given by Americans who have participated in arms control negotiations is that the Soviet Union is unwilling to recognize explicitly the legitimacy of US intelligence activities based in third countries, while the USA would accept no definition that did not legitimate such activities.[7] It is also reasonable to assume that the Soviet Union has its own intelligence-gathering methods that it would prefer not to discuss with the United States.

Allowing the definition of NTM to remain vague has definite advantages. It avoids long and contentious haggling over details and limits which would inevitably be highly arbitrary and artificial. It also allows for flexibility in the application of new technologies of verification and the exploitation of the synergisms among different technologies.

However, vagueness also has disadvantages and can lead to serious problems for the compliance process. In particular, if a monitoring activity or technology is not recognized by one party as a legitimate NTM it does not come under the protection afforded to NTM in all treaties which rely on them. This protection is embodied in the commitment in all of the above-mentioned treaties that the parties will refrain from either directly interfering with the NTM of other parties or deliberately using concealment measures which impede the ability of NTM to carry out verification tasks. At the same time states reserve the right to interfere with attempts to gather military intelligence on matters unrelated to specific treaty obligations. This makes the boundary between legitimate NTM and illegitimate intelligence gathering a very sensitive one, especially when the parties are engaged in an intense military competition and are deeply distrustful of each other's intentions.

Satellite photo-reconnaissance

An interesting and highly significant historical example of such a dispute involved the legitimacy of satellite photography. The reaction of the Soviet Union to President Eisenhower's Open Skies proposal and the ultimate shooting down in 1960 of a United States U-2 aircraft on a photo-reconnaissance mission over Soviet intercontinental ballistic missile installations made unmistakably clear the Soviet attitude towards aerial surveillance. It was therefore not at all surprising that the initial Soviet reaction to the launching of US photo-reconnaissance satellites was intensely negative.[8] Such surveillance was seen as a violation of the principles of international law,[9] no different in essence from the violation of their airspace by US reconnaissance planes. Such a reaction was fully anticipated by the United States when plans were being made to launch the first reconnaissance satellites, and a number of parallel efforts were undertaken to mitigate it. One effort involved advertising the international benefits to be gained from satellite surveying of Earth resources and climate by such systems as Landsat. Another involved a total prohibition of official statements which might embarrass the USSR by revealing the extent of US capabilities for photographing their territory. Finally, the USA began research and development on an anti-satellite (ASAT) system, one of whose functions was to deter Soviet attacks on US satellites by the threat of retaliation in kind.[10]

It is interesting that in its attempts at legitimating satellite photo-reconnaissance the USA often drew an analogy between outer space and the high seas, the freedom of which was guaranteed to all states by international law.[11] The Soviet Union preferred, at least in the early days of the space age, a less liberal analogy, referring to all of the space 'above' the territory of the Soviet Union as its airspace. This is an intriguing semantic problem that has no obvious solution. For example, while the atmosphere above any portion of the Earth rotates along with that portion, the rest of space remains stationary. Therefore the 'space' above any state is constantly changing, and it is not at all clear that it can be thought of as equivalent to airspace.

An exception to this rule occurs in the use of 'geosynchronous' orbits, in which a satellite does remain in a fixed location relative to the Earth and therefore continuously occupies what could be called the 'airspace' of a state located on the Earth's equator. The Outer Space Treaty of 1967 gives free access to all states to "outer space" and has 85 signatories (see table 1, p. 4). However a number of equatorial countries stated in 1977 that: "The Outer Space Treaty 'cannot be considered as a final answer to the problem of the exploration and use of Outer Space' because it was 'elaborated when the developing countries could not count on adequate scientific advice' and were thus unable to participate effectively in its drafting".[12]

While such problems will remain to plague international lawyers for many years to come, the problem of Soviet acceptance of the legitimacy of satellite photo-reconnaissance was solved without fanfare in 1963 when the Soviet Union simply dropped its objection to the practice.[13] There has never been an official Soviet explanation of this change of heart. From one point of view it seems quite illogical to oppose overflights by aircraft and permit them by satellites, when the coverage and resolution of the latter are in many ways as good as or better than those of the former. And satellite photography and signal-detection capabilities are the most important sources of data for US strategic target planning,[14] just as aircraft would have been in the 1950s if the Open Skies proposal had been accepted. Yet satellite reconnaissance has become legitimate and accepted while aerial reconnaissance remains illegitimate and unacceptable, a contrast dramatically emphasized by the destruction of a South Korean airliner which violated Soviet airspace in 1983.

The most likely explanation of this difference in attitude is the realization by Soviet authorities that the use of such satellites would be as highly advantageous to them as it is to the USA, and that the possession of such capabilities by both sides would not only contribute to stabilizing the competition between them but provide excellent means for observing the activities of other states. Indeed, Soviet photo-reconnaissance satellites are very active in monitoring crisis and conflict situations in all parts of the world as well as US and NATO military exercises and deployments.[15]

An extremely important feature of this acceptance of satellite photography by the Soviet Union was its informal nature. It followed closely on the heels of the Cuban missile crisis during a period when the USA and USSR were anxious to reduce tensions and prevent the repetition of such a crisis.[16] No agreement or treaty was ever discussed formally between the parties on legitimating satellite photography, and in fact none of the treaties which rely on NTM for their verification mentions satellites specifically. The legitimacy of satellite photography therefore remains tacit and not explicit in international law.

A major reason for the success of this informal agreement may have been the refusal of US officials to publicly discuss, or even admit, the extent of US photo-reconnaissance capabilities. This 'black-out' of public announcements and discussions was first ordered in 1961 by the Kennedy Administration[17] and remained in effect until 1978, when President Carter admitted that the USA was photographing the territory of the Soviet Union from satellites.[18] By maintaining this official silence in the early years of satellite reconnaissance the USA probably made it easier for Soviet advocates of satellite reconnaissance to overcome the resistance of those who wanted to deal with satellites in the same way as aircraft.

This official secrecy has now outlived its usefulness, but unfortunately it has had over 20 years to embed itself in the bureaucratic mentality of the US intelligence community, and resistance to change is intense. If not for this resistance President Carter's announcement might have been followed by the release of satellite photographs to support his attempt to gain ratification of the SALT II Treaty.[19] Unless this deeply entrenched opposition to greater openness can be overcome it is difficult to see how public confidence in the arms control process can be regained (see chapter 3).

The informal nature of the legitimacy of satellite photo-reconnaissance has some drawbacks. Since the limits of this legitimacy have never been agreed upon and codified, each side is free to attach whatever limits or reservations it chooses. This is most significant in the case of the Soviet Union, which maintains that there is a difference in principle between reconnaissance carried out for verification purposes and for the gathering of military intelligence, even if it is not feasible to distinguish these two missions in practice. For example a 1979 Soviet article on space law stated: "If supervision by means of space equipment goes beyond the purpose of monitoring provided by the treaty and, for example, is carried out for purpose of getting some intelligence information, this activity must be regarded as unlawful".[20] A more recent Soviet assessment begins with the clear assertion that "the use of observation satellites is within the norms of existing international law. The space treaty of 1967... does not impose any restrictions on the use of satellites". Yet this same author concludes with a sentence that can only be interpreted as a reservation: "But not a single international legal document directly approves the use of such satellites for monitoring and control".[21]

Such reservations may be interpreted as keeping open the option of interfering with or attacking satellites which are perceived to be exceeding their legitimate functions. The Soviet Union continues to develop, albeit fitfully, an anti-satellite capability, even though it was hoped by some that acceptance of the legitimacy of reconnaissance satellites would make such a capability unnecessary.[22] The Soviet testing programme has been interrupted several times in the past and is now observing a unilateral moratorium declared by Secretary Andropov in 1983. Nevertheless work continues on a large phased-array radar which, according to one analyst, may contribute to an ASAT battle management capability.[23] And the United States, which has never doubted the legitimacy of satellite reconnaissance, is also moving forward in the development of an ASAT system whose only plausible functions are to attack Soviet photo-reconnaissance, ocean-surveillance or electronic-reconnaissance satellites.[24] So while reconnaissance satellites have come to be accepted almost totally as legitimate intruments for monitoring, the 'almost' is significant, and even this relatively stable and secure situation could be weakened in a time of heightened political tension.

It must be kept in mind, however, that an attack on a satellite of another state would certainly constitute an aggressive act, similar to firing on a ship in international waters.[25] Such an action is likely only when the threat of war is already at a high level. It is extremely unlikely that attacks on satellites would be contemplated in peace-time, whatever formal reservation a state might have about their legitimacy.

Telemetry encryption

In contrast to the high degree of legitimacy now accorded to the use of photo-reconnaissance satellites, another national technical means of verification has come under increasing pressure in recent years and is now facing a genuine crisis of legitimacy. This is the use of land-, sea- and satellite-based antennas to monitor the telemetry from missiles during test flights (see chapter 2, section VIII, p. 79).

The interception of electronic communications is not generally recognized as a legitimate NTM, and most states devote considerable effort to encrypting or otherwise concealing sensitive messages from the intelligence agencies of other states. It is only in one narrow area that the interception of telemetry has been recognized as legitimate, and this recognition is embodied in the following Common Understanding regarding the SALT II Treaty:

> Each party is free to use various methods of transmitting telemetric information, including its encryption, except that, in accordance with the provisions of Paragraph 3 of Article XV of the Treaty, neither Party shall engage in deliberate denial of telemetric information, such as through the use of telemetry encryption, whenever such denial impedes verification of compliance with the provisions of the Treaty.[26]

Several comments and qualifications must be made about this clause. First, the SALT II Treaty has never been ratified by the USA, which means that the understanding has no force in international law. Second, the understanding does not confine its limitation to the encryption of telemetry, but prohibits *all* forms of "deliberate denial of telemetric information" which "impede" verification. For example, a state testing a missile might decide to dispense entirely with telemetry transmissions and instead record flight-test data on magnetic tape aboard the missile. The tape could then be recovered after the test, thereby denying access to the data to anyone other than the state conducting the test. Another method would be to use low-power, highly directional transmitters on the missile so that the telemetry could only be received by those ground stations for which it is intended.

A third complication arises from the heavy dependence of the US telemetry monitoring on ground stations based in third countries (see chapters 2 and 3). But the Soviet Union has never accepted the legitimacy of such third-country monitoring sites as legitimate national technical means,[27] implying that they need not respect limitations on interfering with the operation of such stations. Finally, it is important to emphasize that the common understanding legitimates *both* the interception of telemetry *and* its encryption, providing only a poorly defined criterion for distinguishing acceptable from unacceptable encryption. It is this attempt to have it both ways that has led to one of the most serious of the compliance issues currently dividing the USA and the USSR.

The monitoring of telemetry is very similar to satellite photography in the high degree of overlap between its verification and military intelligence functions. The same information which is needed to obtain an accurate measure of the throw-weight of a missile, a property controlled by SALT II, is very helpful in estimating the accuracy of the missile, a property not regulated by the Treaty but of great interest to military planners. Telemetry information can be important in determining whether an anti-aircraft missile is being tested in an anti-ballistic missile mode in violation of the SALT I Treaty, but it can also help to assess the effectiveness of the anti-aircraft defences of the state doing the testing, something which is not covered by a treaty and which any state would consider highly sensitive information.

There is also an important difference between telemetry monitoring and satellite photography in the relative ease with which each can be interfered with, either actively or passively. In order to interfere actively with a photo-reconnaissance satellite it must be physically attacked, but active interference with a telemetry monitoring antenna requires only a jamming signal. Passive interference with a photo-reconnaissance satellite requires elaborate and often unreliable camouflage or a degree of mobility which is impracticable for many weapons. On the other hand, as chapter 2 shows, the concealment of information in telemetry is a relatively simple matter of combining the signal with a one-time encryption key, producing a message which is indecipherable by even the most powerful computers. It is reasonable to assume that one of the reasons why satellite photography achieved acceptance was the technical difficulty involved in interfering with it. Such inhibitions are not present in telemetry monitoring.

The unlimited monitoring of telemetry clearly conflicts with the basic principles the Soviet Union has used to evaluate past verification proposals. One statement of these principles is given in chapter 3, and the two most relevant to the issue of telemetry encryption are numbers 1 and 3 (see p. 140). Under these principles the conduct of verification should not prejudice the sovereign rights of states, one of which is certainly the right to keep sensitive military information secret from potential enemies. Nor should the scope and forms of verification be any greater than those which are needed for assuring compliance with the specific obligations agreed to in the treaty. This is generally interpreted by Soviet negotiators to mean that the gathering of information should be confined strictly to information relevant to verification of specific treaty provisions; presumably no less, but certainly no more.

For this reason, and possibly for other reasons as well, the Soviet Union began encrypting the telemetry from its missile tests in the mid-1970s, when they learned through espionage of the extent and sophistication of US satellite monitoring capabilities.[28] Since 1977, when the process began in earnest, reports of Soviet telemetry encryption have steadily increased in the US media and in congressional speeches and testimony. Finally, in January 1984 President Reagan included charges of Soviet violation of the common understanding on encryption in a long list of alleged Soviet violations of arms control treaties which he submitted to Congress.[29]

More recently there have been unconfirmed reports in the US press that the Soviet Union has gone beyond the encryption of telemetry and has begun the active jamming of US reconnaissance satellites.[30] If these charges are true, then it would represent a far more direct and less ambiguous Soviet challenge to the legitimacy of electronic satellite reconnaissance. Article XV, paragraph 2 of the SALT II Treaty explicitly forbids interference with the national technical means of the other party as long as the latter are operating "in a manner consistent with generally recognized principles of international law".[31] According to one US interpretation, the legitimacy of satellite photography can be extended to include all "passive sensors" deployed in space.[32] The active interference with such a passive sensor (that is, a receiving antenna) would represent a clear rejection of this interpretation by the Soviet Union.

Soviet encryption of telemetry was already going on at the time when the SALT II Treaty was being negotiated in the late 1970s, but the USA found it difficult to gain a bureaucratic consensus behind a demand for a complete ban on encryption as part of the Treaty.[33] The strongest advocate of a complete ban was the CIA, which over the years has invested vast sums of money and talent in a series of sophisticated satellite monitors such as the Rhyolite, Chalet and Aquacade programmes.[34] Soviet encryption practices make these assets highly vulnerable, and the CIA has a powerful interest in protecting them. At the same time other US bureaucratic interests were less enthusiastic about banning telemetry encryption, suggesting that the USA might also want to use it on some occasions. Although one US negotiator has stated flatly that "the US does not encrypt telemetry",[35] another has suggested that "a lot of people in the US armed forces would substantially object to the loss of the ability to encrypt telemetry in certain areas".[36] Although these statements are not strictly contradictory, the latter one seems more plausible given the natural desire of the developers of new weapon systems to keep the capabilities and limitations of the systems secret as long as possible.

In the end the USA never did formally propose to the Soviet Union that telemetry encryption be totally banned, ostensibly because the US delegation believed that the Soviets would never accept such a proposal,[37] but also possibly because the US delegation could not itself reach a consensus on the demand. For most of the negotiations the Soviet side resisted any implication that the encryption of telemetry was less than proper or could actually impede verification. The final common understanding therefore represented a Soviet concession that there might possibly be ways in which encryption would impede verification,[38] but at the same time Soviet Defence Minister Ustinov made it clear that Soviet encryption practices in no way violated the understanding. He stated emphatically in 1979: "as far as telemetry goes, I don't think there is any sense in discussing this problem. The information essential to verification of the provisions of the Treaty will not be encrypted. Agreement in this has been reached".[39] This statement is difficult to reconcile with reports in the US press that Soviet encryption has on several occasions included 100 per cent of the telemetry data from tests of the allegedly illegal new ICBM, called the SS-X-25 by the USA.[40]

There are a number of possible motivations for the Soviet encryption activities. The most obvious, of course, is the desire to conceal as much information as possible from the USA on the capabilities of the various missiles being tested. It has been alleged by the USA that the Soviet Union is in fact developing two new ICBMs, the SS-X-24 and SS-X-25, in violation of the SALT II restriction to a single new type of ICBM. If the purpose of the Soviet Union is really to conceal a violation of the SALT II limits on new types of ICBM, one can hardly imagine a more clumsy and politically counterproductive means of accomplishing this goal than to try to cover it up by an even more blatant and obvious violation of the Treaty.

Because these "violations" are so blatant and easily recognized they cannot be called "cheating" in the usual sense of carrying out some clandestine activity in order to gain a surprise military advantage. Even without access to telemetry there are other ways for the USA to get information about the properties of the new missiles,[41] information which, although possibly not as complete or precise as that available from telemetry monitoring, is still useful in determining necessary countermeasures. Meanwhile the political consequences are clearly negative, and the Soviet Union has every reason to expect that the USA will put the worst possible interpretation on these activities and use them to justify activities of its own which cut away at the boundaries of the Treaty.

Other possible explanations for the Soviet actions are that they are a response to what the Soviet Union perceives to be US violations, that they are a result of political conflicts within the Soviet hierarchy, or that they are designed to create an incentive for the USA to ratify the SALT II Treaty and to use the Standing Consultative Commission (SCC) to clarify the encryption limits. In fact, all of these motivations may be present simultaneously, and the only effective means of dealing with them is through negotiations. Even internal Soviet bureaucratic conflicts can probably only be resolved as part of the process of domestic consensus building that both sides must go through during US–Soviet negotiations.

One possible response of the USA to the Soviet challenge to the legitimacy of telemetry monitoring would have been to bring the problem to the Standing Consultative Commission for a confidential resolution. This has apparently been attempted, but not with much enthusiasm or success. One source of US reticence in using the SCC has been the reluctance of the Reagan Administration to recognize the legitimacy of a commission associated with the SALT process.[42] The few complaints which have been lodged have reportedly been reponded to by Soviet requests for a detailed description of the data the USA needs in order to verify the Treaty and what necessary data the USA believes are being encrypted. The US delegation has been understandably reluctant to respond to this request, since it would involve revealing highly sensitive US techniques for collecting and analysing telemetry data. The Soviet Union would also acquire a much clearer picture of the limitations of US monitoring capabilities and some insight into the degree of dependence of US intelligence agencies on telemetry data.[43]

The dispute over telemetry encryption has all the earmarks of an impasse which could persist for many years. There seem to be three possibilities for breaking through this impasse, but all three have some genuine difficulties. One possiblity is for the two sides to agree on a total encryption ban. This would certainly be the simplest and most reassuring kind of agreement, and there is a reasonable probability that the USA could get a bureaucratic consensus behind such a proposal. But such a total ban would represent a major change in position by the Soviet Union, a change similar to its acceptance of satellite photography 20 years ago. This historical precedent gives some hope that such a resolution could be achieved, but it is also reasonable to assume that before it acceded to such a ban the Soviet Union would want appropriate compensation in the form of US concessions of similar magnitude. Just what those might be is very difficult to imagine at this time.

A second possible resolution would be to eliminate from future arms control treaties provisions which require telemetry monitoring for their verification.

This would have the advantage of eliminating squabbles over encryption but would have the great disadvantage of preventing agreements limiting a wide range of qualitative improvements in weapon systems. The testing of missiles is essential to the great majority of nuclear weapon developments, and the access of each side to the other's test data is an excellent source of information with which to monitor compliance with limits on such developments. Only if all missile testing could be stopped entirely, or possibly limited drastically to some small number of tests per year, could telemetry monitoring be dispensed with entirely. Such an agreement would represent, in effect, the end of the arms race and would undoubtedly be the most desirable result. However, it does not appear to be a likely outcome of any negotiations in the foreseeable future.

The third way around the telemetry encryption impasse is for the USA to ratify the SALT II Treaty and for the US and Soviet representatives on the SCC to work out a mutually acceptable definition of the limits on encryption. This would be a difficult, sensitive and continuous task, requiring the detailed specification of what kinds of data are essential for verification and what it means to 'impede' verification. One can imagine a situation in which one side decides that a particular data channel is no longer useful for its own testing procedures and drops it from the telemetry programme, only to encounter a protest from the other side that that channel was important for verification. It would be wrong to assume that just because these problems are complicated they are insoluble, but at the same time the combination of technical ambiguities and bureaucratic sensitivities inherent in this issue makes a satisfactory negotiated compromise seem out of reach, at least until the political climate improves considerably.

Of the above possibilities the one which appears to offer the best combination of simplicity, significance and achievability is a complete ban on telemetry encryption. While this would certainly be a difficult decision for the Soviet Union to make, those Soviet leaders who supported it could point to a historical precedent as well as to the potentially substantial political gains to be made in other areas if US hostility on this issue can be neutralized. For its part, the USA could greatly improve the chances of such a resolution by ratifying the SALT II Treaty, returning the SCC to its past important status, and ceasing activities which threaten the SALT Treaties. Among the latter are the development of a space-based ballistic missile defence, planning for both the MX and Midgetman missiles (the analogues of the SS-X-24 and SS-X-25), and the prospective launching of the seventh Trident submarine which, if no other missile launchers are retired, will violate the SALT II launcher limits.[44]

The next section shows that technical violations of treaties can serve as a form of communication between the parties. The case of telemetry encryption seems to be a particularly clear instance of this kind of communication, and both sides will have to listen more carefully to the messages being sent by the other if any resolution is to be achieved.

III. Non-compliance

A typology of non-compliance

It is very difficult to identify and isolate a set of factors unique to the problem of non-compliance. The problem is in fact implicit in much of the discussion in chapter 3, especially in the analyses of adequacy and trust. On top of this there is the myriad of individual charges and countercharges of specific acts of non-compliance with arms control treaties which have been made in the past and are being made in the present with alarming frequency. While the vast majority of these come from the USA, the Soviet Union has occasionally responded with its own charges of US violations, and there have also been charges of violations of various treaties and conventions directed against other states.

An attempt to analyse all or even a significant fraction of these specific charges of non-compliance would require a book of its own and no such comprehensive review will be attempted here. It is more in keeping with the theoretical approach of this study to focus on some general principles.

It is first necessary to define what is meant by a 'violation' of a treaty or agreement. As might be expected, there is no single, unambiguous definition of this term; instead there is a spectrum of definitions which covers the wide range of actions that could be construed as non-compliance. One such spectrum is as follows:[45]

1. A deliberate violation aimed at increasing a state's military capability in ways which the agreement was intended to preclude. Example: The Iraqi use of chemical weapons in the war against Iran.[46]

2. An action inconsistent with the sense or spirit of the agreement and tending to undermine its viability even though it is not prohibited by the agreement. There can be borderline situations in which the activity strains the interpretation of particular provisions. Example: The Soviet Union has charged that continuing research and development by the USA on ballistic missile defence systems along with President Reagan's open commitment to a full-scale space-based defence imply intentions which if implemented would lead to undermining the ABM Treaty of 1972.[47]

3. Unintended violations, occurring, for example, through negligence of higher officials responsible for ensuring compliance by their subordinate organizations. Example: The discovery in 1975 that some samples of biological toxins were hidden by CIA researchers in contradiction to the explicit order by President Nixon that all such toxins be destroyed to bring the USA into compliance with the Biological Weapons Convention of 1972.[48]

4. Actions not banned by an agreement but which complicate verification of the agreement. Example: US charges of Soviet encryption of missile test telemetry may fall into this category, or if 100 per cent encryption and jamming are taking place this would be an example of category 2.

5. Ambiguous activities resulting from differing interpretations of the provisions of the agreement. Example: Soviet deployment of the SS-19 ICBM in spite of the unilateral US interpretation of this missile as a 'heavy missile' prohibited by the SALT I Interim Agreement.[49]

6. Activities assessed as ambiguous due to inadequate information or misinterpretation of information which suggest a violation where in fact none exists. Example: Although it is never possible to state categorically that no violation in fact exists, a good candidate for an example of this last type of 'violation' is the accusations by both the USA and USSR of violations by the other of the Threshold Test Ban Treaty.[50] Another strong candidate for this group is US charges of the use of 'yellow rain' by the Soviet Union or its allies in Indo-China and Afghanistan.[51]

This spectrum shows that 'violations' come in many shapes and sizes. Some of these are intentional and can have as their purpose anything from the conscious attempt to gain a military advantage to the desire to underline a unilateral interpretation of an ambiguous treaty provision or to test the intelligence capabilities of the other side. Other violations are unintentional or 'technical', resulting from misunderstandings, failures of execution or insubordination. Still others cannot be called violations in any meaningful sense since they result from poorly drafted treaty provisions or the inability of the monitoring side to perceive accurately what is going on.

The most important of the intentional violations is, of course, the first one on the list: the attempt to gain a military edge or 'break-out' by clandestine violation of the treaty. In order to be effective such violations must be of substantial military significance and must be kept secret until the time when the new capability is to be employed.

The other forms of intentional activity, the attempt to exploit loopholes or assert unilateral interpretations, are not violations in the literal sense of the word and are in fact a form of military-political communication. Presumably these activities are perceived as having military value or they would not be undertaken, and while they may be hidden or disguised to protect military secrets, they do not have to be clandestine in the same sense as purposeful violations intended to gain a surprise advantage. In fact, the nature of the US–Soviet arms race is such that attempts to gain a perceptual edge by exploiting weak treaty provisions (many of which were put into the treaty precisely to allow for such flexibility) are more effective if the adversary is aware of their existence.

One example of this kind of communication, Soviet encryption of telemetry, has already been discussed in the previous section. Another important example can be found in the ways the USA and USSR carry out nuclear weapon tests. The excellent capabilities of each side to monitor the underground explosions of the other opens up the possibility for a kind of political communication. A number of US and Soviet tests have been timed for maximum political impact on the other side, and the Reagan Administration has increased the testing rate in spite of the development of a number of techniques for acquiring information about weapon effects without testing. Presumably this is being done because: "There's nothing that wakes up the Soviets more than a blip on a seismograph".[52]

Break-out scenarios

So far in the history of US–Soviet arms control there have been no discovered violations of the first type described above. This is hardly surprising given the great technical and political obstacles standing in the way of such violations. The high weapon levels on both sides of the arms race imply that to gain significant military advantage a violation would have to be very large and therefore very difficult to hide. It would have to be carried out over many years and involve many people from many professions and backgrounds. It is almost inconceivable that such a massive effort could be carried on clandestinely in the face of the extensive intelligence surveillance to which both major powers are subjected.

It is very difficult to pose a convincing scenario for such a massive violation. One attempt (such scenarios are a uniquely American cultural phenomenon) postulates that the Soviet Union hides 500 MIRVed ICBMs in nondescript buildings widely spread out over the country. These buildings are made to look like thousands of so-called 'light manufacturing' structures routinely catalogued as innocuous by US photo-interpreters.[53] The secret missiles would then be used in a surprise attack against the United States land-based ICBM force, which would leave the USA in a deeply inferior position with respect to the Soviet Union, and therefore effectively inhibited from carrying out a retaliatory strike.[54]

This scenario is a variation of a theme which has haunted US strategic planners for many years: the presumed vulnerability of the land-based ICBM force and the impact of this vulnerability on the credibility of the US 'deterrent'. The above scenario differs from others of its type only in its use of a secret cache of missiles to carry out the surprise attack. Others have postulated the same sort of attack or threat with known Soviet ICBM forces.[55]

How technically and politically feasible is this scenario? How likely is it that 500 MIRVed ICBMs (objects with lengths of 25–30 metres and diameters of 2–3 metres) could be assembled in secret in widely dispersed sheds? (Transporting them assembled from a central factory is clearly too risky.) How likely is it that the warheads, the command-control system, and the multitude of personnel could be assembled, distributed and controlled all in secret? And even if the secrecy succeeds and the moment arrives to carry out the surprise attack, what will be the political objective of such an attack and how confident will the attackers be that their intimidation will work and that the remaining US retaliatory force will not be used?

If this scenario is looked at from the point of view of the political and military leaders who must bear the responsibility for the enormous risks involved at every step, it makes no sense whatsoever. At every stage there is an unknown probability that the secret will be exposed, and at the final stage there is an incalculable probability that the result will be a total disaster. There is not a shred of evidence to suggest that the Soviet Union or any other state would take such risks. Yet this scenario and its many variations are the backbone of the 'ICBM vulnerability' problem in US political discourse and constitute the most probable massive cheating scenarios. All others are even less plausible.

The invocation of weird and irrational evasion scenarios is not confined to a handful of zealots; it is a common currency in the debate over verification in the USA. One US official, in explaining why a ban on anti-satellite weapons could not be verified, suggested that "for all we know there are antisatellite weapons up there now. We can't rule it out".[56] The vast apparatus possessed by the USA for monitoring and tracking not only every Soviet rocket launch, but every piece of junk still in Earth orbit from satellites launched more than 20 years ago, is not mentioned by this official.

Another US official has argued that the proposed use of control posts to monitor movements of troops into and out of the Mutual Force Reduction (MFR) zone in Central Europe is a 'farce' because the Soviet Union could evade them by flying in troops dressed in civilian clothes in Aeroflot airliners.[57] Just how many tens of thousands of such phony tourists would be needed to upset the military balance in Central Europe was not specified by the official.

Many more examples could be given of this genre, but these will suffice to show how empty and detached from technical and political reality these scenarios are. Despite such inept attempts to discredit it, the proposition still appears to hold true that the greater the military significance of a possible violation the less the likelihood that it could be kept a secret. This relationship has at least the virtue of plausibility, and until reasonably plausible counter-examples are suggested it must stand as a useful working hypothesis in designing verification systems.

The politics of accusation

Most of the accusations of Soviet cheating which have flooded the US mass media in the past few years have not involved massive clandestine 'break-out' scenarios. Indeed, if the Soviet Union has been trying to cheat secretly these past 10 years it has done an exceptionally poor job. Veritable catalogues of alleged Soviet violations can be found in US Congressional sources,[58] and new reports of US intelligence discoveries of Soviet cheating are leaked almost daily to receptive US newspapers and journals.

If it is assumed for a moment that even a fraction of these allegations represent real Soviet violations of existing treaties, the serious question arises as to why the Soviet leadership would act in such a way. What would it hope to gain by blatantly and systematically violating treaties it has signed with the United States and many other states? The answer according to the accusers can be summarized as follows:

> Under present and foreseeable circumstances, the last thing the U.S. government would want to be confronted with is evidence of a major Soviet violation of SALT. The Soviets have been all too aware of this aversion and they have exploited it with a strategy of selective SALT violations that create just enough ambiguity to give the U.S. Administration some leeway in rationalizing Soviet actions. . . .
>
> Optimistic assessments of U.S. verification under SALT II are based in large part on the presumption that the Soviets will be deterred from violations by an acute fear of detection and its consequences. Quite the contrary can be assumed: namely, that the Soviets know full well what they have gotten away with under SALT I and that they will act accordingly under SALT II. [59]

Just what it was that the Soviet Union has "gotten away with" in SALT I has been graphically described by another critic of SALT and its verifiability: "under SALT I the United States has traded away its ABM in return for a tripling or quadrupling of the Soviet strategic threat against it, all the while tolerating Soviet negotiating deception and massive operational concealments and ruses in Soviet strategic deployments". [60] In short, according to this view the Soviet Union does not have to go to elaborate lengths to hide its cheating. A compliant, fearful and even complicit US government will look the other way and try to cover up the evidence anyway.

This is not the first time in US history that political debate over arms control has sunk to such a primitive level. Nor is it necessary to point out that the Soviet Union has suffered its own spasms of irrational fears, bizarre suspicions and bitter rhetoric. At such times it is easy for verification to serve as a fig leaf to cover much deeper attitudes of hostility and suspicion, but it is crystal clear that the arguments themselves have virtually nothing to do with verification. They are premised on the assumption that the threat of detection of violations is no deterrent in any event. The real target of these attacks is arms control itself, and attempts to counter arguments like these with assertions about the capabilities of monitoring instruments and data analysis are doomed to futility. In an atmosphere in which these positions have achieved prominence and widespread influence, a balanced discussion of the capabilities and limitations of verification is very much whistling into the wind.

Nevertheless one can hope that the debate will someday return to reality, and then there will still be the question of how to deal with all the other kinds of 'violation' in the above list, that is, those which are not purposeful and blatant, but which are ambiguous, inadvertent or the result of errors in monitoring and interpretation. In such cases the nature and handling of the evidence are extremely important in determining the response, and the response itself should be carefully tailored to the magnitude and significance of the violation. For example, if there is any reason to suspect that an apparent violation is the result of inadvertent or unauthorized behaviour on the part of subordinate officials, it would be a serious error to make public accusations of violation. No state enjoys admitting to incompetence or insubordination, and public accusations by foreigners will generally produce a closing of ranks behind the perpetrators rather then a quiet and speedy correction of the problem.

The evaluation process

There is no more critical point in the entire process of verification than the boundary at which the technology of detection encounters the politics of evaluation and response. However precise and comprehensive the monitoring techniques, there is no escaping the need to evaluate all evidence within some political context which must include as coherent and accurate as possible a model of the "behavioural style and approach to calculating political action" of the state being monitored.[61] But while such a model is indispensible, it is also dangerous, because it inevitably biases the receptivity of those who subscribe to it in favour of evidence which reinforces the model and against evidence which contradicts it.[62] This problem has already been pointed out in chapter 3 in connection with the problem of adequacy in verification, but some further elaboration on it is essential for an understanding of the nature and effects of treaty violations.

It has been a basic assumption of arms control advocates that violations of treaties would be strongly inhibited by the potential political consequences of detection and exposure. According to one US advocate of SALT II: "Evidence of non-compliance is a strong signal. Without an agreement, there can be neither cheating nor the indicator of a barrier crossing that results if cheating is detected. Verification has at least this modest importance".[63] There are two criticisms which can be made of this assertion. First it should be noted that while 'signal' is given an adjective (strong), 'evidence' is given no adjective. Does the statement suggest that weak evidence is also a strong signal? What, in fact, constitutes evidence? Such questions are often begged in discussions of verification, yet the quality of the evidence supporting charges of non-compliance is critical to the credibility of any arms control treaty. And disputes over the quality of the evidence are certain to arise. For example, one highly placed US official, when asked about the allegations by the Reagan Administration of Soviet violations of various treaties, replied: "It's not alleged cheating; it's cheating—period. We have hard evidence of a number of major violations".[64] But a careful analysis of the charges, by the Federation of American Scientists, states: "Given the ambiguity of some of the treaty provisions as well as the inconclusive nature of U.S. evidence, few, if any, of the alleged violations can be proven".[65]

A second criticism derives from the psychological insight that "it is incorrect to think that a signal will be detected simply because it is strong relative to the background noise. The rewards which a person gets if he detects the stimulus, and the cost he must pay if he fails or gives a false report, are as important as the signal's strength in determining whether the person will perceive the stumulus".[66] Notice that the signals could as well be signals of compliance as opposed to non-compliance. The problem of detection against a background of entrenched ideological and institutional biases is no different in the two cases.

Institutional biases can act in different ways at different levels of an intelligence bureaucracy.[67] At the lower levels, close to the stream of monitoring data, there is a high premium on thoroughness and a severe penalty for failure to report a signal. This creates a high noise level as many false signals are passed up to intermediate levels. At these intermediate levels there is a high cost attached to annoying the actual decision makers by passing on false or unsubstantiated reports. Therefore the middle levels act as a 'filter', typically passing on evidence that reinforces existing biases and rejecting that which does not. This filter can act as it did in the USA during the 1970s to screen out ambiguities and reinforce the institutional belief that the Soviet Union was in essential compliance with SALT and other agreements. Or it can act as it has under the Reagan Administration to place negative interpretations on such ambiguities and generate a picture of widespread and systematic non-compliance. This example supports the hypothesis that "the entire communications system is biased by the ideas and plans of the top decision makers".[68]

This biasing is made easier by the fact that the filtering at intermediate levels is done by people who generally have neither the close familiarity with the capabilities and limitations of the monitoring process possessed by those at lower levels, nor the larger world view and policy-making responsibility of those at higher levels. It is little wonder that such a filtering process can often lead to poor intelligence and unpleasant surprises, yet it must also be accepted that such imperfect mechanisms are probably inevitable in any organization as large and complex as a national intelligence apparatus.[69]

Neither of the obvious remedies of moving the filter higher up or lower down is necessarily any better than leaving it where it is. When Henry Kissinger was National Security Advisor to President Nixon an attempt was made to move the filter all the way to the top, and while this solved some problems in the negotiation of the SALT I Treaty it created others (see chapter 3, pp. 155–56). To move the filter downwards would be to place the burden of evaluation of evidence on the professional intelligence analysts themselves, a demand which also raises serious problems of professional competence and responsibility (see chapter 3, pp. 154–55).

A number of analysts have suggested that the problem of bias could be reduced by including within the intelligence bureaucracy groups whose task it is to play the 'devil's advocate', that is, to challenge the prevailing assumptions and policies and to call attention to evidence which contradicts them.[70] These proposals differ in significant details. For example, one suggests that the devil's advocate group should have nothing to do with particular treaties and that "It should not start with intellectual baggage or emotional investments that need protection".[71] Its purpose would be to devise strategies that an adversary might use to successfully evade detection by US monitoring processes of strategically significant violations.

There are some similarities between this suggestion and the actual employment of 'Team-B' during the Ford Administration to challenge the prevailing CIA assessment of Soviet military capabilities and intentions (see chapter 3, p. 132). The major similarity is the fact that the challenging group was made up entirely of people from outside the CIA who had no organizational interests to protect. But that this group carried no "intellectual baggage or emotional investments" cannot be seriously argued.[72] In fact, the exercise was seen to have clear political motivations, a long way from the objective and dispassionate attitude demanded by the author of the suggestion.

An alternative is to construct the group using people within the agency and to provide them with institutional protection and support for their adversary role.[73] One specific suggestion would have the IAEA safeguards agency explore scenarios for diversion of sensitive nuclear materials in which a state would attempt to hide the diversion by making it difficult for the IAEA to apply safeguards effectively. Current IAEA scenarios consider the problem of diversion only under the assumption that safeguards are operating effectively.[74]

These are important suggestions, and the creation of such internal mechanisms for challenging entrenched assumptions could have very beneficial effects on the alertness and quality of analysis of intelligence agencies. Still, there are real problems with such suggestions, the major one being the great difficulty in preventing political and ideological pressure from corrupting the adversary system. There are real risks that internal pressures will circumscribe the freedom of the challengers to make their challenge effectively, or that frustrated challengers will become 'whistle blowers' and take their challenge outside the agency into the political arena. In either case the process will be damaged. Despite these risks the potential benefits seem great enough to make such an experiment worthwhile as long as it is kept in mind that the essential ambiguity of the verification process can never be fully removed.

This ambiguity is best understood by picturing an arms control treaty as a central "core" of clearly prohibited behaviour, represented by item number 1 on the above list, surrounded by a "penumbra of doubtful conduct",[75] which, in effect, encompasses all the other items on the list. This grey area at the edges of violations is where the vast majority of possible disputes will arise, and the behaviour of states in this area will be closely tied to their overall attitudes towards arms control and each other. A national leadership strongly committed to a particular treaty will be inhibited from engaging in activities inside this penumbra for fear of creating suspicion or concern on the other side. At the same time it is likely to give the benefit of the doubt to activities in this doubtful area by the other side. These biases are a natural result of the desire to preserve a treaty in which the leadership has had to invest much effort and take many political risks to gain the domestic consensus necessary to ratify it.

However, inhibitions against activities in the penumbra are not consistent with the legalistic premise that everything not prohibited by an arms control agreement is allowed. Such a premise is actually implicit in the concept of arms control (as opposed to disarmament), which recognizes that the control of certain weapons and activities is taking place in the context of continuing competition in other areas that are often closely related. For example, the restriction on anti-ballistic missile systems has coexisted for over 10 years with an absence of prohibitions against anti-satellite weapons. But much of the technology is very similar, so that a large Soviet radar which looks to US analysts like a prohibited ABM radar, and may very well be able to serve that function, can be explained by the Soviet Union as a space-tracking radar, possibly designed for battle management functions in its anti-satellite programme.[76]

The attempt to regulate activities in the penumbra must run up against this difficulty. The Soviet Union has often been characterized as having a "strict constructionist"[77] approach to arms control treaties (or for that matter all treaties), in which any behaviour not specifically forbidden is permitted. Restraints on activities in the penumbra would then be seen by the Soviet Union as a form of unilateral restraint, something which is always difficult for a leadership to achieve in the face of bureaucratic opposition. But the Soviet Union is not alone in this interpretation. The United States sees arms control treaties as contracts, and it is a basic principle of US contract law that: "The very meaning of a line in the law is that anyone may get as close to the line as he can if he keeps on the right side".[78] Therefore the same problem with charges of unilateral restraint can be expected to arise in the USA, and has in fact arisen[79] in connection with a number of arms control agreements.

It is no answer to this problem to design monitoring equipment and procedures which are sensitive only to activities in the core area and somehow capable of filtering out or ignoring activities in the penumbra. This is highly unrealistic because intelligence data generally only make sense when interpreted against the full context of the activities of another state.[80] No responsible decision maker could willingly ignore the possibility of acquiring as much information as possible about the activities of a potential adversary, even if it were feasible (and it most certainly is not) to make clear dividing lines between activities which are strictly prohibited by treaties and those which are merely dubious, not to mention the problem of distinguishing information relevant to militarily important activities from information on unimportant activities.

Political versus military significance

Since ambiguities, errors, false alarms, suspicious activities, and misunderstandings are inevitable companions of arms control treaties, the only practical question one can ask is how they should be responded to when they occur. Here again the answer depends on one's basic evaluation of the arms control process. If it is considered important and worth protecting, then extreme caution is indicated in responding to apparent incidents of non-compliance. If, instead, one is unimpressed by the value of ongoing arms control negotiations and agreements and convinced of the insincerity and malign intentions of the other side, then some domestic political capital can be made by making accusations of violations.

There is no point in attempting to have it both ways. It has been pointed out quite correctly that: "Governments cannot logically carry on negotiations with a nation it [*sic*] has just accused of violating existing agreements on the very same issue".[81] The logic of the situation demands that issues of non-compliance be settled before productive negotiations can be resumed. But public accusations are certainly the least promising avenue for satisfactory resolution of compliance problems, especially when the latter involve, as they invariably do, complex, ambiguous and secret evidence. It does not require a sophisticated political awareness to understand that the making of such charges will erect major obstacles in the path of further negotiations as well as undermine the credibility of existing treaties.

In spite of this obvious difficulty, the Reagan Administration contrived to submit to the Senate its public accusations of Soviet violations during the very same week that President Reagan called for renewed negotiations in a conciliatory speech addressed to both US and European audiences on the opening day of the Stockholm Conference on Confidence- and Security-Building Measures and Disarmament in Europe.[82] For most of 1984 the conflict between the two approaches seemed to be resolved in favour of downplaying the charges of violations as pleas for reopening negotiations have intensified. A later, more comprehensive report on Soviet compliance practices prepared by the President's General Advisory Committee (GAC) on Arms Control and Disarmament was released with the disclaimer that: "Neither the methodology of analysis nor the conclusions reached in this report have been formally reviewed or approved by any agencies of the US Government".[83]

Such a disclaimer could be interpreted as an attempt by the Reagan Administration to distance itself from the extremely negative conclusions the report made about Soviet compliance practices. An official report to the Congress was delayed for several months, but when it was finally submitted in February 1985 it recapitulated all of the charges contained in the original report and the GAC report.[84]

Both the charges themselves and the inconsistent and confusing behaviour of the Reagan Administration towards them have done considerable damage to the credibility of the arms control process and it is not at all clear that the damage can be easily repaired, either in relation to the Soviet Union or to US and West European public opinion.

There are, of course, many alternatives to public denunciations. One process of resolving ambiguities and minor infractions of treaty provisions has been developed by the IAEA in its nuclear safeguards programme. The Agency maintains a high level of secrecy with respect to safeguarding of nuclear facilities in many states. Although instances of discrepancy and ambiguous evidence arise often,

> It would be counterproductive to point a finger at a particular government for a relatively minor safeguards transgression or in regard to a minor anomaly that has not yet been resolved. The cooperation of governments is essential to the operation and it should not be lightly jeopardized. The charge of non-cooperation should only be made when the government's performance seriously impairs the ability of the IAEA to verify that no diversion is taking place. Moreover, there are so many minor transgressions and anomalies that naming names in public would soon lose any positive effect! [85]

Another confidential mechanism for resolving ambiguities and minor infractions is the Standing Consultative Commission created by the USA and the USSR as an integral component of the SALT process (see section IV). This Commission seemed to work quite effectively during the 1970s and even survived some breaches of confidentiality deemed necessary by the Carter Administration to promote ratification of the SALT II Treaty. But the Reagan Administration has made much less use of the SCC, choosing instead to make its accusations public[86] because, according to one Administration official, the violations are "serious issues" and appear to have been premeditated many years in advance. [87]

In both the nuclear safeguards and SCC instances the crucial criterion seems to be the seriousness of the violation. While 'minor' ambiguities and infractions may be handled confidentially, it would appear that 'serious' issues may require public exposure either to force the violator to reform or to brand him as a conscious violator of an agreement. It is in fact the threat of such exposure and the resulting condemnation of world public opinion which are supposed to provide one of the major deterrents to violation of arms control treaties. If the deterrent is to be credible, it is argued, then there can be no alternative to carrying out the threat of exposure when it is warranted by a serious premeditated violation.

Again the inevitable question arises—how serious? Is it possible to specify the criteria which determine the seriousness of a violation and a threshold beyond which public exposure and other forms of retaliation are called for? One interesting attempt to define an appropriate criterion has been made in the context of the highly artificial model referred to in chapter 3 (see chapter 3,

p. 163). The model involves the rotation of some number of ICBMs among some much larger number of silos and includes provisions for the monitoring state to see sample populations of open silos in order to determine on a statistical basis whether a violation of the missile limit has occurred. The author of the model divides possible violations into 'politically significant' and 'militarily significant' categories, defined as follows: "Politically, the deployment of one 'extra' ICBM would be significant, raising doubts about purposes, intentions, trust, etc. Militarily, the significance of cheating would closely depend on aggregate strategic force sizes and perceptions of the existing strategic balance".[88] The purpose of these definitions was to provide a clear definition of 'adequacy' based on a military criterion and to determine the parameters of a monitoring system which would be able to detect militarily significant violations. The simplicity of the model ensures that when the monitoring system is designed in this way, the system is by definition incapable of detecting violations which are politically significant but militarily insignificant. Of course, this renders moot the supposed political significance of such minor violations.

Unfortunately the world is not as simple as this model and it is not possible in real cases to design monitoring systems which automatically filter out politically troublesome but militarily innocuous information. That filtering process must be done by fallible and biased human beings working in political environments which are strongly affected by all sorts of influences beyond the particular compliance problem under consideration. Under such conditions, according to one analyst:

> Verification and compliance arrangements should not only protect U.S. security; they should also instill confidence in the American public that its interests are being protected and that the agreements are functioning fairly and effectively. And public confidence will often depend less on esoteric assessments of whether possible violations are militarily significant than on simple perceptions of whether the Soviets are cheating, regardless of the military significance.[89]

These are heavy demands to place on verification and compliance 'arrangements' if the latter word refers only to the processes of monitoring and analysis this book has discussed so far. It has been amply demonstrated that modern verification systems will regularly turn up many 'possible violations', and recent experience has shown how easy it is for a change in political leadership to switch public attention away from 'esoteric assessments' of military significance to 'simple perceptions' of widespread cheating. What the author of the statement leaves out is the predominant role of the political leadership of any state in defining the psychological and political climate in which the significance of possible violations is evaluated. Such leadership can in no sense be abdicated to some set of technical and administrative 'arrangements': it is in fact the one irreducible ingredient of any compliance mechanism. Whether or not a militarily insignificant 'violation' or ambiguity will be seen as politically significant is very much a matter of political choice. This is not an absolute statement; events can move beyond the control of political leaders. But the contrast in behaviour in regard to ambiguous evidence between the Reagan Administration and those that preceded it illustrates very clearly the wide latitude available to political leaders for influencing public attitudes towards treaty compliance.

This argument strongly suggests that no stable criteria can exist for defining politically significant violations. Any definition of a violation which is going to be strong enough to survive the inevitable swings in political attitudes must be based on more objective criteria, and the only others available are military criteria. Along with this must come a strong recognition of the essential difference between a 'violation' and a 'possible violation'. The frequency of the latter can be expected to far exceed the frequency of the former, and unless the compliance process includes powerful and essentially apolitical means for distinguishing one from the other it can never maintain its credibility over time. Simply put, the concept of innocent until proven guilty must be an integral part of the process, this concept in turn deriving from the element of trust shown to be necessary in the previous chapter.

If military criteria are to be adopted for assessing the significance of violations then there must be a workable political consensus, both domestic and international, on perceptions of the existing strategic balance and on the relative importance of deviations from this balance. In effect, the requirement is for a consensus on military doctrine, precisely the consensus which does not now exist, either between the USA and USSR or within the USA itself. This consensus can only be achieved through informed debate and compromise, but the debate must be about weapons, strategies and goals, not about verification. Far too often verification has served as a surrogate for the more fundamental debate over doctrine, a classic case of setting the cart before the horse.

If a military criterion could be established and if the word 'violation' were in fact used only in cases where violation had been proven beyond reasonable doubt, there would still remain the somewhat arbitrary division into significant and insignificant violations. This separation could be combined with the earlier separation into intentional and unintentional (i.e., either unauthorized or accidental) violations to produce a classification scheme like that of table 8.

The category of significant, intentional violations would contain all efforts to achieve a genuine military advantage by clandestine violations of a treaty. Such violations would call for the most serious response, up to and including abrogation of the treaty and even pre-emptive attack if the violation were sufficiently threatening.

The category of intentional but militarily insignificant violations is one for which a number of examples have already been seen. Such violations can be

Table 8. Classification of violations according to military significance and degree of intent

	Violation	
	Intentional	Unintentional (accidental, unauthorized)
Militarily significant	Clandestine acquisition of clear military advantage ('break-out')	Highly unlikely to be unintentional
	Response: Major diplomatic or military initiative	Response: SCC or direct contact of political leaders
Militarily insignificant	Probe of intelligence capabilities or political resolve ('communication')	Great majority of cases; no threat
	Response: Uncertain, depends on situation	Response: SCC

used as a form of political communication to probe the intelligence capabilities or political resolve of other parties. The party that uncovers such a 'message' can choose to ignore it, presumably to protect intelligence assets, or to respond firmly but confidentially in a forum like the SCC. Or the charges and evidence can be made public, inevitably leading to an even further worsening of the political atmosphere. Any state considering such a probe must take into account the possibly serious political repercussions it could produce. In an already ugly political atmosphere such game playing may seem to carry little cost. However, one suspects that the inhibitions against such behaviour would rise rapidly as the political atmosphere began to improve. This is closely related to the mechanism of trust building described in chapter 3. Given a real commitment by all sides to a building of such trust, the political risks involved in making intentional insignificant violations would come to seem very high, and the tactic would make no sense.

It is virtually impossible to think of an entry for the upper right-hand corner of the table. One can certainly not imagine a militarily significant violation occurring by accident, and it seems highly dubious that such a thing could be carried out by unauthorized persons somehow managing to evade the intelligence agencies of all parties to the treaty, including their own. Of course, this problem could become somewhat more serious at very low levels of armaments, depending on the precise criteria for military significance that were applied. This, however, is a problem that optimists might look forward to dealing with sometime in the future.

Finally, the lower right-hand corner will contain the vast majority of violations, those which are technical, accidental or unauthorized as well as non-threatening, and which can be dealt with easily and confidentially in a consultative body.

The neatness and clarity of this scheme should not be overrated. It depends for its success on clear criteria for military significance and the willingness to presume innocence until guilt is proven. Neither of these preconditions will be easy to achieve, but to place the burden on them has at least the virtue of removing an impossibly heavy burden from the compliance process.

The essential conclusion of this analysis of the many forms of non-compliance is that the single most important determining factor in the significance of a violation is the political atmosphere in which it occurs. This is perhaps most vividly illustrated by an arms control agreement which has survived more than 165 years in spite of repeated violations by both sides, many of which were judged militarily significant by the standards of their time. The agreement is the Rush–Bagot Treaty whose purpose was to demilitarize the Great Lakes separating the USA and Canada, the latter being at the time still a British colony and very much the object of US expansionist ambitions.[90]

The Rush–Bagot Treaty limits each state to "one vessel, not exceeding 100 tons burden, and armed with one 18 pound (8.2 kg) cannon"[91] on each lake. Since its entry into force in 1818 it has been violated by both the US and Canadian governments, even to the point of a rumoured US proposal in the early 1960s to deploy nuclear-armed intercontinental missiles on the Great Lakes. According to the author of the study,

> Even the most seasoned manipulators of the *clausula rebus sic stantibus* might blush while pronouncing the presence of scores of weapons, each of the destructive equivalent of 50 million tons of TNT, to be consistent with the spirit of an Agreement forbidding the presence of anything in excess of the normal amount of ammunition for four 18 pound cannon. But that is not to say they could not have done it.[92]

There are no violations of the SALT or other US–Soviet treaties that are anywhere near as blatant or obvious as those that have threatened the Rush–Bagot Treaty over more than 150 years. Yet relations between the USA and the USSR remain hostile and unproductive while those between the USA and Canada are cordial and mutually beneficial. This should leave little doubt as to the controlling variable in the process. The recognition of mutual interest and the shared commitment to achieving relaxation of tension are far more critical to the success of arms control than the absence of treaty violations. It is far too easy to forget this basic truth in the face of the obsessive concern for verifiability which exists today.

IV. Co-operative measures

Far too often in discussions of verification the term "co-operative measures" serves as little more than a "euphemism for on-site inspection".[93] However, it is shown in chapter 1 that there are many more ways for states to co-operate in reassuring each other of their compliance with arms control agreements, and it is important that these other methods get the attention they deserve. Therefore this section focuses on those co-operative measures which do not require the presence of foreign inspectors on the territory of a state, and the special case of on-site inspection is treated separately in the next section.

Measures involving direct communication

There are a number of ways in which states can communicate with each other to reduce suspicions and monitor compliance with agreements. These range from the need for rapid, unobstructed contact in times of serious crisis to the need for a continuous diplomatic and technical dialogue to anticipate and resolve problems which arise in the arms control process.

At the crisis end of the spectrum is the concept of the 'hot line', a direct telecommunications link between the highest political officials in the USA and the USSR. The need for such a device was clearly demonstrated by the difficulties in communication between Moscow and Washington during the Cuban missile crisis of October 1962, and by June 1963 a working hot line between the two capitals was in operation.[94] This link has been upgraded twice since that time, once in 1971 when satellites were added to telephone cables as the transmitting devices,[95] and in July 1984 when a facsimile transmission capability was added. The current system is capable of transmitting teletype text at a rate of 67 words per minute as well as pages of text, maps or charts in facsimile form.[96] It should be emphasized that the communication link uses teletype machines and printed text or graphics, not telephone conversations as is often suggested in popular or fictional accounts. There have been recent suggestions by a number of US Senators to further improve the hot-line system by creating 'risk-reduction' or 'crisis' centres which would permit instantaneous voice communication between US and Soviet political and military leaders.[97]

There can be no question that the hot line is an important innovation and that even more opportunities for effective communication in times of crisis would be desirable. However, the primary value of such arrangements is their ability to reduce tension, suspicion and misunderstanding in dangerous crises, not their contribution to the day-to-day task of monitoring compliance with arms control treaties. For example, it does not make sense to think of the hot line as a means by which a US president and a Soviet general secretary might resolve a problem of compliance such as an ambiguous radar under construction or a series of suspicious seismic events. Since these kinds of problem often involve sensitive and complex intelligence information and the skills and interests of a number of military, diplomatic and intelligence agencies, they can only be resolved by a mechanism which takes into account such bureaucratic interconnections and operates on a longer time-scale and on a more formal diplomatic level. Any attempt by the leadership of the two states to resolve such issues by informal exchanges might produce some short-term benefits, but would soon encounter powerful bureaucratic opposition, and could lead to serious or embarrassing errors. While such an assumption of discretionary power by the top leadership is acceptable in a crisis, it is not a characteristic operating procedure in a modern bureaucratic state.

Exchange of data

Proposals for the international exchange of information are one of the most common types of verification mechanism suggested for a wide variety of arms control measures.[98] The actual form of the information exchange could be an open public declaration of existing stocks of weapons or materials, confidential submissions to an agency empowered to monitor a treaty, or direct exchange between states. But all such proposals have in common the assumption that each state will assemble the necessary data unilaterally, submitting it voluntarily to whatever agency or other states are specified in the treaty.

A number of existing treaties incorporate various forms of information exchange. The SALT Treaties require each side within the context of the Standing Consultative Commission to "provide on a voluntary basis such information as either Party considers necessary to assure confidence in compliance with the obligations assumed".[99] During the negotiations for SALT II the United States insisted on, and eventually succeeded in achieving, a so-called "agreed data base".[100] The Soviet Union agreed to provide its own numerical data on those weapons covered by the Treaty, a concession both sides considered to be of historic significance (see chapter 3, p. 123).

Far more elaborate provisions for information exchange are included in the US–Soviet Peaceful Nuclear Explosions Treaty (PNET). In addition to the usual specification of national technical means of verification, this Treaty requires each of the parties to "provide to the other Party information and access to sites of explosions and furnish assistance in accordance with the provisions set forth in the Protocol to this Treaty".[101] The information specified in the Protocol is quite extensive, amounting to an essentially full disclosure of the purpose, location, yield and geological environment of the explosion.[102] The Threshold Test Ban Treaty (TTBT) also contains provisions for significant information exchange, including detailed data on two nuclear weapon tests at each distinct test site for the purpose of calibrating the seismological detectors of the other side.[103]

These provisions represent significant advances over previous treaties and point to one clear advantage of information exchange mechanisms: they are considerably more acceptable politically than such intrusive measures as on-site inspection. Their acceptance by both sides (assuming that the United States finally ratifies the treaties) would indicate that both sides accept the premise that voluntary provision by a state of information on its military capabilities provides a significant degree of reassurance that the state is complying with its commitments.

There are two major factors which act to inhibit states from supplying false information in violation of a treaty. First, the state itself needs accurate information on its own military capabilities, so if it is to supply false information to others it must in effect keep two sets of accounts. If this is to be done for a militarily significant violation then it will almost certainly require the active involvement of a substantial number of people in various agencies. The risk of exposure of the fraud would therefore be strongly correlated with its military importance. Second, it must be assumed that other states will continue to use their own intelligence apparatus to get an independent check on the data provided. To submit false data would be to risk exposing a discrepancy with data gathered by others.

These advantages are important, and they constitute a strong argument for including mechanisms for information exchange in future arms control treaties. But some reservations are in order, mostly in connection with inescapable problems of ambiguity which plague virtually all compliance mechanisms.

One source of ambiguity lies in the definitions of items to be counted or characteristics to be measured. Unless there is an agreement on precise definitions, even honest reporting by one side can be subject to challenge by the other. The importance of clear and mutually acceptable definitions makes them worth some struggle to achieve, but the process can be carried to counterproductive extremes. A good example of the latter is the exchange of troop data in the MFR talks in Vienna. NATO and the Warsaw Treaty Organization long ago began to exchange data on troop deployments, but after much argument the USA and USSR have still not been able to agree on what constitutes deployed military forces.[104] While it would be wrong to attribute the lack of progress in the negotiations to this argument alone, it is still true that such a dispute over definitions can provide a very convenient excuse for stalling the process.

A second problem is the inevitability of errors, either by the state doing the reporting or by the intelligence apparatus of the other side. Such errors would show up as disagreements in the data of the two sides, and it could be very difficult to find a way to reconcile the discrepancy. In order to confront the reporting state with the discrepancy the other state would have to reveal the extent of its knowledge of the reporting state's capability and could thereby compromise valuable intelligence assets. But in the absence of such a confrontation the error might go uncorrected and suspicions persist that the false report was intentional, either as an attempt at concealment or as an attempt to probe the other side's intelligence capabilities.

Neither of these difficulties is insurmountable, but they imply that information exchange can never by itself provide an adequate level of assurance of compliance.[105] Not only must it function in co-operation with other methods, but it is particularly vulnerable to changes in the political atmosphere. The kinds of ambiguity and potential for manipulation which are an inevitable part of an information exchange process make it far too fragile to survive a hostile political environment and incapable on its own of acting as a confidence-building measure.

In addition to the direct exchange of information there are a number of other co-operative measures which work to facilitate the monitoring process (see chapter 1). These include agreements not to engage in deliberate conceal-ment activities or interfere with the national technical means of other states in such a way as to impede verification. Other such measures included in the SALT Treaties are agreed counting rules (e.g., the number of warheads on a MIRVed missile is taken to be the largest number with which the missile has been tested), and common understandings on so-called 'functionally related observable differences' which allow one side to distinguish similar systems which serve different purposes (e.g., bombers and aerial refuelling tankers).

All of these measures derive from the inherent limitations of national technical means. They are genuinely co-operative in that they represent an at-tempt by two parties to reassure each other that these limitations will not be exploited. But they are also extremely vulnerable to changes in the political climate and to honest differences in interpretation. For example, because of the effectiveness of satellite monitoring, states will want to use camouflage and other forms of deception to conceal military activities uncontrolled by treaties. Such activities are quite legitimate, yet it is inherent in the nature of camouflage that the observer be deceived about the true nature of what is being hidden. How can the suspicious observer be reassured that what is being hidden is *not* a violation of a treaty? This is the crux of the current dispute over Soviet encryption of missile telemetry (see above), but the paradox applies to a wide variety of other verification problems and demonstrates the self-fulfilling quality of the assumption that states party to a treaty will cheat whenever the probability of detection can be reduced to a low level. This one-sided view of the monitoring process neglects both the mutual recognition of common interest inherent in a treaty and the genuinely inhibiting effect on a state which has publicly committed itself to such a treaty of even a small prob-ability of being detected in a major violation or a pattern of minor violations. It is the factor of common interest in preserving the treaty that motivates the kinds of co-operative measure discussed here. If for any reason this recog-nition of common interest is lost, co-operative measures become the first casualties to suspicion and ambiguity.

Standing Consultative Commission

It was realized early in the SALT negotiating process, in November–December 1969, that some kind of 'special arrangement' would be required to address problems of implementation of any agreements that might be achieved.[106] The arrangement ultimately took the form of a standing commission made up of diplomatic, military, technical and intelligence personnel of both parties and required to meet in Geneva at least twice each year to:

(*a*) consider questions concerning compliance with the obligations assumed and related situations which may be considered ambiguous;

(*b*) provide on a voluntary basis such information as either Party considers necessary to assure confidence in compliance with the obligations assumed;

(*c*) consider questions involving unintended interference with national technical means of verification;

(*d*) consider possible changes in the strategic situation which have a bearing on the provisions of this Treaty;

(*e*) agree upon procedures and dates for destruction or dismantling of ABM systems or their components in cases provided for by the provisions of this Treaty;

(*f*) consider, as appropriate, possible proposals for further increasing the viability of this Treaty, including proposals for amendments in accordance with the provisions of this Treaty;

(*g*) consider, as appropriate, proposals for further measures aimed at limiting strategic arms. [107]

This list of duties, in particular items (*c*) and (*e*), was elaborated somewhat in the SALT II Treaty as other weapon systems besides ABM were brought under limitations.

The above list makes clear that the responsibilities of the SCC extend far beyond the handling of compliance issues. Such complex technical agreements as the SALT Treaties require a great deal of detailed definition of procedures for implementation. For example, the SALT II Treaty (article XI) requires that weapons in excess of agreed limits "shall be dismantled or destroyed under procedures to be agreed upon in the Standing Consultative Commission". [108] This means that neither side has the right unilaterally to determine the means of getting rid of excess weapons—the process has been made co-operative. [109]

In spite of this important implementation function it has been the role of the SCC in handling compliance issues that has received the most public attention. According to a former SCC Commissioner from the United States the essence of the SCC task in compliance-related questions is: "to head off potential gross dislocations or irretrievable circumstances by acting early enough and finding mutually-acceptable clarifications and implementing understandings, as well as inducing unilateral changes in troublesome activities, to sustain intact the agreements". [110]

The essential intent of this procedure is to *preserve the agreement*. Members of the SCC must "operate on the assumption that the agreement is to be sustained as negotiated, and ... it is their task to resolve any problems that arise for the continued functioning of the agreement". [111]

It is important to emphasize this conservative role of the SCC. It is in no sense intended as a device for detecting and prosecuting violations, but in fact must operate on the assumption that ambiguities or apparent violations are 'problems' to be resolved by discussion and compromise. This places a high premium on early identification and discussion of problems before they get out of hand, on confidentiality to prevent the premature imputation of culpability, and on a continued mutual commitment to the preservation of the treaty despite the inevitable problems which arise in its implementation.

The Standing Consultative Commission is probably the single most creative and significant product of the SALT process. It was used during the 1970s to resolve a continuous series of compliance issues and was judged by most observers to be generally successful as long as its limited mandate to deal only with ambiguities and misunderstandings is kept in mind. [112] Not only has the SCC resolved many problems of implementation, [113] it has also been used to clarify and specify detailed rules for future conduct to prevent disputes from recurring. [114]

The SALT SCC is now under serious political pressure, as are all aspects of the SALT process. The SCC is no more immune to the effects of a corrosive political atmosphere than any other co-operative measure. Yet the concept is a solid one and the experience gained with the SALT SCC has led many to suggest that this model can be adapted to other arms control treaties as well, [115] and even extended from a bilateral to an international context. [116] It is safe to predict that the great majority of future arms control agreements will be accompanied by something resembling the SALT SCC.

V. On-site inspection

From the earliest days of the nuclear arms race the problem of on-site inspection has been one of the major obstacles to the achievement of arms control or disarmament agreements. Indeed, in the 1940s and 1950s, before the arrival of reconnaissance satellites, sensitive seismic networks and other national technical means, 'inspection' was the word generally used to refer to what is now called verification. [117] It is interesting to note that the change to the modern term 'verification' coincided quite closely with the advent of artificial Earth satellites. [118]

It is pointed out in chapter 3 that on-site inspection has been primarily a preoccupation of the United States. Soviet leaders have always been sensitive to criticism of their society as 'closed' or excessively secretive and have generally seen proposals for on-site inspection as polemic devices used by the United States to score points in world opinion. [119]

It is certainly true that when the USA proposes on-site inspection, and the Soviet Union rejects it, a contrast is suggested between the 'openness' of Western societies and the 'closedness' of Eastern. For example, US Secretary of Defense Casper Weinberger asserted in a radio interview: "We need a lot better verification methods than we've had in the past. We need on-site verification which we've always offered, which the Soviet Union has always refused, which says quite a lot about the difference between the two societies".[120] Such statements are intended to highlight the differences between the two societies and to imply that a reluctance to accept on-site inspection is tantamount to an admission that one cannot be trusted to live up to agreements. However, such statements are never accompanied by a careful examination of the many technical, legal and political difficulties inherent in on-site inspection proposals.

It is remarkable, given the frequency with which elaborate on-site inspection schemes are proposed, how little such careful analysis has been made by the proposers. For example, the current US proposal for an 'open invitation' system of compulsory on-site inspection in connection with a chemical weapons treaty (see chapter 3) does not appear to have behind it a thorough (or even superficial) analysis of how such a scheme might work in practice. Without such an analysis the proposal is effectively empty, having all the earmarks of an attempt to gain the high ground in the propaganda battle.

This book is not the place for an analysis of the many specific proposals for on-site inspection. Instead, the following discussion will focus on a number of inherent problems in the concept of on-site inspection, focusing on its technical, legal and political feasibility as a realistic verification tool, using specific proposals as illustration.

Forms of on-site inspection

The analysis must begin with the recognition that on-site inspection can take many forms. It can be bilateral or international and it can be conducted in a variety of ways. One attempt at a comprehensive list has been made in the context of the chemical weapons treaty negotiations in the CD. On-site inspection might be conducted:

> (*i*) 'on an immediate basis', i.e., involving the presence of inspectors as soon as feasible,
> (*ii*) 'on a continuous basis', i.e., involving the presence of inspectors at all times during an operation,
> (*iii*) 'on a periodic basis', i.e., involving regular visits to an operation at fixed intervals,
> (*iv*) 'on a quota basis', i.e., involving an agreed number of regular visits ... on the basis of agreed criteria and data communicated by States,
> (*v*) 'on a random basis', i.e., involving an agreed number of visits which follow an irregular pattern with limited advanced warning,
> (*vi*) on any other agreed basis.[121]

This list includes inspections which would be conducted as a matter of routine (e.g., continuous, periodic) or on a non-routine basis requiring some sort of demand or challenge (e.g., immediate or quota). From a practical point of view routine inspections must be limited to so-called 'declared' sites and facilities, that is, those which are named specifically in a treaty or agreed to in some other way by the parties concerned. Challenge or demand inspections might also be confined to declared sites, but could in principle also be extended to any facility if such a provision were written into a treaty. Random inspections might be applied either to declared or undeclared sites.

The difference between routine and non-routine inspection has proved to be a crucial one historically. Routine inspections such as those carried out under IAEA safeguards have proved acceptable to many states, and even the nuclear weapon states which are not required to submit to such inspections have volunteered to do so in order to strengthen the system's legitimacy. All parties to the chemical weapons negotiations have now accepted the principle of continuous on-site verification of destruction of declared chemical weapon stockpiles, removing an important obstacle to the conclusion of a ban on chemical weapons.

Routine on-site inspection mechanisms are inherently more acceptable for a number of reasons. They are technically easier to carry out because they focus on a limited number of known sites for which standard monitoring devices and operative procedures can be implemented. They are politically easier to accept because they carry no accusatory connotations and because they strictly limit the freedom of movement and access to information by foreigners in the state under inspection.

However, such routine inspections do not prevent possible violations of treaty provisions at undeclared or clandestine sites. For example, IAEA safeguards inspectors have no authority to visit undeclared facilities which they suspect might be engaged in activities associated with nuclear materials or devices, even in states which have signed the Non-Proliferation Treaty. This means that in principle it is possible for a state to produce a nuclear weapon clandestinely while outwardly demonstrating full compliance with the NPT.

Another contingency not covered by the routine inspection of declared facilities is the possibility that the initial declarations were inaccurate or intentionally misreported. For example, a facility dedicated to the destruction of a declared stockpile of chemical weapons could perform exactly as required by the Treaty, but because some stocks of such weapons were not declared initially, the objective of complete chemical disarmament of the state would not be achieved.

It is the possibility of such activities that has led many people to advocate on-site inspection measures which would be instigated on a challenge or demand basis. In some such plans it is sufficient for one party to demand an inspection on the basis of evidence which it believes suggests the possibility of a violation. Other plans would require some kind of independent or neutral commission to review the evidence before recommending or refusing a challenge inspection. The latter procedure would tend to inhibit the making of capricious or politically motivated challenges as well as those for which the gathering of intelligence is a more important objective than monitoring compliance.

Legal problems

So far in the history of arms control efforts no such non-routine on-site inspection system has been adopted, and the prospects for any such scheme becoming acceptable in the foreseeable future are virtually nil. However, it would be wrong to attribute the unacceptability of such plans to a lack of a sincere desire for meaningful arms control agreements. In fact, much of the resistance to non-routine on-site inspections derives from their genuine legal, political and technical difficulties.

The legal problems are best illustrated by the US 'open invitation' proposal for a chemical weapons treaty.[122] In the US proposal only government-owned facilities were at first to be subject to inspections, and this was later amended to include private industries operating under government contracts. However, this still left most of the US and other Western chemical facilities uncovered, making the treaty highly unequal in its treatment of private enterprise and socialist economies.

When questioned about this asymmetry US officials conceded that it gave an advantage to the USA, but they claimed that such inequality was unavoidable because of the prohibition embodied in the Fourth Amendment to the United States Constitution against "unreasonable search and seizure" of private property.[123] This objection was analysed carefully many years ago, and a number of arguments were suggested as to why it should not prove to be an insurmountable obstacle to a realistic and effective inspection plan, even if unannounced searches of industrial plants without warrants were involved.[124] The only kind of facility which might remain immune from inspections under the Fourth Amendment would be the so-called 'button factory', that is, a plant nominally engaged in activities unrelated to the treaty and for which insufficient evidence of illegal activity exists to allow the foreign inspectors to obtain a search warrant from a US court.

As interesting as such legal niceties might be, they are not truly relevant to the problem of adequate verification of arms control agreements. Even if it were shown to be legally possible for Soviet inspectors to drop in unannounced on US button factories to look for chemical weapons, no one seriously imagines that such things would be done. It is highly unrealistic to imagine a scheme involving hundreds of foreign inspectors roaming about a country searching random industrial facilities without good reason to expect they will find something incriminating. And if such random searches are indeed illegal under the US Constitution, then it makes no sense, either logically or politically, to demand that the Soviet Union submit to them anyway.

If instead of focusing on remote and irrelevant hypothetical cases, attention is focused on inspection schemes that are politically realistic and technically feasible, then the difficulties do not appear to be insurmountable. The US Constitution seems to be flexible enough to permit a significant amount of on-site inspection by foreigners. [125]

Analogous studies of the Soviet legal system also reveal some potential obstacles to the implementation of an on-site inspection system but conclude that "Soviet law... presents a generally suitable framework for overcoming a great many of these obstacles" [126] and that "the Soviet leadership has at its disposal the necessary means to ensure full compliance with an arms inspection policy". [127]

It is important to emphasize that these assessments of the adaptability of the two legal systems assume the desire on the part of the national authorities to implement a system of inspection. All of the above studies also point out that if the leadership is opposed to or ambivalent about such a system, the legal systems can provide any number of means of interfering with it. On the one hand the Soviet system "contains inherent obstacles that could be unobtrusively set in motion by opposing factions to inhibit the inspection process without officially denouncing the arms control agreement". [128] On the other hand, in the United States the Congress must pass laws implementing any inspection scheme, [129] and there is ample evidence in US history to show how this Congressional process can delay and even destroy the implementation of a law or treaty.

But these are not legal problems; they are political problems deriving from the difficulty in establishing a domestic consensus in support of something so unprecedented and controversial as the inspection of the territory and economic and military assets of a sovereign state by foreigners, at least some of whom might be representatives of hostile states. Such yielding of sovereign powers to foreigners or international bodies is not a normal activity of national leaders, who tend to see their purpose in life as implementing and extending the power of their nation, not giving it away. Without a clear and stable national consensus on the desirability of such a yielding of national sovereignty, it would take a rare act of political courage for a national leader to take the risks involved in such a step. It is difficult to find such a consensus in any state, let alone in the two great powers.

Political resistance

It is instructive to look back in history to some earlier efforts to establish on-site inspection. When such suggestions were made in connection with enforcing the naval disarmament treaties of the 1920s, the position of the US government was made crystal clear by Secretary of State Kellogg: "The United States will not tolerate the supervision of any outside body in this matter nor be subjected to inspection or supervision by foreign agencies or individuals". [130]

Although the publicly expressed attitudes of the US government have obviously changed substantially since the 1920s, there still remain doubts as to the ease with which even a relatively non-intrusive inspection scheme could be implemented.

Concern over the relinquishing of national sovereignty is also quite prevalent in the US Congress. This became evident in the early negotiations over a comprehensive test ban treaty when it was proposed that an international commission be set up to make independent judgements on the evidence used to support on-site inspection challenges. Influential members of Congress were very reluctant to agree that any international body could have the power to overrule a determination by US experts that an inspection was warranted by the evidence.[131]

Whatever powers might be given to an international body to deny inspections, it is a certainty that no international body will ever have the power to force a state to submit to an inspection it does not want. And it is also obvious that no state will voluntarily submit to an inspection it anticipates will expose a violation. The bank robber does not invite observers from the police to certify his crime. Therefore the real signal for a violation must be the refusal by a state of an inspection deemed by other states to be warranted by the evidence, and it is safe to conclude that the United States has understood this for a long time: "United States planning proceeded on the basis that in such a case the other party would probably refuse to permit the exercise of inspection rights, *and that in itself would be the treaty breach*. In other words, inspection would operate not as an information-getting device but as a trigger mechanism".[132] But there are other reasons for refusing an inspection besides an attempt to hide illegal activity, for example, the protection of legitimate, military or commercial secrets or the knowledge that the demand for inspection is motivated more by a desire to harass and embarrass than by a real suspicion of misbehaviour.

If such legitimate refusals to permit inspection are automatically to be interpreted as *prima facie* treaty violations, then there are substantial risks involved in signing a treaty to be verified by challenge inspections. False challenges could also be used by a state desiring to abrogate the treaty but at the same time wanting to shift the blame for the abrogation to the other side.

Such concerns are evident in the Soviet approach to on-site inspections. At one point in the SALT I negotiations the United States

> raised the possibility of *ad hoc*, on-site inspections, on a 'request' basis, called selective direct observation (SDO). The Soviets objected. They had no trouble with the concept of inspection if a nation invited it, but they were concerned with the political consequences of denying inspections requested by the other side, *even though it would be understood that this did not constitute a violation of the agreement*.[133]

The proviso at the end of this quote is, of course, in direct conflict with the similarly emphasized segment of the previous statement. Since both quotes are from active and knowledgeable participants in the US arms control establishment, the contradiction perhaps indicates some ambivalence in US thinking on this issue. Nevertheless, the first statement has a more authentic and plausible ring, while the second smacks of the kind of hypothetical conjecturing that often takes place in negotiations. The prevailing US view was clearly expressed by a US Senator as follows: "I want to make that clear. No other nationality, no other group of people can overrule any decision made by our scientists that a given location is the epicenter. If for any reason at all the Russians decide we can't go in there then we know it is about time to call the whole thing to an end".[134]

The problem of equating a denied inspection with a violation is most acute in bilateral treaties. It can be alleviated to some extent in international treaties by the use of an impartial commission to evaluate challenges before they are formally made. Even if no formal veto power is given to such a commission, its refusal to certify a challenge as warranted by the evidence would be a significant inhibiting factor against capricious or poorly documented challenges.

In conclusion, there can be no question that the acceptance by a state of a treaty provision involving non-routine or challenge on-site inspections is a genuine signal that the state intends to live up to its obligations under the treaty. Such signals are very significant and greatly to be desired from all states. But at the same time an acquiescence to such a provision represents an assumption of trust that other parties will not abuse the challenge process by using it to gain military or political advantage. This second factor is rarely mentioned in discussions of on-site inspection, but it is crucial to their acceptance and emphasizes again the fundamental role of trust in the verification process. On-site inspection, the mechanism which might produce the greatest degree of confidence building, demands for its acceptance an already relatively high level of mutual confidence. If the logic of this is taken just a bit further it might be concluded that as on-site inspection becomes more feasible it becomes correspondingly less necessary. While such a neat conclusion may be somewhat oversimplified, it is certainly more realistic than the idea that elaborate challenge schemes for on-site inspection are feasible in an early stage of arms control.

Technical obstacles

To the legal and political constraints on non-routine on-site inspection methods must be added a pragmatic appraisal of their technical feasibility. What can actually be learned from on-site inspections with a reasonable investment in instruments, personnel and time? As is shown in chapter 3 there has been a growing recognition in the United States that the potential benefits of on-site inspection have been exaggerated. For example, both US and Soviet experts have criticized as easily evadable early US proposals for on-site inspections in connection with limitations on MIRV deployments.[135] More recently a former US negotiator has argued that "on-site inspection is vastly over-rated for everything except the Comprehensive Test Ban Treaty".[136]

The tendency to exaggerate the usefulness of on-site inspection has its political and propaganda aspects, as has already been noted. But it can also be attributed partly to hopes that such inspections would provide useful 'collateral information' (precisely the objection the Soviet Union has traditionally raised against US on-site inspection proposals) and partly to "exaggerated analogies drawn from on-site inspection's unquestionably substantial potential role in monitoring Soviet compliance with any potential Comprehensive Test Ban Treaty".[137]

It is significant that two of the above criticisms of on-site inspection exempt the comprehensive test ban from their negative evaluations. The US insistence on on-site inspections on demand as part of a comprehensive test ban (CTB) goes back to the earliest days of test ban negotiations and seems still to be a precondition to ratifying the treaty.[138] Belief seems to be widespread in the arms control community that this is one area in which the concept is both necessary and practical. Therefore it is worth examining it in more detail here from the point of view of its technical feasibility and usefulness in monitoring compliance, assuming that some day on-site inspection proves acceptable to all parties to a CTB.

There is surprisingly little in the way of technical assessment of on-site inspection of a CTB in the open literature. One tends to assume that careful technical studies have been made on the way in which such a system would operate, but if such studies exist they have not been made public. Instead one finds only a few very sketchy, almost offhand, references to the problem, most of which generate considerably more scepticism than confidence.

The problem faced by a CTB on-site inspection system is to identify a small seismic event as either an earthquake or nuclear (or possibly chemical) explosion by visiting the site where the event occurred and making various kinds of observation. It must be assumed that the event is of small magnitude ($m_b \leqslant 4$), since a network of remote seismographs is generally argued to be capable of reliably identifying events larger than this (see chapter 2). It can also be assumed that the event will occur in a seismically active area where small earthquakes are common. It would make no sense to conduct a clandestine nuclear explosion in a seismologically quiet area where it would immediately attract attention.

One relatively detailed description of how an inspection would be carried out envisages a team of about 20 people who would carry out visual inspections of the areas, sample radioactivity, set up seismometers to monitor aftershocks and take rock samples. The 'host' nation would be expected to provide transportation to, at and from the site as well as indigenous labour at the site.[139] The make up of the team is summarized in table 9. This inspection team must be well trained, have its equipment available and be ready to spend roughly six weeks at the site. Several tonnes of equipment would be necessary,

Table 9. Typical inspection team composition and functions

Inspection tasks	Personnel	Functions performed, etc.
Visual inspection (air and ground)	3 natural scientists	Team leadership; aerial and surface conventional photography; scientific detective work
Gamma spectrometry (air and surface)	2 engineers (plus 2 local labourers)	Aerial radioactivity survey followed by surface inspection
Broad-spectrum photography and magnetometer survey	1 photo interpreter, 1 geophysicist, 1 helicopter pilot	Coverage flown during airborne visual inspection; data reduced on ground; pilot is operations officer
Seismic monitoring	1 seismologist, 2 technicians	Seismic monitoring of aftershock signals
Shocked rock sampling	1 physicist (plus 1 local labourer)	Gathering and inspection of rock samples for crystal deformation
Technical support and maintenance	2 mechanics/technicians, 2 radio men, specialists	Maintenance of equipment and power units; communications and record keeping
Logistic support	1 interpreter, 1 medical technician, 2 cooks and bakers	Provide liaison, administration, health services; assist on inspections; provide familiar food, etc; receive and use 1 000 kilograms of food and fuel per week
Host nation support		Transportation to, at and from the site; indigenous labour at site; permit courier communication service

Source: Developments in Technical Capabilities for Detecting and Identifying Nuclear Weapons Tests, Hearings before the Joint Committee on Atomic Energy, US Congress, 5–12 March 1963 (US Government Printing Office, Washington, DC, 1963), p. 424.

especially if the team were required to visit a remote Arctic site, and something like one tonne per week of supplies, rock samples and other cargo would have to be flown in and out.[140]

However, it remains unlikely that the evidence uncovered by such a team would provide conclusive evidence that a nuclear explosion had taken place. Such an explosion would be small and buried deep underground precisely to prevent easy detection by surface observations. Although it is possible that radioactive gases from the explosion could seep to the surface through small rock fractures, the host country would surely monitor this on its own and, if such incriminating evidence had leaked to the surface, find some way to delay or refuse the inspection.

The unlikelihood of finding incriminating evidence on the surface means that the inspecting states must retain the option of drilling beneath the surface, since such drilling "remains the only way to get incontrovertible evidence of a fully contained nuclear explosion".[141] But a decision to drill for evidence would involve a far more substantial commitment of equipment and personnel as well as an extension of the inspection period by four to six months, according to one estimate.[142]

Some idea of the magnitude of the drilling operation can be obtained by comparing the size of the area to be searched with the size of the cavity created by a nuclear explosion. The size of the area to be searched depends on the precision with which remote seismographs can locate the epicentre of the event. The size of this area has decreased as the quality and quantity of seismographic data have increased. In 1963 the assumed area to be searched was of the order of 500 km^2,[143] and in 1971 it was 250 km^2.[144] A more recent estimate claims an accuracy in position of 10–25 km using a network of stations and selecting those which produce high-quality seismic data.[145] This suggests a minimum area of uncertainty of roughly 100 km^2, although a recent Swedish proposal contemplates searches over areas 10 times as large.[146]

A 5 kt nuclear explosion, certainly the largest that might be mistaken for an earthquake if detonated without special provisions to disguise it (see below), would be set off at a depth of at least 200 m and would create a cavity with a diameter of 30–40 m in granite.[147] However, the cracking of rocks and other effects might spread out to 20 times this distance, that is, a diameter of 700 m.[148] The collapse of rock into the cavity would create a 'chimney' with a height 4–6 times the cavity radius, roughly 80 m.[149] This would put the top of the chimney more than 100 m beneath the surface, thereby preventing to a high level of confidence both the formation of a subsidence crater and leakage of radioactivity to the surface. If it is assumed that drilling anywhere into the full 700 m diameter of the fractured region will produce the necessary evidence of a violation, then the area in which a successful drilling must be localized is roughly 0.4 km^2. The most optimistic estimate for the area in which test drillings must be made is 100 km^2. Therefore the probability that a single drilling will find the evidence is at best 1 in 250, probably considerably less. So 125 holes would have to be drilled to be 50 per cent certain that no test had occurred, and 225 holes to be 90 per cent certain. If the project is to take only 4–6 months then this means that at least one hole per day would have to be drilled to a depth of 100–200 m.

This simple calculation should not be taken too seriously. It probably underestimates the area which would have to be covered by an inspection, but overestimates the density of holes that would have to be drilled. The explosion would create an extended period of aftershocks, so it might be possible to establish the existence and location of the cavity by sensitive seismic monitoring. The inspection team might also employ active local seismic methods such as those used to locate oil deposits or other distinctive subterranean features.

However, depending on the area of uncertainty, these could still involve considerable drilling and the use of underground explosions.

In any event, the size and expense of such an operation would be substantial, to say the least. Ambassador Averell Harriman, who represented the USA in negotiations of the Partial Test Ban Treaty in 1963, was deeply impressed by the technical demands of such an inspection effort. As he testified in 1973:

> At the same time some of our experts thought three inspections would be adequate because it would give us a spot check which would make the Soviets unwilling to run the risk of detection... But then when I saw the details of what our experts would demand in the way of the kind of inspection..., the large area over which we would have helicopters range, and the number of holes we would have to drill, and that sort of thing ... I am satisfied they would never have agreed to it... The Russians accepted onsite inspection as a principle, but I am satisfied we would never have come to an agreement on what was really needed in the way of onsite inspection.[150]

Not only would these inspections have constituted a vast intrusion on Soviet territory, demanding substantial Soviet co-operation in transport, labour and logistical support, but they would almost certainly have had to take place in Soviet Central Asia where earthquakes are frequent. But this area of high seismicity happens to coincide with one of the most sensitive military-strategic areas in the Soviet Union.[151] How such inspections might be managed without the Soviet Union risking the disclosure of collateral information was apparently not thoroughly analysed.

The point of this argument is not to determine whether the Soviet Union or any other state would ever permit such a massive intrusion on its territory by foreigners, but whether, even if it were permitted, it makes any sense. There is ample reason to conclude that it does not. One professional assessment of on-site inspection concluded that "visual inspection and radiochemical analysis are the only useful techniques" and that "sufficiently deep burial will preclude surface effects and seepage of radioactive gas to the surface".[152] Another study employing analytical decision theory and published data on nuclear explosions concluded that the use of the $m_b : M_s$ discriminant based on seismic network data (see chapter 2) was more reliable in deterring violations than a scheme involving one or more on-site inspections per year.[153] Advances in seismic technology since 1970, when this assessment was made, have undoubtedly added strength to this conclusion. Even better identification capabilities could be obtained with seismic stations, manned or unmanned, deployed at selected locations in the states to be monitored. The Soviet Union agreed to the use of such stations on its territory at an early stage of the test ban negotiations.[154]

A number of techniques have been suggested for disguising or hiding nuclear tests from a seismic network.[155] These include exploding the device in a large cavity in order to reduce the intensity of the seismic wave produced (decoupling), hiding the explosion in the seismic background created by a natural earthquake, or setting off multiple explosions in such a way as to simulate the seismic-wave pattern of an earthquake. Whatever the potential utility of such schemes may be, and careful analysis indicates that it is likely to be very small, on-site inspection has very little to do with deterring or detecting them. The first two evasion techniques are designed to prevent detection of the event, and it is only when an event is detected but not unambiguously identified that on-site inspection would be called for. The third technique, simulating an earthquake, is assumed to be detectable but not properly identifiable. But there is no experimental evidence that such a simulation can be conducted,[156] and seismological theory is far too uncertain to give any potential violator the confidence that such a trial could fool a sophisticated seismic network, not to mention the satellite observations that could detect the preparations for the test.

This analysis raises very serious doubts about the "unquestionably substantial potential role" for on-site inspection in monitoring a CTB (see above).[157] In fact the utility of on-site inspection in such a treaty is highly questionable on both political and technical grounds. For most professional seismologists "it is difficult to see why on-site inspection, in the way it has been proposed, is regarded as a necessary verification method to achieve an adequate verification of a CTB".[158]

Conclusion

It is important to keep in mind that this critique of on-site inspections is directed to non-routine, challenge inspections, not to routine on-site monitoring (either by people or instruments) of declared facilities, or to *ad hoc* inspections at the invitation of an offended party as, for example, when Iran invited an international expert group to verify its charges that Iraq had used chemical weapons. Such inspections have also been agreed to as part of the Environmental Modification Treaty.[159] It is only the concept of demand on-site inspections which appears to pose insurmountable obstacles, at least as long as the world continues to be made up of sovereign states.

VI. Internationalizing verification

Introduction

The strong focus in this book on unilateral and bilateral verification mechanisms reflects the historical and political realities of their evolution. Nevertheless, table 1 (pp. 4–5) lists a number of multinational or international treaties which contain significant verification provisions, and it is noted in chapter 3 that many states have made serious efforts to promote a more international approach to verification.

It is therefore important to examine both the existing and proposed international verification mechanisms to assess both their virtues and limitations. In keeping with the theme of this chapter the assessment deals with both technical and political factors as well as with their interaction. Also in keeping with the more general theoretical approach of this book there is no attempt to examine the many treaties and verification provisions in detail. Instead the aim is to identify the major problems and trends with a view towards anticipating how well future efforts at internationalizing verification are likely to succeed.

It is possible to identify three major trends, or what might be called 'traditions', in the development of international verification measures. One such tradition can be seen originating in the Antarctic Treaty of 1959 and progressing through the Outer Space Treaty of 1967, the Sea-Bed Treaty of 1971, the Biological Weapons Convention of 1972 and the Environmental Modification Treaty of 1977. Current negotiations in the Geneva Conference on Disarmament towards a chemical weapons treaty can be identified as an outcome and potential propagator of this tradition. A second tradition began with the earliest attempts to control the spread of nuclear explosive technology by monitoring the testing of nuclear weapons and the inventories of nuclear explosive materials in the non-military nuclear fuel cycle. The third tradition has been focused on the regional security problems of Europe and has proceeded along the parallel tracks of the Mutual Force Reduction negotiations in Vienna and the so-called Helsinki Process which involves continuing negotiations on security- and confidence-building measures in Europe. These three traditions are analysed separately for the particular verification problems they present as well as for the contributions they have made to the evolution of international verification techniques and institutions. In reading the following analyses the reader may find it helpful to refer to table 1.

The chemical–biological–environmental tradition

The characteristic that most distinguishes this tradition from the others is the relatively low military significance of the regions and weapons controlled and the relatively low priority placed on verification in their implementation. At the same time it is also possible to see a gradual increase in the military significance of the agreements over time, and a correspondingly slow increase in the extent and effectiveness of verification arrangements. The progression in both military significance and the need for effective verification are quite evident when one compares the problem of chemical weapons control to the problem of preventing military activities in Antarctica, a region few if any have ever believed to be of military significance to anyone.

In one sense the Antarctic Treaty achieves the ideal verification system.[160]

All parties to the treaty are entitled to appoint observers who will have free access to all areas, installations, ships, aircraft, and so on in Antarctica as well as the right to inspect them without interference (article VII). These observers also remain under the control and protection of their national governments at all times and places in Antarctica (article VIII). A similar openness characterizes the Outer Space Treaty[161] which requires that: "All stations, installations, equipment and space vehicles on the moon and other celestial bodies shall be open to representatives of other States Parties to the Treaty on a basis of reciprocity" (article XII).

The political equality implied by these provisions is, of course, illusory because of the vast technological and economic inequalities among the parties to the treaties. That the United States and Mauritius (both parties to the Outer Space Treaty) should agree to open their installations on the Moon to each other on the basis of reciprocity unfortunately lends itself more to mocking equality than to enhancing it, as well as to providing evidence in support of the proposition that agreement on verification is always easiest to achieve when it is most irrelevant. Further evidence for the proposition can be found in the failure of the Treaty to mention bodies in Earth orbit under the reciprocal inspection provision. The military significance of objects in Earth orbit is well established, so the concept of open inspection is considerably less attractive to states who control such satellites. This has the effect of making the major provision of the Treaty—that nuclear weapons are prohibited from being placed in orbit (article IV)—essentially unverifiable.

Compared to this situation, the Sea-Bed Treaty, which was signed four years later, represents measurable progress[162]. This treaty not only gives the right to each party to observe on its own the activities of other states on the ocean floor but provides for consultations and co-operation among parties in the verification process as well as "through appropriate international procedures within the framework of the United Nations and in accordance with its Charter" (article III, paragraph 5). This last clause is significant in that it represents the seed from which the concept of international consultative committees has grown.[163] So, while the Sea-Bed Treaty differed little from the Antarctic or Outer Space Treaties in its military significance or practical contribution to international equality (see chapter 3, pp. 137–38), it at least represented a small evolutionary step towards a more effective international approach to verification.

The convention on biological and toxin weapons was signed in 1972 and entered into force in 1975.[164] It contains a vague and ineffectual verification clause (article V) which includes the right to "consult one another" if problems arise and also includes the "appropriate international procedures within the framework of the United Nations" clause of the Sea-Bed Treaty. These procedures are not further defined except to specify that any state which finds another state guilty of a violation can lodge a complaint with the UN Security Council (article VI). However, the language implies that the state bringing the complaint must have sufficient evidence to demonstrate guilt; it does not provide for an independant investigation on the basis of suggestive evidence to determine if a violation has in fact occurred.

This weakness in the Biological Weapons Convention has led to serious problems in connection with allegations of violations, both in the case of the so-called 'yellow rain' incidents in Indo-China and an outbreak of anthrax near the city of Sverdlovsk in the Ural Mountains of the Soviet Union.[165] Both of these incidents are highly controversial, and in neither case is the evidence of violation at all convincing. Yet in both cases it is clear that if an 'appropriate international procedure' had existed to gather and evaluate evidence and receive relevant data and testimony from the concerned parties, a more satisfactory resolution of the problem would have been obtained. As it happened, an investigation of the 'yellow rain' incidents was ordered by the UN Secretary General after an intense debate in 1980, but the expert group was not able to make its first interviews of witnesses before October 1981 and never was allowed to visit the sites of the alleged attacks.[166] Their report was, not surprisingly, inconclusive.[167]

Despite this result the appointment of a commission of experts to investigate charges of misconduct was an important precedent. Based on this precedent the Secretary General was able to respond promptly to a request by Iran in 1984 to investigate the alleged use of chemical weapons by Iraq in the war between the two states. A committee of experts on chemical weapons was appointed and allowed by Iranian authorities to visit the sites of the alleged attacks and take necessary samples and data. The result of this investigation was far more conclusive, stating unequivocally that chemical weapons had been used and identifying two distinct types. The expert commission could not identify the state which had carried out the attacks.[168]

Seven years before this successful use of a "consultative committee of experts", a provision for just such a body was included in another international arms control treaty, the Environmental Modification (Enmod) Convention.[169] In article 5 of the Enmod Convention the phrase "appropriate international procedures" is amplified by suggestion of the use of "appropriate international organizations" as well as a Consultative Committee of Experts to be appointed at the request of any party by the Secretary General within one month of the request.

The responsibilities and rules of procedure for the Consultative Committee are spelled out in an annex to the Treaty. Members are required to confine themselves to making appropriate "findings of fact" and to provide "expert views" relevant to the problem under investigation. The full committee is permitted to decide procedural questions but not "matters of substance".

These restrictions are clearly intended to ensure that the Consultative Committee confines its work to the gathering and analysis of data and stops short of making judgements about the guilt or innocence of various states or even the degree of seriousness of the violation.[170] Similar restraint is evident in the report of the committee investigating the charges of chemical weapon use against Iraq (see above). This attempt to separate the analytical and evaluative functions is quite similar to that made by many national intelligence agencies and is seen as the best way to maintain a high level of confidence in the objectivity and integrity of the committee (see chapter 3, pp. 154–56). It would be all too easy for the work of such a committee of experts to be undermined by disputes over "matters of substance", that is, those questions which require political judgement.

The consultative committee envisaged in the Enmod Convention is an *ad hoc* committee appointed only when there is reason to believe that a violation has occurred. There have been suggestions that the committee be made a permanent one charged with handling routine exchanges of information on research and development in environmental modification techniques as well as monitoring the many applications of these techniques. However, considering the marginal significance of the Enmod Convention it does not seem worth the political and administrative effort required to create such a permanent committee.[171]

In contrast, a treaty banning chemical weapons would certainly require not only a permanent consultative committee, but a large, well equipped and highly diversified one as well. The need for such a commission in a chemical weapons treaty has been recognized for many years by both the USA and the USSR,[172] and recent versions of such a treaty retain and amplify the concept of a consultative committee as well as provide for a wide variety of other co-operative measures, such as exchanges of information and a carefully worded procedure to be followed when demanding an on-site inspection.[173]

The emergence of the concept of a consultative committee has a complex history, but certainly one of the major stimuli for its promotion came from the apparent success of the Standing Consultative Commission created by the US–Soviet SALT I agreement. In fact, the first proposal for such a committee, in a speech by the Netherlands representative in the CCD (the predecessor of the CD) in 1975, referred to the SALT SCC explicitly.[174] This serves as one more example of the important impact the SCC concept has had on arms control.

International monitoring

Nuclear test bans

The second major tradition in international arms control is the sequence of treaties controlling the testing and proliferation of nuclear weapons. In this tradition there are no analogues to Antarctica, Outer Space and the Sea-Bed on which to conclude marginal treaties, and consequently verification has been a prominent and constant concern from the beginning. This tradition has evolved from the earliest effort to control the spread of nuclear weapons, and the preoccupation of Western states with effective verification can be seen clearly in the original proposals for international control of atomic energy presented to the United Nations in 1946 by Bernard Baruch.[175]

This tradition also shows an evolution of co-operative measures, but these emphasize on-site inspection instead of consultative committees. Here it is also possible to see progress as testing limits have progressed from the Partial Test Ban Treaty (PTBT) of 1963, through the Threshold Test Ban and Peaceful Nuclear Explosion Treaties of 1974 and 1976 respectively, to current negotiations for a comprehensive test ban treaty. The concept of on-site inspection was incorporated from the beginning in the 1967 treaty prohibiting nuclear weapons in Latin America (Treaty of Tlatelolco) and the Non-Proliferation Treaty of 1968.

The Partial Test Ban Treaty banning nuclear explosions in the atmosphere, in outer space and under water was first agreed to by three of the four nuclear weapon states—the USA, the UK and the USSR.[176] France did not join the Treaty, and in 1964 China indicated its attitude towards the Treaty by conducting its first nuclear explosion in the atmosphere, where it has conducted the great majority of its nuclear tests ever since.[177] France stopped testing in the atmosphere in 1975 but has still never signed the PTBT.[178] However, a great many other states have signed it, and the PTBT ranks second only to the Non-Proliferation Treaty in its number of signatories (112 as against 124 on 31 December 1984).[179]

There is no explicit verification provision in the PTBT, but it was implicit that national technical means were to be used by the parties. These means included satellites and various ground-, air-, space- and sea-based radiation monitors for detecting fall-out (see chapter 2), and since the vast majority of the parties to the PTBT do not possess such means, the lack of verifiability is for them a genuine limitation. Most states who have reason to fear the possible development of nuclear weapons by a rival have no or only very limited independent means of detecting a nuclear test in that state and must therefore depend for such crucial information on those states who do possess these technologies. This problem was highlighted when the Soviet Union and the United States detected and monitored apparent preparations for an underground nuclear test by South Africa in 1977[180] and ambiguous flashes of light somewhere over the South Atlantic in 1979 and 1980.[181] States such as Angola, Zimbabwe or Mozambique, which presumably would have the most reason to be concerned about such a test, had no means to detect these activities on their own.

The alleged South African tests are particularly relevant to the issue of internationalizing the verification process. The data suggesting an atmospheric nuclear explosion were picked up by a US Vela satellite (see chapter 2) and have been kept secret. At least two analyses were carried out by panels of US experts, one convened by the President's Science Advisor, concluding that the satellite "probably did not see a nuclear explosion".[182] Another group at the US Naval Research Laboratory concluded that "there was a 'nuclear event' on 22 September near Prince Edward Island, South Africa or Antarctica".[183] The dispute over the proper interpretation of the data divided US scientific and intelligence analysts into 'believers' and 'non-believers' and was characterized by charges of "a political motive to ignore uncomfortable facts".[184]

Who is correct in this controversy is not as important for the present discussion as the total inability of other states to make an independent analysis of the data. If suspicions of political motivation could surface within the US intelligence community, then it would not be surprising to find such suspicions in states whose relationship to South Africa is less secure than that of the United States. If the data had been recorded by an internationally controlled satellite and made available to all interested states, then independent analyses would have been possible, and any state would have been free to draw its own conclusions based on the best available data. As it is there is no way to dispel the residual suspicion of political manipulation by the USA even if such suspicion is unwarranted.

The Threshold Test Ban Treaty[185] and the Peaceful Nuclear Explosion Treaty[186] are both bilateral treaties, and their contribution to increased acceptance of co-operative measures by the two leading nuclear weapon states is discussed above. Here it is necessary to emphasize two important reservations concerning the significance of this apparent progress for internationalization. First, the USA has not yet ratified either Treaty and the prospects for ratification do not look bright. This indicates that strong reservations persist in the USA against accepting these arrangements even in a bilateral context. Second, even if the USA did ratify the Treaties, the acceptance of these co-operative measures on a bilateral basis would not necessarily imply a willingness to accept them on an international basis. The need for equal treatment and reciprocity in any such international treaty would qualitatively alter the administrative, technical and political issues which would have to be dealt with, and the process of resolving these issues could take many years and prove to be unwarranted by the benefits to be gained from internationalizing either Treaty, especially since this effort would distract the international community from working towards a comprehensive test ban which would make both the TTBT and PNET unnecessary.[187]

The effort to achieve an international CTB is certainly worthwhile, and here there are considerable grounds for optimism that solutions to its verification problems are well within reach, both technically and politically. An ongoing research programme led by the Swedish delegation to the CD has demonstrated the feasibility of an international seismic network and data exchange system which would allow all states to have access to seismic data on an equal basis.[188] Further experimentation is necessary to improve the capabilities of the system and the quality of the data which can be transmitted, but there appear to be no insoluble technical problems. The real obstacles that still remain in the path of a CTB are political and have little or nothing to do with verification.

Safeguards

Closely connected with the efforts to ban nuclear tests have been the efforts to prevent the horizontal proliferation of nuclear weapons. Here the effort is by its very nature international, although bilateral agreements between nuclear technology suppliers and recipients also play an important role. [189] The treaties which make up this tradition are (in addition to the PTBT of 1963) the Treaty of Tlatelolco (1967) prohibiting nuclear weapons in Latin America, [190] the Non-Proliferation Treaty of 1968, [191] and the Convention on the Physical Protection of Nuclear Materials adopted in 1980 but not yet entered into force. [192]

Verification of all these agreements is carried out under the Safeguards Programme of the International Atomic Energy Agency (see chapter 2, section IX). At present there are 76 non-nuclear weapon states who have safeguards agreements with the IAEA, [193] and which have therefore agreed to submit their nuclear facilities to inspection by international inspectors. The IAEA safeguards operation in 1984 involved 434 personnel and a budget of almost $34 million, 35 per cent of the total budget of the Agency. [194] While it is easy to criticize the IAEA safeguards programme for its many gaps and weaknesses, and some such criticisms are made below, it is important to keep in mind that this programme represents an unprecedented and remarkable achievement in international arms control, whose benefits considerably outweigh its shortcomings. In its annual report for 1983 the Agency was able to state, as it has in all previous years, that it "did not detect any anomaly which would indicate the diversion of a significant amount of safeguarded nuclear material—or the misuse of facilities or equipment subject to safeguards". [195]

As it stands this record demonstrates the accumulation of much evidence of compliance with the NPT and other non-proliferation agreements. Unfortunately, this record cannot be used to demonstrate conclusively the effectiveness of safeguards. In the words of an IAEA official: "Paradoxically, effective safeguards contribute to the difficulty of measuring safeguards effectiveness by the most simple indicator, namely the percentage of diversion acts or related events during a given period". [196] This paradox is always associated with the attempt to evaluate measures designed to prevent inherently improbable but potentially dangerous events. For example, it shows up clearly in the concern over the safety of nuclear power plants, where those who are favourably disposed towards nuclear power can point to the complete absence of catastrophic meltdown accidents as powerful evidence for the safety of such plants, while those opposed to nuclear energy can argue that it is precisely the absence of such events which makes it impossible to say how safe reactors really are, and that the potential consequences of a catastrophic accident are too serious to permit the operation of power plants with such ignorance of the risks.

If nuclear power plants melted down at measurable rates the risks could be adequately assessed, as they can be, for example, for car or aircraft accidents. But such a frequency of nuclear accidents would obviously make nuclear power plants socially and economically unacceptable and they would not be built. Similarly, if a safeguards system routinely turned up some low frequency of diversions for weapons or for purposes unknown, the system would be politically insupportable and effectively useless. According to one perhaps excessively pessimistic IAEA official: "Even the diversion of 100 grams of plutonium could result in political disaster because of hysterical reactions from a misinformed public".[197] Although this may overstate the argument somewhat it remains true that the survival of the safeguards system depends critically on its extremely low probability of turning up violations.

This inherent fragility of the safeguards system would be problem enough if safeguards were applied uniformly to all states. Unfortunately this is not the case, and there are at least 14 nuclear facilities in five states which are not subject to safeguards under any agreements,[198] and four of these states (India, Pakistan, South Africa and Israel) have either demonstrated a capability to build nuclear weapons or are generally believed to have or to be within reach of such a capability.

There is nothing the IAEA or its safeguards system can do about this. The IAEA "is not an international police agency. It cannot protect nuclear materials and facilities against misuse. Its safeguards cannot control the future policies of states, but only verify present activities. The Agency cannot physically prevent anything, but only report diversions".[199] These limitations derive from historical and political factors which are important to understand in order to appreciate the obstacles which would have to be overcome before the safeguards system could be significantly extended or before a similar system could be applied in other contexts, for example to a complete ban on the production of nuclear explosives or to a chemical weapons treaty.

To extend the IAEA safeguards programme to cover a ban on production of plutonium or highly enriched uranium for weapons, the following changes would have to be made:

1. The current requirement of safeguards only for non-nuclear weapon states would have to be extended to include *all* states.

2. The current application of safeguards only to commercial facilities would have to be extended to military facilities as well.

3. The current emphasis on material accounting techniques would have to be shifted to a much greater dependence on more sophisticated containment and surveillance techniques.

All of these changes are quite feasible in principle, but they would represent a major change in the operation of the Agency. Making such changes in an international regime involving dozens of states is extremely difficult. For example, any substantive changes in safeguards requirements for one or a few states would require that the changes be applied equally to *all* states. One estimate suggests this would require the renegotiation of some 50 NPT safeguards agreements concluded since 1970,[200] a bureaucratically and diplomatically long and tedious process.

Extension of the safeguards system to a chemical weapons treaty raises even more difficult problems. If it were only a matter of monitoring the flows and inventories of certain well defined and highly specialized chemical agents and precursors at declared facilities, then the problem would probably be manageable. All countries engaged in the production of lethal substances have a strong interest in keeping good inventory records, and an international monitoring agency could use these national records in much the same way as the IAEA uses national accounts of nuclear materials.[201] Depending on how many chemical substances and facilities were monitored such a scheme could involve a great many inspectors and heavy demands for information storage and processing. But technically it should be manageable.

The politics of the situation is another matter, and here it is important to look at the particular political factors associated with nuclear energy that made the IAEA possible in the first place. Historically the IAEA and its safeguards system grew out of the US Atoms for Peace programme, first proposed by President Eisenhower in 1953.[202] The purpose of this programme was to promote the international development of atomic energy for peaceful purposes, and a simultaneous application of safeguards was seen as necessary to prevent the diversion of nuclear technology and materials for military purposes. The USA was able to enforce a system of safeguards because it had control of a technology that other states wanted and were willing to make some political sacrifices to obtain. For example, the Euratom Treaty of 1957 was designed to "constitute a framework for obtaining technological support from the United States"[203] and "to assure the United States that the nuclear materials it supplies are not being diverted to military use".[204]

This same principle, under which the controllers of nuclear technology agree to supply it to others in return for guarantees that it will not be misused, is embodied in the NPT, which promises all states in return for their signature on the Treaty "the fullest possible exchange of equipment, materials and scientific and technological information for the peaceful uses of nuclear energy".[205]

The creation of a safeguards system was possible because it seemed at the time a relatively small price for states to pay in order to gain access to US nuclear technology. The original emphasis of Atoms for Peace was on *development*, with control clearly subordinate. This gave the Agency time to create a safeguards system slowly and relatively free from outside criticism. By the time the NPT was signed in 1968 a certain amount of experience and credibility had been achieved for the safeguards system, and it could be chosen as the primary instrument for verifying the NPT.

This description of the historical process of adoption of safeguards makes clear the differences between the problems of control of nuclear materials and facilities and of chemical or biological materials and facilities. There is no centralized supplier for these latter technologies which can demand controls in return for information or equipment. The knowledge and raw materials for producing chemical or biological weapons are widely spread throughout the world, and the technological/industrial base required to make them already exists in the great majority of states. Indeed, many fear that current trends in the spread of knowledge and technical capability in the *nuclear* field may eventually overwhelm and destroy the effectiveness of the existing safeguards system.[206]

Simply stated, if safeguarding nuclear energy against the proliferation of nuclear weapons had been the only task of the new IAEA in 1957, it is unlikely that the Agency would have been created. Similarly, if preventing the spread of nuclear weapons to new states had been the only purpose of the NPT in 1968 it is unlikely that the Treaty would have been agreed to. This historical lesson must be kept in mind in thinking about institutional arrangements for verifying a chemical or biological weapons treaty.

The political lessons to be learned from the safeguards system relate to the degree to which states are willing to yield on matters of national sovereignty, even when they perceive they have much to gain from such concessions. On its face the acceptance by non-nuclear weapon states of on-site inspections of their nuclear industry represents a significant sacrifice of national sovereignty, especially when one reads the IAEA Statutes which authorize the agency "To send into the territory of the recipient State or States inspectors . . . who shall have access at all times to all places and data and to any person who by reason of his occupation deals with materials, equipment or facilities which are required by this Statute to be safeguarded".[207]

The reality, however, is far from the ideal envisaged in this statute. In fact, any investigations beyond routine inspections can only proceed with the permission of the state to be investigated, and any refusal to accept an investigation can be dealt with only by arbitration, which may be quite lengthy, or sanctions, which involve at most a report of the state's unwillingness to cooperate and suspension of the state from membership in the Agency and of any assistance the state may be receiving. Other limitations allow states to invoke "unusual circumstances" to limit access of inspectors and to complain if inspections are "being deployed with undue concentration on particular facilities". Another provision allows states to refuse to accept particular inspectors for whatever reasons they choose.[208]

These restrictions are often frustrating, and one former IAEA inspector has expressed his frustration as follows: "The difficult part of the job is that you must prepare yourself mentally to ignore the many signs that may indicate the presence of clandestine activities going on in the facility adjacent to the reactor, facilities that you were not permitted to inspect".[209]

At the same time it must be noted that the restrictions on IAEA inspections are not static, and improvement is possible. For example, it was assumed for many years that the operators of gas centrifuge enrichment facilities would not permit inspectors to enter the 'cascade' area, that is, the hall where the centrifuges are located.[210] This restriction derived from the desire on the part of the plant operators to protect industrial secrets, but it seriously undermined the credibility of the safeguards system at centrifuge facilities because of the possiblity of modifying the cascade to produce highly enriched uranium without the inspectors' knowledge. Fortunately, there has been some progress in solving this problem, and those NPT states that have centrifuge facilities are showing a greater willingness to consider inspections of the cascade halls.[211] Such progress is important in helping to sustain and improve the credibility of the safeguards system, but much more needs to be done to lift the many restrictions which now prevent inspectors and containment/surveillance devices from applying the most effective possible safeguards to nuclear facilities.

The lesson to be drawn from the safeguards experience is clear: even the most comprehensive and intrusive on-site inspection system yet devised has not succeeded in infringing in any significant manner on the traditional sovereign rights of states.[212] That such infringements are also unlikely in the future can be seen, for example, in the 'first basic principle' of the Soviet approach to verification (see chapter 3, p. 140) which rejects any form of verification that would "prejudice the sovereign rights of states or permit interference in their internal affairs". Any future international verification system will have to do the best it can within the limits established by this principle, which history has shown is not held solely by the Soviet Union.

Satellite monitoring

The previous argument does not prove that progress towards effective international verification of arms control is impossible, only that it will be slow and will depend strongly on the difficult process of relaxing jealously defended concepts of national sovereignty. But these concepts do evolve, and one significant evolutionary change has already been described earlier in this chapter: the acceptance of the legitimacy of satellite reconnaissance as a national technical means of verification. The question immediately arises: if this activity is acceptable as a *national* technical means, why not as an *international* technical means?

Just such a question has been posed by the French proposal at the 1978 UN Special Session on Disarmament to create an International Satellite Monitoring Agency (ISMA).[213] The French proposal noted the international significance of recent and potential technological progress in this field and proposed that "within the framework of current disarmament efforts, this new monitoring method should be placed at the service of the international community".[214] Such an agency could offer its services to any group of states who needed it to monitor arms control or non-aggression agreements, much in the way that the IAEA offers to implement safeguards agreements between nuclear suppliers and purchasers.[215]

A study of the ISMA concept was commissioned by the UN Secretary General, and a report was published in 1983. Its essential conclusions were:

1. An ISMA is technically feasible and could be built up in stages to include image processing, data transmission and satellite facilities.

2. Nothing in existing international law would prohibit an international agency from carrying out monitoring activities from satellites.

3. The costs, while uncertain and certainly greater than any previous international/technical undertaking, would still be less than one per cent of total annual expenditures on armaments.[216]

As might be anticipated, both US and Soviet reactions to this proposal have been negative. The objections were very similar, both noting that arms control or disarmament agreements must deal with individual weapons and conditions and that the verification measures emphasized must be tailored to fit the special needs of each treaty. Therefore, according to the Soviet representative, "the formation of any supervision and monitoring organs not connected with the implementation of various practical disarmament measures would simply create the appearance of doing something in this sphere".[217] To the US representative, "An agency created to verify arms-control agreements not yet in existence would be premature ... It would be a mistake to create costly capabilities which could prove ill-suited to their tasks".[218] It is ironic that these comments should come from the two states who have deployed vast numbers of nuclear weapons, weapons which "simply create the appearance of doing something" in the military sphere and which have proven singularly "ill-suited to their tasks".

These objections can be characterized as political, arising from a reluctance on the part of the two leading space powers to relinquish any of their dominance in this field. But even if these arguments are discounted there remain serious problems with the concept of an ISMA which must be addressed before much progress can be expected. Many of these problems arise from the fact that the technology required to operate such an agency is highly sophisticated and expensive and requires many skilled and dedicated personnel. This, coupled with the knowledge that the effort to create such an agency can expect little or no help from the two states with the greatest technical and financial resources in this area, means that any ISMA will have to begin on the initiative and resources of smaller, less technically competent states and will have to overcome the wide variations in technical and financial capabilities in the international community. The IAEA safeguards system gives evidence that these difficulties can be overcome to some extent, but the safeguards system has enjoyed the full support of the superpowers and still suffers from serious difficulties in recruiting qualified personnel from the developing states.[219]

Another problem in creating a fully international satellite monitoring agency would be the absence of any existing international institutional and scientific base on which it could be constructed. This can be contrasted, for example, with the concept of an international seismic monitoring agency which is greatly aided by the long history of international co-operation among seismologists. Such co-operation was from the beginning inherent in the nature of the field in which they did their research.

There is no comparable international scientific community for satellite monitoring. In fact, the institutional base for satellite monitoring has evolved from the field of military intelligence, probably the least international field one can imagine. While one can easily envisage co-operation within the international community of astronomers in looking *away* from the Earth, it is much more difficult to imagine co-operation among intelligence agencies in looking *towards* the Earth. Decades of accumulated bureaucratic habits of secrecy would need to be overcome to make such collaboration possible.

While these problems argue persuasively against any early creation of an ISMA, it has been argued that some activity can at least be started in the form of *regional* satellite monitoring agencies, and here the prospects seem somewhat more promising.[220] The argument here is that some infrastructure for co-operation in space already exists in Europe in the form of the European Space Agency in the West and the Intercosmos Council in the East. There is also the historical precedent of Soviet–French co-operation in space. Of course, any such agency which included Soviet or Warsaw Treaty Organization participation would have to overcome the political objections of the Eastern bloc noted above. These objections have not noticeably softened since 1979, and the WTO states voted as a bloc against a UN General Assembly resolution in 1982 to request a further report on practical measures to implement an ISMA.[221]

A possibly more hopeful development is the embryonic French–West German collaboration on a photographic reconnaissance satellite.[222] Discussions of such a project have already taken place between high-level officials of France and FR Germany, and French research and development on the imaging system is at a relatively advanced stage.

A collaboration on such a militarily sensitive venture between two states whose histories have been marked by frequent wars and deep distrust would be a highly significant step in establishing the credibility of international co-operation in verification. Its success would very likely attract other West European states into participation and thereby ease the considerable financial burden such a system would impose on its members. Even more interesting is the possibility that the potential success of such a project leading to a diffusion of political control over satellite monitoring data may cause the USA and USSR to reconsider their opposition and attempt to retain their influence on developments in this area by collaborating with the project rather than ignoring or opposing it. [223] There is a historical precedent for this kind of behaviour in the Atoms for Peace programme (see above, p. 232) in which the United States recognized the failure of its attempt to prevent nuclear weapon proliferation by a policy of secrecy and chose instead to attempt to control proliferation by offering collaboration in nuclear energy development. Whether or not the Soviet Union could be drawn into such a collaboration is an entirely different question, but the overall point seems clear: if an international collaboration in satellite monitoring is to be created, the first steps in demonstrating its feasibility and credibility will have to be taken at the initiative and at the expense of non-superpower states. Such a demonstration will be difficult and expensive but it could serve a historically important function if it succeeded in opening up to some degree the field of satellite reconnaissance to participation by a greater number of states.

If such a multinational space reconnaissance effort is to succeed the problems of data dissemination and secrecy will have to be confronted. The problem of data dissemination and interpretation is already controversial in discussions on the feasibility of an ISMA. [224] One dilemma has been summarized as follows:

> The mere dissemination of data, including auxiliary data, without any interpretation by the Agency, would tend to promote confidence in the accuracy and impartiality of the findings, because no human evaluation would be involved. However, the adoption of this format for the ISMA reports would produce unintelligible information for those users who do not possess appropriate technology and skills to do their own interpretation. This method would clearly discriminate in favour of the technologically more advanced states. It therefore seems that an ISMA's role would be to provide a factual report based on the processing and analysis of the data available to it. The Group also recognized that inconclusive or contradictory interpretation could emerge in the course of analysis of data by teams at the Image Processing and Interpretation Centre (IPIC) and was of the view that in such cases it might be necessary to provide the users with more than one analysis together with data used for such analyses. [225]

This problem is familiar from the earlier discussion of the credibility problem for national intelligence and verification agencies, and there are good reasons to believe it would be at least as difficult to solve in an international context.

Another set of contradictory forces are the legitimate requirements of confidentiality and the need for openness and freedom of access to information by all interested parties. In this case the experiences in applying IAEA safeguards and in designing an international seismic information exchange give some hope that a solution can be found. The former system has found ways to confine inspectors to certain well defined areas and tasks, sufficient to carry out their safeguards duties while still protecting commercial and technical secrets. The seismic information network contemplates a very open information exchange, but in this area the collateral information acquired beyond what is needed for verification purposes is neither militarily nor commercially sensitive and would in fact be highly useful for scientific research activities.

While such experiences are encouraging they cannot be extrapolated directly to an ISMA. The collateral information collected by high-resolution satellite photography (and the system would have to have a high-resolution capability to be an effective verification tool) can be extremely sensitive both militarily and commercially. An international staff handling and interpreting such information would have to have a high degree of integrity and protection against the inevitable pressures from unauthorized parties or states to obtain information. Data might be encrypted for transmission,[226] and employee clearance systems might be used to limit access to sensitive material, but the more this is done the more cumbersome and opaque the process of analysis and evaluation becomes. The balance, if and when it is found, will be a delicate one just as it is in any intelligence agency.

Confidence-building measures

The two traditions so far discussed began in very different ways and have evolved different mechanisms for international verification, yet they have begun in recent years to converge as problems of greater military significance, such as banning chemical weapons or underground nuclear weapon tests, have been tackled. Alongside this slow convergence, the even slower evolution of a third tradition has taken place, born in the European context but also potentially applicable in a wider international arena. These are the so-called confidence-building measures (CBMs)—now generally referred to as confidence- and security-building measures (CSBMs)—which first appeared as part of the Final Act of the Conference on Security and Co-operation in Europe (CSCE) signed in Helsinki in 1975.[227] In the same tradition, and closely associated with the CSCE process both historically and politically, are the Mutual Force Reduction negotiations which have been going on in Vienna since 1973.[228] The CSCE process has evolved since 1975 through a review conference in Belgrade in 1978, and another in Madrid, which lasted from 11 November 1980 to 6 September 1983.[229] The latter accomplished little more than to arrange for another Conference on Confidence- and Security-Building Measures and Disarmament in Europe, which began its work in Stockholm in January 1984.[230]

Many of the verification issues already discussed in other contexts have arisen in the course of the MFR talks and there is no need to repeat or amplify what has been said before. Suffice it to say that the parties to the talks have managed to agree on an impressive list of verification provisions which would be included in a future agreement (see table 1, p. 5):

(a) periodic exchanges of data after force reductions;

(b) notification of the beginning and end of reduction steps;

(c) prenotification of large military movements into and out of the reduction zone;

(d) permanent observation posts at the exit and entry points of the reduction zone;

(e) non-interference with national technical means of verification;

(f) the use of on-site inspections; and

(g) establishment of a consultative commission to resolve ambiguities about compliance.[231]

This list of agreed verification provisions, and in particular the agreement in principle to on-site inspections, can be taken as a good measure of the convergence in attitudes of the two major European alliances which have taken place over the years on the issue of verification. Virtually all the crucial elements for an adequate verification regime are present, but, while some have suggested that an agreement is now quite close,[232] others suggest that serious problems still remain and cite verification as the major stumbling block.[233]

The only remaining verification problem which seems at all serious is the amount of on-site inspection which will be acceptable to all parties. The Western side is demanding an annual quota of up to 18 on-site inspections, using both ground and aerial techniques.[234] As usual it is the Eastern side which is most obviously resisting this concept, asking instead for on-site inspections only by invitation in response to challenges by the other side. But it is not only the Warsaw Treaty Organization states who have such reservations. It has been reported that "Some Western countries were already not comfortable with the idea of on-site inspections by the East ... with the more stringent measures, Western agreement on the associated measures was going to be even more difficult".[235] This again illustrates, if any further illustration is necessary, that resistance to on-site inspection is not a uniquely Eastern phenomenon. It also illustrates that, whatever the issue, multilateral negotiations are more difficult than are bilateral ones. In the MFR talks, for example, even if the USA and USSR could agree on an on-site inspection scheme which suited their needs, much political work would remain to be done to convince the central European states, on whose territories and in whose military installations the inspections would take place, that such inspections were in their interests as well.

An even stronger example of the agonizing slowness with which such multilateral negotiations proceed is the CSCE process in which 35 states are participating. The focus of these negotiations has been more political than military, so that verification issues are not prominent. But the process also recognizes that political progress is far more difficult when military threats are made and/or perceived by the negotiating parties. Hence the recognition of the need for confidence-building measures designed to reduce the perception of military threat in Europe and facilitate political accommodation.

After 11 years of work the CSCE process has produced the following set of confidence- and security-building measures: (*a*) prior notification (minimum of 21 days) of military manoeuvres exceeding a total of 25 000 troops; (*b*) exchange of observers at military manoeuvres on a voluntary basis; and (*c*) voluntary prior notifications of smaller manoeuvres and major military movements.[236]

These are, to say the least, modest beginnings towards a reduction of the perception of military threat in Europe, and the experience of the first eight months of the Stockholm Conference, whose mandate is to strengthen and expand these measures, suggested that progress will continue to be slow and modest.[237]

The record of notification of military manoeuvres under the CSCE stands as a good example of the problematic relationship between verification and confidence building. From 1975, when the agreement entered into force, until the end of 1983 there were 130 notifications of 100 manoeuvres involving a total of several million troops.[238] Yet there was one instance of a failure to notify properly: the Soviet Union's 'Zapad-81' manoeuvres, which were allegedly carried out "to improve co-ordination and co-operation between units from different branches" and which took place in the Byelorussian and Baltic military districts and the Baltic Sea.[239]

The prior notification provision of the CSBM document requires not only that the purpose and location of the manoeuvres be included in the notification but also the 'designation' of the manoeuvre (which seems to mean nothing more than its code name) and the number of troops to be involved.[240] The Soviet Union did not provide the latter two pieces of information and was therefore in technical violation of the treaty.[241] When the USA requested the information through diplomatic channels the Soviet Union is reported to have argued that the provision of such information was voluntary and that the CSBM notification measures in the agreement are 'guidelines', not requirements.[242] While it is true that the Helsinki Final Document emphasizes the voluntary nature of these notifications, the word 'guidelines' does not appear in the Document, and the specification of the information to be provided seems quite unambiguous.[243] If the Soviet Union does view these specifications only as guidelines, it is still remarkable that the Zapad-81 manoeuvre was the only one of many in which the guidelines were violated.

The manoeuvres took place between 4 and 12 September 1981 at a time when political developments in Poland were moving in a direction unpalatable to the Soviet Union, and given the location of the manoeuvres it is difficult to escape the suspicion that the Soviet Union was conscious of their potential political impact on Poland and Europe in general. The purpose of the prior notification provision is to remove any possible perception of threat in such manoeuvres, and the failure to notify properly, especially in time of political tension, is a serious matter. The United States government has seen it as serious enough to warrant inclusion of this incident in its list of alleged Soviet violations submitted to the Senate in January 1984.[244]

There is no question that a technical violation did occur, but this is not the place to speculate either on the reasons for its occurrence or its overall political significance. What must be noted here, however, is the unpleasant fact that one such technical violation at a politically sensitive moment can go far towards undermining the confidence built up by the record of compliance in more than 100 other cases. Such is the fragility of any verification effort built on the assumption that heavily armed adversaries can somehow gain a sense of security by being allowed a slightly better look at the forces of the other side. As long as a verification system is constrained to operate under such an assumption its role as a confidence-building mechanism will be deeply problematic.

An international verification agency

The three traditions evaluated here evolved towards different forms of international institution for verification. Monitoring of a comprehensive test ban would require an international seismic network; a chemical weapons ban would require a permanent consultative commission; the NPT already uses the services of the IAEA. To this can be added the suggestions for regional or international satellite monitoring agencies.

In view of this proliferation of verification agencies and of the important role played by interactions or synergisms among them, it is reasonable to ask whether it would not be more equitable, effective and efficient to combine all such international verification responsibilities and place them under the auspices of an international verification agency. There have been a number of proposals for the creation of such an agency,[245] one example being the 'International Disarmament Control Organization' suggested by Alva Myrdal in 1974.[246] If such an organization were to be created, "Its immediate function should be to act as an intermediary, or a clearing house, for providing knowledge about the implementation of disarmament agreements".[247] Other possible functions for the organization might be to collate knowledge from scientific journals, production statistics and other open sources and develop standardized techniques of reporting information and data relevant to verification problems.

In order for the organization to function free of political influence, "It would be important ... to maintain a strict separation of powers: the International Disarmament Control Organization should never itself pronounce verdicts. It should only assemble, collate, coordinate and transmit data."[248] In this respect it would resemble such other successful international collaborations whose purpose is to improve communications and international co-operation in fields such as health (World Health Organization), civil aviation (International Civil Aviation Organization) and telecommunications (International Telecommunications Union) and others.[249]

Yet it must be kept in mind that the data and information such an organization would handle are the most sensitive kind—they relate to the national security of states. It is not realistic to imagine that the process of verification can so clearly be divided into an objective component (i.e., assembly, collation, co-ordination and transmission) and a subjective or political component (i.e., analysis, evaluation and response).

Even the act of assembling information has political content, since not all possible information can be assembled and choices must inevitably be made as to what kinds of information are important and what kinds not important. Imagery data from satellites, for example, are inherently selective—it is impossible to photograph the whole Earth at high resolution at regular intervals—which implies that choices must be made as to where to take pictures and what sort of picture to take. Imagery data from states involved in disputes with other states cannot have the same non-political character as other imagery data.[250]

These criticisms do not invalidate the concept of such an organization, and certainly there are powerful moral and political reasons for exploring the possible benefits to be gained from creating it. But the historical record and the current international political climate provide little basis for optimism that it could be created in the foreseeable future. It may well be that once some multinational verification mechanisms have demonstrated their effectiveness and have created a useful record of experience, an organization like the one described would become feasible. But unless it is accompanied by progress in solving the more fundamental problems of war and militarism—the problems that make verification necessary—it could not hope to be very effective.

Conclusion

While the achievements of international verification measures are considerably less than one might hope for, they are at the same time more positive and useful than perhaps one has the right to expect. The three traditions examined in this chapter have been evolving for many years, and in that time a substantial number of creative and useful innovations have appeared and have remained to develop experience and institutional momentum.

Institutions such as the IAEA safeguards system, the Conference on Disarmament, the International Seismic Data Exchange and a number of standing consultative commissions or expert committees, all represent a level of cooperation and concern unprecedented in history. Experience with these institutions is cumulative, and each has produced innovations which not only improve its own performance but which provide models for adaptation in other arms control contexts. While the centre of gravity of the arms competition still sits squarely between the two great powers, the centre of gravity of pressure for disarmament is substantially displaced into a more international location. It is important that international verification efforts continue to develop and that states other than the USA and the USSR continue to take initiatives and develop creative alternatives to bilateral treaties and national technical means of verification.

Notes and references

1. Treaty between the USA and the USSR on the limitation of anti-ballistic missile systems (ABM Treaty), article XII, in Goldblat, J., *Agreements for Arms Control: A Critical Survey* (Taylor & Francis, London, 1982), p. 198 [a SIPRI book].
2. Article V, Interim agreement between the USA and the USSR on certain measures with respect to the limitation of strategic offensive arms (SALT I Agreement), in Goldblat (note 1), p. 202.
3. Article II, Treaty between the USA and the USSR on the limitation of underground nuclear weapon tests (Threshold Test Ban Treaty), in Goldblat (note 1), p. 211.
4. Article IV, Treaty between the USA and the USSR on underground nuclear explosions for peaceful purposes, in Goldblat (note 1), p. 218.
5. Article XV, Treaty between the USA and the USSR on the limitation of strategic offensive weapons (SALT II Treaty), p. 280.
6. Brown, H., *Report of the Committee on Foreign Relations* (SFRC Report), United States Senate, 19 November 1979 (US Government Printing Office, Washington, DC, 1979), p. 194.
7. Brown (note 6).
8. Steinberg, G.M., *Satellite Reconnaissance: The Role of Informal Bargaining* (Praeger, New York, 1983).
9. Steinberg (note 8), p. 28.
10. Steinberg (note 8), pp. 29-35.
11. Steinberg (note 8), p. 60.
12. *The Implications of Establishing an International Satellite Monitoring Agency,* Department for Disarmament Affairs, United Nations, New York, 1983, p. 52.
13. Steinberg (note 8), p. 64.
14. Ball, D., 'Targeting for strategic deterrence', Adelphi Paper No. 185 (IISS, London, 1983), p. 26.
15. Jasani, B., 'The military use of outer space', in SIPRI, *World Armaments and Disarmament, SIPRI Yearbook 1984* (Taylor & Francis, London, 1984), pp. 352-56.
16. Steinberg (note 8), p. 98.
17. Steinberg (note 8), pp. 40-45.
18. Cohen, S.A., 'The evolution of Soviet views on SALT verification: implications for the future', in Potter, W.C. (ed.), *Verification and SALT: The Challenge of Strategic Deception* (Westview Press, Boulder, CO, 1980), p. 54.
19. Cohen (note 18).
20. Cohen (note 18), p. 72.
21. Zheleznov, R., 'Monitoring arms limitation measures', *International Affairs* (Moscow), July 1982, p. 79.

244 *Verification: how much is enough?*

22. Steinberg (note 8), p. 4.
23. Pike, J., *FAS Public Interest Bulletin*, FAS, Washington, DC, March 1984, pp. 3-9.
24. Pike J., *FAS Public Interest Bulletin*, FAS, Washington, DC, November 1983, pp. 8-12.
25. Bunn, G., 'Legal context of arms control verification', in Tsipis, K., Hafemeister, D. and Janeway, P. (eds), *Arms Control Verification: The Technologies that Make it Possible* (Pergamon, Elmsford, NY, 1985).
26. SALT II Treaty, Second Common Understanding to paragraph 3 of article XV, in Goldblat (note 1), p. 280.
27. *Military Implications of the Treaty on the Limitation of Strategic Offensive Arms and Protocol Thereto (SALT II), Hearings before the Committee on Armed Services* (SASC Hearings), US Senate, 96th Congress, First Session (US Government Printing Office, Washington, DC, 1979), Part 1, p. 228.
28. Ball, D., 'The Rhyolite program', Reference paper No. 86, Strategic and Defence Studies Centre, The Research School of Pacific Studies, Australian National Univerity, Canberra, November 1981, p. 15.
29. White House Office of the Press Secretary, *The President's Report to the Congress on Soviet Non-compliance with Arms Control Agreements*, Press Release, Washington, DC, 23 January 1984.
30. Andrews, W., 'Soviets reportedly are jamming US satellites used as monitors', *Washington Times*, 4 June 1984, p. 3.
31. SALT II Treaty (note 26).
32. Bunn (note 25).
33. Talbot, S., *End Game: The Inside Story of SALT II* (Harper & Row, New York, 1979), p. 201.
34. Ball (note 28), p. 7.
35. Rowney, E., SASC Hearings (note 27), Part 2, p. 686.
36. Seignious, G., *The SALT II Treaty, Hearing Before the Committee on Foreign Relations* (SFRC Hearings), US Senate, 96th Congress, First Session (US Government Printing Office, Washington, DC, 1979), Part 1, p. 267.
37. Talbot (note 33), p. 199.
38. Talbot (note 33), p. 238.
39. Cohen (note 18), pp. 50-51.
40. Ulsamer, E., 'The Soviets test a new ICBM', *Air Force Magazine*, Vol. 67, No. 1, January 1984, p. 17.
41. Brown, H., SASC Hearings (note 27), Part 1, p. 52.
42. Pike, J. and Rich, J., 'Charges of treaty violations: much less than meets the eye', *FAS Public Interest Report* (Washington), Vol. 37, No. 3, March 1984, p. 15.
43. Ulsamer (note 40).
44. Gwertzman, B., 'US may defy '79 arms pact terms', *New York Times*, 30 March 1984, p. A3. As this book was going to press the Reagan Administration announced a decision to extend its compliance with the numerical limits in SALT II by dismantling a Polaris submarine when the new Trident is launched.
45. Kissinger, H., Press Conference, Washington, DC, 9 December 1975, in Labrie, R.P. (ed.), *SALT Handbook: Key Documents and Issues 1972-1979* (American Enterprise Institute for Public Policy Research, Washington, DC, 1979), p. 346.
46. 'Chemical warfare in the Iraq–Iran War', SIPRI Fact Sheet: Chemical Weapons I, SIPRI, Stockholm, May 1984.
47. 'The United States violates its international commitments', News and Views from the USSR, Soviet Embassy Information Department, Washington, DC, 30 January 1984, p. 4.

48. Towle, P., 'The Soviet Union and the Biological Weapons Convention', *Arms Control*, Vol. 3, No. 3, December 1982, p. 36.
49. Sullivan, D.S., 'The legacy of SALT I: Soviet deception and U.S. retreat', *Strategic Review*, Vol. 7, Winter 1979, pp. 33-35.
50. White House Office of the Press Secretary (note 29), p. 5; Soviet Embassy Information Department (note 47), p. 5.
51. Boffey, P.M., 'Evidence is fading as US investigates use of "yellow rain"?' *New York Times*, 15 May 1984, p. 1.
52. Broad, W.J., 'Expanding the underground A-war', *Science*, Vol. 218, No. 4570, 22 October 1982, p. 360.
53. Katz, A.H., *Verification and SALT: The State of the Art and the Art of the State* (Heritage Foundation, Washington, DC, 1979), p. 33.
54. Katz (note 53), p. 37.
55. Nitze, P., 'Assuring strategic stability in an era of detente', *Foreign Affairs*, Vol. 54, No. 2, January 1976, pp. 207-32.
56. 'Antisatellite ban called unsound', *New York Times*, 16 March 1984, p. 8.
57. *The Arms Control Reporter*, M(B)FR Vienna Talks, Institute for Defense and Disarmament Studies, Brookline, MA, March 1984, p. 401.B.59.
58. McClure, J. (Senator), *Congressional Record*, US Senate, 1 February 1984, pp. S647-S652.
59. Garn, J. (Senator), 'The SALT II verification myth', *Strategic Review*, Vol. 7, Summer 1979, pp. 17-18.
60. Sullivan (note 49), p. 27.
61. George, A.L. and Smoke, R., *Deterrence in American Foreign Policy: Theory and Practice* (Columbia University Press, New York, 1974), p. 582.
62. de Rivera, J.H., *The Psychological Dimension of Foreign Policy* (Merrill, Columbus, OH, 1968), pp. 53-57.
63. Harris, W.R., 'A SALT safeguards program: coping with Soviet deception under strategic arms agreements', in Potter (note 18), p. 130.
64. Iklé, F., 'A "Sea Change" in U.S. approach to arms control', *US News and World Report*, 16 April 1984, p. 53.
65. Pike & Rich (note 42), p. 1.
66. de Rivera (note 62), p. 56.
67. de Rivera (note 62), p. 56.
68. de Rivera (note 62), p. 57.
69. de Rivera (note 62), p. 576.
70. de Rivera (note 62), pp. 61-64; Katz, A.H., 'The fabric of verification: the warp and the woof', in Potter (note 18), p. 217; Grümm, H., 'Safeguards verification—its credibility and the diversion hypothesis', *IAEA Bulletin*, Vol. 25, No. 4, December 1983, pp. 27-29.
71. Katz (note 70).
72. Sanders, J.W., *Peddlers of Crisis* (South End Press, Boston, MA, 1983), pp. 197-204.
73. de Rivera (note 62), p. 62.
74. Grümm (note 70).
75. Chayes, A., 'An inquiry into the workings of arms control agreements', *Harvard Law Review*, Vol. 85, No. 5, March 1972, p. 937.
76. Pike & Rich (note 42), pp. 3-9.
77. Chayes (note 75), p. 937.
78. Chayes (note 75), p. 937.
79. Sullivan (note 49).
80. Freedman, L., 'Assured detection: needs and dysfunction of verification', in

Nerlich, V. (ed.), *Soviet Power and Western Negotiation Policies, Vol. 2: The Western Panacea: Containing Soviet Power Through Negotiation* (Ballinger, Cambridge, MA, 1983), p. 252.

81. 'Soviet treaty violations and U.S. compliance policy', *National Security Record*, No. 63, Heritage Foundation, Washington, DC, December 1983, p. 2.

82. Weisman, S.R., 'President urges Soviet to return to arms talks', *New York Times*, 17 January 1984, pp. Al, A9.

83. Reagan, R., Letter of transmittal to Thomas P. O'Neill, Speaker of the House of Representatives, for the report *A Quarter Century of Soviet Compliance Practices under Arms Control Commitments: 1958–1983*, 10 October 1984, p. 1.

84. White House Office of the Press Secretary, *The President's Unclassified Report to the Congress on Soviet Non-compliance with Arms Control Agreements*, Washington, DC, 1 February 1985.

85. Fischer, D. and Szasz, P., *Safeguarding the Atom: A Critical Appraisal*, Goldblat, J. (ed.) (Taylor & Francis, London, 1985), p. 83 [a SIPRI book].

86. Jackson, W.E., Jr, 'The sacking of SALT', Fulbright Institute of International Relations, University of Arkansas, Fayetteville, 20 January 1984, p. 3; Pieragostini, K., 'Soviet cheating? Reagan's rush to judgement', *ADIU Report*, Vol. 6, No. 1, January/February 1984, Science Policy Research Unit, University of Sussex, Brighton, p. 2.

87. Perle, R., Transcript of testimony before Senate Armed Services Committee, 14 March 1984, p. 2.

88. Meyer, S.M., 'Verification and the ICBM shell game', *International Security*, Vol. 4, No. 2, Fall 1979, pp. 47-48.

89. Einhorn, R.J., 'Treaty compliance', *Foreign Policy*, No. 45, Winter 1981–82, p. 34.

90. Eayrs, J., 'Arms control on the Great Lakes', *Disarmament and Arms Control*, Vol. 2, No. 4, Autumn 1964, pp. 373-404.

91. Eayrs (note 90), p. 374.

92. Eayrs (note 90), p. 402. *Clausula rebus sic stantibus* is a tacit condition said to attach to all contracts meaning that they cease to be obligatory as soon as the state of facts out of which they arose has changed—*Black's Law Dictionary*, 5th edition (West Publishing Company, St Paul, MN, 1979), p. 226.

93. Earle, R., II, 'Verification issues from the point of view of the negotiator', in Tsipis, Hafemeister & Janeway (note 25).

94. Memorandum of understanding between the USA and the USSR regarding the establishment of a direct communications link, in Goldblat (note 1), pp. 155-56.

95. Agreement between the USA and the USSR on measures to improve the direct communications link, in Goldblat (note 1), pp. 190-92.

96. Pincus, W., 'US, Soviet agreement on new hot line', *International Herald Tribune*, 18 July 1984, p. 1.

97. Knickerbocker, B., 'US Senators look beyond hot line to "crisis centers"', *Christian Science Monitor*, 19 July 1984, p. 3.

98. Crawford, A. *et al.*, *Compendium of Arms Control Verification Proposals*, 2nd edition, ORAE Report R81, Department of National Defence, Ottawa, March 1982, p. 337.

99. SALT I Treaty, article 13, paragraph b, and SALT II Treaty, article 17, paragraph 2b, in Goldblat (note 1), pp. 198, 281.

100. Talbot (note 33), pp. 95-98; SALT II Treaty, article 17, paragraph 3, in Goldblat (note 1), p. 281.

101. Treaty between the USA and the USSR on underground nuclear explosions for peaceful purposes, article 4, paragraph 1b, in Goldblat (note 1), p. 218.

102. Goldblat (note 1), pp. 219-21.
103. Protocol to the treaty between the USA and the USSR on the limitation of underground nuclear weapon tests, in Goldblat (note 1), pp. 211-12.
104. Barton, D., and Pöllinger, S., 'Negotiations for conventional force reductions and security in Europe', in SIPRI, *World Armaments and Disarmament, SIPRI Yearbook 1983* (Taylor & Francis, London, 1983), pp. 595-605.
105. Crawford *et al.* (note 98).
106. Buchheim, R.W. and Caldwell, D., 'The US–USSR Standing Consultative Commission: description and appraisal', Working Paper No. 2, Center for Foreign Policy Development, Brown University, Providence, RI, May 1983, p. 2.
107. SALT I Treaty, article 13, in Goldblat (note 1), pp. 198-99; Memorandum of understanding between the USA and the USSR regarding the establishment of a Standing Consultative Commission, in Goldblat (note 1), pp. 206-207.
108. Goldblat (note 1), p. 279.
109. Kincade, W.H., SFRC Hearings (note 36), Part 5, p. 207.
110. Buchheim & Caldwell (note 106), p. 6.
111. Buchheim & Caldwell (note 106), pp. 7-8.
112. *Challenges for U.S. National Security, Final Report, Vol. 4: Verification*, Carnegie Endowment for International Peace, Washington, DC, 1983, p. 53.
113. *Compliance with SALT I Agreements*, US Department of State, Bureau of Public Affairs, Special Report No. 55, Washington, DC, July 1979.
114. Slocombe, W., 'Verification and negotiation', in *The Nuclear Weapons Freeze and Arms Control*, Proceedings of a symposium held at the American Academy of Arts and Sciences, 13–15 January 1983, Washington, DC, 1983, p. 85.
115. Buchheim & Caldwell (note 106), p. 15.
116. See for example 'Draft treaty banning any nuclear weapon test explosion in any environment', Protocol III, Swedish Mission for Disarmament, Geneva, 21 June 1983.
117. Melman, S. (ed.), *Inspection for Disarmament* (Columbia University Press, New York, 1958).
118. *Verification and Response in Disarmament Agreements*, Woods Hole Summer Study, 1962 (Institute for Defense Analysis, Washington, DC, November 1962).
119. Smith, G., *Doubletalk: The Story of SALT I* (Doubleday, New York, 1980), p. 168.
120. Weinberger, C., Transcript of radio interview 'From the editors desk', Public Broadcasting System, 30 January 1983.
121. Report of the *Ad Hoc* Working Group on Chemical Weapons to the Committee on Disarmament, Committee on Disarmament document CD/446, Geneva, 22 August 1983, Annex I, p. 5.
122. Bush, G., Address before the CD on banning of chemical weapons, Geneva, 18 April 1984, US Department of State, Bureau of Public Affairs, Washington, DC.
123. Smith, R.J., 'A novel proposal on chemical weapons', *Science*, Vol. 224, No. 4648, 4 May 1984, p. 474.
124. Henkin, L., *Arms Control and Inspection in American Law* (Greenwood Press, Westport, CT, 1958), pp. 64-75.
125. Henkin (note 124), pp. 153-54.
126. Berman, H.J. and Maggs, P.G., *Disarmament Inspection under Soviet Law* (Oceana, Dobbs Ferry, NY, 1967), p. 46.
127. Zile, Z.L., Sharlet, R. and Lore, J.C., *The Soviet Legal System and Arms Inspection* (Praeger, New York, 1972), p. 309.
128. Zile, Sharlet & Lore (note 127).

129. Henkin (note 124), p. 154.
130. Towle, P., *Arms Control and East–West Relations* (Croom Helm, London, 1983), p. 134.
131. *Developments in Technical Capabilities for Detecting and Identifying Nuclear Weapons Tests*, Hearings before the Joint Committee on Atomic Energy, US Congress, 5–12 March 1963 (US Government Printing Office, Washington, DC, 1963), p. 424.
132. Chayes, A., (note 75), p. 954 [emphasis in original].
133. Smith (note 119), p. 134 [emphasis added].
134. Hearings (note 131), p. 419.
135. Scoville, H., 'A leap forward in verification', in Willrich, M. and Rhinelander, J.B. (eds), *SALT—The Moscow Agreements and Beyond* (Free Press, New York, 1974), p. 176; Smith (note 119), p. 103.
136. Slocombe (note 114), p. 86.
137. Note 112, pp. 45-46.
138. Clines, F.X., 'Reagan, rebutting Russians, says he's in summit mood', *New York Times*, 22 June 1984, p. 3.
139. Long, F.A., Hearings (note 131), p. 414.
140. Hearings (note 131), p. 415.
141. Hearings (note 131), p. 415.
142. Hearings (note 131), p. 420.
143. Hearings (note 131), p. 421.
144. Lukasik, S.J., 'Status of current technology to identify seismic events as natural or man made', *Hearing before the Subcommittee on Research, Development, and Radiation of the Joint Committee on Atomic Energy*, 27–28 October 1971 (US Government Printing Office, Washington, DC, 1971), p. 65.
145. Sykes, L.R. and Evernden, J.F., 'Verification of a Comprehensive Nuclear Test Ban', *Scientific American*, Vol. 247, No. 4, October 1982, p. 48.
146. Note 116, Protocol II, p. 1.
147. Glasstone, S. and Dolan, P.J., *The Effects of Nuclear Weapons*, 3rd edition, US Department of Defense and Energy Research and Development Administration (US Government Printing Office, Washington, DC, 1977), p. 261.
148. Dahlman, O. and Israelson, Y., *Monitoring Underground Nuclear Explosions* (Elsevier, Amsterdam, 1977), p. 42.
149. Glasstone & Dolan (note 147).
150. Seaborg, G.T., *Kennedy, Khrushchev and the Test Ban* (University of California Press, Berkeley, 1981), p. 191.
151. Seaborg (note 150), pp. 191-92.
152. Lukasik (note 144).
153. Ericsson, U.A., 'Event identification for test ban control', *Bulletin of Seismological Society of America*, Vol. 60, No. 5, October 1970, p. 1545.
154. Sykes, L.R., Evernden, J.F. and Cifuentes, I., 'Seismic methods for verifying nuclear test bans', in Hafemeister, D.W. and Schroeer, D. (eds), *Physics, Technology and the Nuclear Arms Race*, AIP Conference Proceedings No. 104 (American Institute of Physics, New York, 1983), p. 116.
155. Dahlman & Israelson (note 148), chapter 13.
156. Dahlman & Israelson (note 148), p. 312.
157. *Challenges for U.S. National Security* (note 112), pp. 45-46.
158. Dahlman & Israelson (note 148), p. 329.
159. Krass, A.S., 'The Environmental Modification Convention of 1977: the question of verification', in Westing, A.H. (ed.), *Environmental Warfare: A Technical, Legal and Policy Appraisal* (Taylor & Francis, London, 1984), pp. 65-76 [a SIPRI book].

160. Goldblat (note 1), pp. 150-53.
161. Goldblat (note 1), pp. 159-62.
162. Goldblat (note 1), pp. 175-77.
163. Sims, N.A., 'Consultative committees as 'appropriate international procedures'', in disarmament-related treaties', *Transnational Perspectives*, Vol. 4, No. 1-2, 1978, pp. 15-19.
164. Goldblat (note 1), pp. 193-95.
165. Towle, P. (note 48), pp. 31-40; Perry Robinson, J.P., 'The Soviet Union and the Biological Weapons Convention and a guide to sources on the Sverdlovsk incident' (note 48), pp. 41-56.
166. Flowerree, C. C, 'Cloudy treaties', *Foreign Service Journal*, Vol. 60, May 1983, p. 18.
167. 'The conclusions section of the report of the UN Group of Experts to investigate reports on the alleged use of chemical weapons', in SIPRI (note 104), pp. 424-26.
168. *Report of the Specialists Appointed by the Secretary-General to Investigate Allegations by the Islamic Republic of Iran concerning the Use of Chemical Weapons*, Security Council Report S/16433, 26 March 1984.
169. Goldblat (note 1), pp. 228-31.
170. Krass (note 159), p. 70.
171. Krass (note 159), p. 74.
172. Issraelyan, V.L. and Fisher, A.S., Committee on Disarmament document CD/48, 7 August 1979, p. 4.
173. *Report of the Ad Hoc Working Group on Chemical Weapons to the Committee on Disarmament*, Committee on Disarmament document CD/416, Annex II, Contact Group B, pp. 10-17.
174. Sims (note 163), p. 16.
175. The Baruch Plan, Statement by the United States Representative (Baruch) to the United Nations Atomic Energy Commission, 14 June 1946, *Documents on Disarmament 1945–1959*, Vol. I, US Department of State, Publication 7008 (US Government Printing Office, Washington, DC, August 1960), pp. 7-16.
176. Goldblat (note 1), pp. 157-59.
177. Sykes & Evernden (note 145), p. 48.
178. Goldblat (note 1), p. 312.
179. Goldblat, J. and Ferm, R., 'Major multilateral arms control agreements', in SIPRI, *World Armaments and Disarmament, SIPRI Yearbook 1985* (Taylor & Francis, London, 1985), p. 503.
180. Jasani, B. (ed.), *Outer Space—A New Dimension of the Arms Race* (Taylor & Francis, London, 1982), p. 271 [a SIPRI Book].
181. Jasani (note 180), p. 58.
182. 'Debate continues on the bomb that wasn't', *Science*, Vol. 209, No. 4456, 1 August 1980, pp. 572-73.
183. Marshall, E., 'Navy lab concludes the Vela saw a bomb', *Science*, Vol. 209, No. 4460, 29 August 1980, pp. 996-97.
184. Marshall (note 183), p. 996.
185. Goldblat (note 1), pp. 211-12.
186. Goldblat (note 1), pp. 218-27.
187. Goldblat, J., 'Multilateral arms control efforts', in SIPRI (note 15), pp. 596-97.
188. Dahiman, O., Committee on Disarmament document CD/448, 9 March 1984.
189. Donnelly, W.H., 'Changing pressures on the non-proliferation regime', in SIPRI (note 104), p. 69.
190. Goldblat (note 1), pp. 162-70.
191. Goldblat (note 1), pp. 172-74.
192. Goldblat (note 1), pp. 291-95.

193. *IAEA Bulletin*, Vol. 26, No. 1, March 1984, p. 36.
194. *The Agency's Budget for 1984*, IAEA, Vienna, August 1983, pp. 9, 93-94.
195. *Annual Report for 1983*, IAEA, Vienna, July 1984, p. 59.
196. Grümm (note 70), p. 27.
197. Grümm, H., 'IAEA safeguards: where do we stand today?', *IAEA Bulletin*, Vol. 21, No. 4, August 1979, p. 37.
198. Donnelly (note 189), p. 80.
199. Donnelly (note 189), p. 72.
200. Fischer & Szasz (note 85), p. 84.
201. United Kingdom of Great Britain and Northern Ireland, 'Verification of non-production of chemical weapons', Committee on Disarmament document CD/353, Geneva, 8 March 1983, p. 4.
202. Address by President Eisenhower to the General Assembly, 8 December 1953, in *Documents on Disarmament 1945–1959* (note 175), pp. 393-400.
203. Krass, A.S., Boskma P., Elzen, B. and Smit, W.A., *Uranium Enrichment and Nuclear Weapon Proliferation* (Taylor & Francis, London, 1983), p. 199 [a SIPRI book].
204. Henken, (note 124), p. 53.
205. Non-Proliferation Treaty, article IV, para. 2, in Goldblat (note 1), p. 173.
206. Donnelly (note 189), pp. 76-78
207. Statute of the IAEA, in Goldblat (note 1), p. 149.
208. *The Structure and Content of Agreements Between the Agency and States Required in Connection with the Treaty on the Non-Proliferation of Nuclear Weapons*, INFCIRC/153, paras 76d, 77, 82, 85b, in Goldblat (note 1), pp. 177-190.
209. 'The IAEA: improving safeguards', *Hearings before the Subcommittee on International Security, Scientific Affairs and International Economic Policy and Trade*, Committee on Foreign Affairs, US House of Representatives (US Government Printing Office, Washington, DC, 3, 18 March 1982), p. 2.
210. Krass *et al.* (note 203), pp. 52-53.
211. Menzel, J.H., 'Safeguards approach for gas centrifuge type enrichment plants', *Nuclear Materials Management*, Winter 1983, pp. 33-34.
212. Imber, M.F., 'Arms control verification: the special case of IAEA–NPT "special inspections"', (note 48), p. 68.
213. Final Document of the Tenth Special Session of the General Assembly, para. 125(d), in Goldblat (note 1), p. 265.
214. *The Implications of Establishing an International Satellite Monitoring Agency*, UN document A/AC.206/14, New York, 1983, p. 1.
215. UN (note 214), p. 66.
216. UN (note 214), p. 4.
217. SMA/WP1, Compilation of excerpts from statements made at the Tenth Special Session and the Thirty-Third Regular Session of the General Assembly, Group of Government Experts on the Implications of Establishing an International Satellite Monitoring Agency, 11 June 1979, p. 18.
218. SMA/WP1 (note 217), p. 19.
219. Imber (note 212), p. 67.
220. Jasani, B., 'A regional satellite monitoring agency', *Environmental Conservation*, Vol. 10, No. 3, Autumn 1983, pp. 255-56.
221. Jasani (note 220), p. 255.
222. 'French to propose satellite imaging system', *Aviation Week & Space Technology*, Vol. 121, No. 2, 9 July 1984, p. 61.
223. Abdel-Hady, M. and Sadek, A., 'Verification using satellites, feasibility of an international or multinational agency', in Jasani (note 180), p. 294.

224. UN (note 214), pp. 71-76.
225. Abdel-Hady & Sadek (note 223), p. 280.
226. UN (note 214), p. 48.
227. Goldblat (note 1), pp. 216-17.
228. Sharp, J., 'Troop reductions in Europe: a status report', *ADIU Report*, Vol. 5, No. 5, September/October 1983, p. 4.
229. Reinius, U., 'The CSCE and a European Disarmament Conference', in SIPRI, *World Armaments and Disarmament, SIPRI Yearbook 1982* (Taylor & Francis, London, 1982), pp. 51-62.
230. Barton, D., 'The Conference on Confidence- and Security-Building Measures and Disarmament in Europe', in SIPRI (note 15), pp. 557-81.
231. Sharp (note 228), p. 5.
232. Sharp (note 228), p. 4.
233. O'Leary, J., 'U.S. offers initiative to reduce numbers of troops in Europe', *Washington Times*, 20 April 1984, p. 6.
234. Sharp (note 228), p. 5; Dean, J., 'Soviet shift in Vienna', *New York Times*, 1 August 1983, p. 15.
235. *The Arms Control Reporter* (note 57), p. 401.B.70.
236. Goldblat (note 1), pp. 216-17.
237. Barton (note 230).
238. Barton (note 230), p. 558.
239. Reinius (note 229), pp. 60-61.
240. Goldblat (note 1), p. 216.
241. Reinius (note 229), p. 61.
242. Voas, J., 'The President's report on Soviet non-compliance with arms control agreements: A discussion of the charges', Report No. 84-160F, Congressional Research Service, Washington, DC, 10 September 1984, p. CRS-71.
243. Goldblat (note 1), p. 216.
244. Note 29, p. 3
245. Jasani, B. and Karkoszka, A., 'International verification of arms control agreements', paper prepared for the Independent Commission on Disarmament and Security Issues (Palme Commission), December 1981, p. 17.
246. Myrdal, A., 'The international control of disarmament', *Scientific American*, Vol. 231, No. 4, October 1974, pp. 21-33.
247. Myrdal (note 246), p. 29.
248. Myrdal (note 246), p. 31.
249. Jasani & Karkoszka (note 245), p. 19.
250. Freedman, L. and Schear, J., 'International verification arrangements', paper prepared for the Independent Commission on Disarmament and Security Issues (Palme Commission), October 1981, pp. 8-9.

Chapter 5. Conclusion

The verification of arms control agreements raises many subtle and complex problems. Some of these problems are technical and can therefore be solved by suitable technical innovation or economic investment. But the most complex and subtle problems are political and psychological and therefore much more dependent for their solution on the creation of an appropriate atmosphere within which the compliance process can function.

At the root of most of the problems faced by verification are the deeply contradictory attempts by two powerful states to negotiate arms control agreements even as they work diligently to maintain or enhance the credibility of their military threats against each other. This military competition will inevitably be the primary determinant of the political/psychological atmosphere, and while verification and intelligence systems will produce vast amounts of detailed evidence on the military activities of the parties, it is far more likely that the meaning of the evidence will be influenced by the context than that the context will be changed by the evidence. Any verification system will have to confront the psychological phenomenon common to both states and individuals: the tendency to use evidence to reinforce existing attitudes rather than to challenge them.

The complexity and essential subjectivity of verification militate against any attempt to draw neat conclusions about the role verification can play in promoting disarmament. There are no general answers to the questions of how much verification is enough or what forms of verification are most effective. Such questions must always be answered by negotiation in the context of specific agreements. At the same time it is possible to extract from the evidence and analyses of chapters 1–4 the following propositions which can serve as guidelines to help the reader form his or her own judgements on specific questions about verification.

1. Verification has two fundamental purposes: to deter violations by posing a credible threat of discovery and to build confidence in a treaty by demonstrating compliance. These two functions overlap to some extent, defining an area within which any verification system should be designed to operate. However, the two purposes can also conflict with each other. Too much

emphasis on guaranteeing detection of violations will cause the system to see too much and become overloaded with ambiguities and suspicions, thereby undermining the confidence-building function. On the other hand too much emphasis on confidence building can lead to complacency and even temptations to exploit the latitude allowed for stretching the limits of the treaty.

There is no formula which can produce the correct balance between these two imperatives, and any balance which is achieved can be all too easily upset by changes in the political atmosphere. This is well illustrated by the fate of SALT which received excellent compliance reports from the Nixon, Ford and Carter Administrations and has on the basis of the same evidence been emphatically rejected by the Reagan Administration. It is very difficult to imagine a verification system which would not be vulnerable to such political shifts, and while the tendency to look for certainty in higher and higher degrees of intrusiveness is a natural one, it will become self-defeating if pushed too far.

2. Arguments about verification are very often surrogates for more fundamental disagreements about military doctrine and the appropriateness of arms control. Concepts of 'adequacy' of verification which evolved in the 1960s and 1970s were closely tied to the doctrine which held that marginal changes in a military balance already at high levels are militarily, and by implication politically, insignificant. Present US concepts of 'effectiveness' of verification are connected to a much more activist military-political doctrine which sees continued value in either the reality or the perception of marginal military superiority.

The evidence of almost 40 years of arms control experience supports the conclusion that the only standard of adequacy capable of maintaining a workable verification system is the ability to detect *militarily significant* violations in time to make an appropriate response. A standard which sees all possible violations as of equal importance or which is based on a legalistic 'contract' approach to arms control cannot survive the political tensions it helps to exacerbate. Acceptance of this conclusion should shift the political debate to an area where it more properly belongs, to the problem of military doctrine, not verification.

Based on a standard of adequacy defined by military significance it is clear that the SALT I and II Treaties are more than adequately verifiable, and that even more comprehensive and significant treaties would pass the same test (see proposition 7 below).

3. Verification will always involve a substantial degree of secrecy. This arises from two causes: first, the intimate connection between verification and intelligence gathering and, second, the added deterrent effect on a potential violator of uncertainty as to the capabilities of those watching him. But it is also essential that considerably more solid information on the scope and capabilities of verification as well as the workings of the compliance process be made available to the public. Granted that the balance between secrecy and credibility is a difficult one to maintain, it is still clear that the emphasis in the

past has been much too heavily on secrecy. This has left the concerned public with little more than leaks and guesswork on which to form a judgement on verification and compliance. Considering the damage done to the credibility of the verification system in the past few years it will take a concerted effort at public information and education to regain a public consensus in the United States on the possibility of adequately verifying future arms control treaties.

4. Verification does have an important deterrent effect against militarily significant clandestine violations, and in fact the demands on such a system in the present military stand-off are not great. Verification does *not* have a significant deterrent effect against unilateral interpretations of ambiguous treaty provisions or the minor stretching of limits to test the response of the other side. The military competition is a vast and complex web, and the job of any given verification system is to watch only a narrow region of this web and somehow to ignore the rest. Because this is often impossible to do, the verification system is always under stress and needs substantial help in the form of restraint by both parties in stretching the limits of treaties and in responding to incidents of limit-stretching. Using the verification system to 'demonstrate resolve' or to 'enhance credibility' in the usual senses of these terms will ultimately destroy the system.

5. Verification is a co-operative process, it is in no sense a unilateral process. Co-operation can be passive in the form of the restraint mentioned in the previous proposition as well as in the agreement not to interfere with or impede the legitimate verification activities of other parties. Co-operation can also be active in the form of exchanges of relevant information and the allowance of certain forms of physical intrusion such as 'black boxes', control posts, observers or inspectors.

Perhaps the most important form of co-operation is a continuing process of consultation among the parties, institutionalized in a consultative commission made up of highly qualified experts. The purpose of such a commission must be entirely on the side of preserving agreements and building confidence by dealing promptly and objectively with any ambiguities, misunderstandings or technical violations which arise. Only after this process has been given its full play should charges of violations be entertained. Once such charges have been made the issue will have passed beyond the competence of a consultative commission and will have to be dealt with diplomatically or even possibly militarily.

6. On-site inspection has been vastly overrated in the history of arms control. It has an important role to play in certain cases as one of the co-operative measures just mentioned, but it is also inherently limited in what it can achieve. The limitations are in some cases technical but in most cases political. In particular, those forms of on-site inspection which demand that states relinquish significant aspects of national sovereignty must still be classified as Utopian. It can be taken as axiomatic that no state will ever knowingly permit the discovery of a treaty violation on its territory by foreigners.

The most promising role for on-site inspection is the routine or continuous monitoring of declared facilities, for production, testing, deployment or destruction of materials or weapons under international auspices. A willingness to declare such facilities and accept inspectors or observers into them is an excellent sign of a state's intention to comply with a treaty. But even these applications will be slow in coming and must be carefully designed to allay fears of military or industrial espionage as well as interference with the effective operation of commercial facilities.

7. There is no necessary connection between the amount or type of verification required and the levels of armaments retained by parties to a treaty. The historical evidence suggests that there is a close correlation between the amount of distrust and suspicion and the levels of armaments. This implies that armaments will not be reduced unless suspicions are reduced and vice versa. But it is not at all clear what role verification can play in sustaining such a reduction process. It seems most likely that if a disarmament 'spiral' were in fact underway, verification demands would at worst stay constant and could very well decrease. But, verification itself cannot be the instigator of such a downward spiral. This can only be an act of political will based on an understanding of common interest in disarmament. The very existence of such an understanding would make fundamental changes in the role of verification, eliminating the present demand that it serve as a substitute for trust and allowing it to act as a true confidence-building measure.

8. From the standpoint of verification, treaties that totally ban specified activities or weapons are preferable to treaties that set quantitative or qualitative limits on them. But it must be kept in mind that verifiability is only one measure of the value of a treaty and that the achievement of other values may require compromise on this issue. On the other hand, there seems to be no reason to believe that broad, comprehensive treaties are easier to verify than narrowly constructed ones. For example, a treaty could be constructed entirely from detailed provisions chosen entirely for their ease of verification. The SALT agreements are a good example of this type of treaty. While such a treaty would obviously be highly verifiable there is no guarantee that it would have beneficial effects in reducing suspicion or slowing the arms race. On the other hand, a more comprehensive treaty might contain provisions of lower verifiability but represent a major step in arms limitation or reduction. The latter type of treaty seems more desirable, but if it contains poorly verified provisions it will be highly vulnerable to shifts in the political winds.

The nuclear freeze proposal is a good example of both of these principles. If the freeze were a *total* ban on the production, testing and deployment of nuclear weapon systems it would be highly verifiable with present national technical means and no more extensive co-operative measures than have already been accepted in other treaties. But such a complete freeze would in fact represent a commitment to nuclear disarmament, since it would eliminate replacement or modernization of defective, obsolete and deteriorating weapons. The nuclear arsenals of all parties to such a freeze would gradually lose their reliability, and pressures would be strong on all parties to seek mutual reductions to prevent the development of dangerous asymmetries resulting from unequal rates of decay.

However desirable it may be, such a freeze is unfortunately unlikely. A less unlikely 'freeze' would be one that allowed for replacement and modernization of weapons, keeping their numbers constant. In this case production and testing facilities would continue to function and new weapons would be deployed. Under such conditions the potential for ambiguous activities and the resistance to significant co-operative verification measures would increase, putting far greater pressure on the verification system. In fact, once exceptions to the freeze begin to be allowed, its susceptibility to verification becomes no more favourable than other proposals to limit activities rather than eliminate them.

9. The technology of verification has made and continues to make rapid improvements in sensitivity, resolution, reliability and comprehensiveness. Some technologies are already at or very near their theoretical limits of performance. These include satellite and aerial photography, seismology, phased-array radars, radiation detectors and communications-monitoring antennas. Another group of technologies are still some distance from their theoretical limits but are the objects of intense research and development efforts and promise to improve rapidly in the near future. In this group are infra-red sensors, image and data processing techniques and synthetic-aperture radar. There is also one group of technologies which is far short of its potential and which could benefit from more attention than it is getting. This group includes the various containment and surveillance devices to be applied under IAEA safeguards. As the world nuclear industry grows the job of applying safeguards will expand with it. This means that it will inevitably be necessary to rely more on technological safeguards methods than on human inspectors, who are already finding it difficult to give adequate attention to all safeguarded facilities. Any effort to extend the current safeguards system to the monitoring of a ban on the production of fissionable materials would require an even greater effort at technological development.

10. The advanced state of the art in many verification technologies implies that if verification were the only concern a number of significant treaties could be signed and ratified immediately. A comprehensive nuclear test ban treaty, a ban on testing of anti-satellite weapons, and a freeze or reduction in deployments of land-based intercontinental and intermediate-range ballistic missiles would all be eminently verifiable. Other treaties such as a chemical weapons ban and a mutual force reduction in Europe require some further convergence in views on the role of on-site inspection, but given a pragmatic approach to this problem by all sides it could be quickly resolved. The signing of all of these treaties would by no means end the arms race, but it would at least signal a badly needed improvement in the political atmosphere.

11. Despite the remarkable achievements and steady growth of monitoring, data processing and analytical capabilities there are trends in weapon system development which if allowed to continue will outrun the ability of technology to monitor them. Incessant military demands for more mobile, flexible, controllable and survivable weapons are leading to new weapons which will be smaller, more mobile, less recognizable and capable of carrying out a variety of missions. Most threatening in this regard are cruise missiles, direct ascent anti-satellite weapons fired from fighter aircraft, binary chemical weapons and all so-called dual-purpose delivery vehicles.

In many cases the most effective way to control such weapons is to ban their testing during research and development. An important historical example was the development of multiple independently targetable re-entry vehicles in the 1960s, and two current examples are the development of anti-satellite weapons and small, mobile ICBMs. In all three cases the verification of a test ban would have been, or would be, a simple matter, while verification of deployment after development becomes extremely difficult, if not impossible.

12. The internationalization of verification will continue to be a slow and frustrating process for a long time to come. The two great powers who control the vast majority of the militarily useful monitoring technologies are no more interested in giving up their monopoly interest in this field than they are in giving up their dominance in nuclear weapons. Any initiatives to create, for example, an International Satellite Monitoring Agency will have to be taken by other states, and these efforts will be limited by lack of economic and technical resources as well as by political pressures from the USA and USSR.

All of the easy international arms control treaties have been signed and now stand as symbols of the shallowness of the *détente* that characterized the relationship of the USA and USSR in the 1970s. Future international treaties will be much more difficult to achieve and will depend heavily on superpower cooperation to achieve them. Until the bilateral arms race can be brought to a halt and reversed the prospects for international arms control and verification will not be bright unless, like the Non-Proliferation Treaty and its accompanying safeguards, they suit superpower interests.

If a genuine *détente* can be established and progress made in bilateral disarmament, then it is inevitable that the problems of disarmament and its verification will eventually become international in scope. One is entitled to hope that once the process had proceeded that far the ultimate goal of genuine international disarmament verified by international means would be within reach.

Verification has a relationship to intelligence gathering which is in many ways analogous to the relationship between arms control and the arms race. Both arms control and military planning require information, and in many cases it is precisely the same information, gathered and analysed by the same devices and techniques. It follows that any attempt to define precisely the boundary between verification and espionage is inevitably artificial and political as opposed to rigorous and technical. And this same essential arbitrariness and negotiability applies to any attempt to define a standard of adequacy for verification.

Historically the Soviet Union has been associated with challenges to legitimacy and the United States with questions about adequacy. While there are legitimate technical and political reasons for these attitudes, there has also been far too great a tendency for each side to exaggerate its concerns as a convenient means of influencing public opinion or rationalizing failure to reach agreements. It will not be easy for the two major powers to break this behaviour pattern. Only when negotiations are based on the mutually shared premise that the military competition has outlived its usefulness and must be ended can the political compromises be made which will establish the foundation for a successful verification system. And both states will have to devote considerable efforts to building the domestic political consensus necessary to support these compromises.

This book has devoted a great deal of space to the difficulties of verification. Such difficulties are real and must be faced honestly. Yet the overwhelming weight of the evidence and analysis presented in this book supports the conclusion that the opportunity exists for the USA and the USSR to make a significant beginning towards meaningful disarmament with agreements that are adequately verifiable. Both states possess elaborate and sophisticated means of gathering and analysing intelligence, and while this does not by any means eliminate uncertainty in their assessments of each other's capabilities and intentions, it does make it virtually impossible that either side could attempt to gain a significant military advantage over the other without incurring a high risk of discovery.

There was evidence that this reality was coming to be understood by both sides as SALT and other negotiations progressed through the 1970s. But the rapid deterioration of the political climate which began in the late 1970s went a long way towards destroying most of the progress that had been made. Quiet diplomacy and technical discussion of ambiguous behaviour were replaced by loud public accusations of bad faith and a renewal of the kind of posturing and provocation around issues of verification that characterized the political climate of the 1940s and 1950s. Verification again became a convenient whipping boy for many whose real purpose was to challenge the entire concept of arms control as it had evolved during the period of *détente*.

Verification is too fragile to serve as the foundation for disarmament in such a political atmosphere. The most that verification can ever be is a tool to aid in the implementation of a process whose foundation is a mutually shared recognition of the futility and danger of the arms race and the will to act politically on this recognition. No amount of verification can substitute for this act of political will or make it easy to take. And too much emphasis on verification, with its implicit message of distrust, can only make the process more difficult.

As these conclusions are being written the USA and USSR have resumed arms control negotiations after more than a year of abstention. This resumption of talks has been accompanied by a noticeable toning down of hostile political rhetoric and a somewhat reduced emphasis on charges of violations of previous agreements. However, it remains to be seen whether these changes are genuine, and even if they are genuine whether the will exists to repair the damage done to arms control in recent years. The manner in which the issues of verification and compliance are dealt with by both sides will be an excellent gauge of the seriousness with which they are approaching these new negotiations.

Index